God Needs No Defense
Reimagining Muslim–Christian Relations in the 21st Century

Thomas K. Johnson & C. Holland Taylor (Editors)

Humanitarian Islam is a global movement that seeks to restore *rahmah* (universal love and compassion) to its rightful place as the primary message of Islam, while positioning these efforts within a broader initiative to preserve and strengthen a rules-based international order founded upon shared civilizational values.

The inspiration for Humanitarian Islam is the unique example of the 15th/16th-century *Wali Songo* ("Nine Saints") who proselytized *Islam Nusantara* ("East Indies Islam") — rooted in the principle of *rahmah* — stressing the need to contextualize Islamic teachings and adapt these to the ever-changing realities of space and time, while presenting Islam not as a supremacist ideology or vehicle for conquest, but rather, as one of many paths through which humans may attain spiritual perfection.

Established by leaders of Indonesia's 90-million-member Nahdlatul Ulama (NU), the Institute for Humanitarian Islam and Center for Shared Civilizational Values work with a group of closely affiliated organizations including Nahdlatul Ulama; the NU's 5-million-member young adults movement, Gerakan Pemuda Ansor; LibForAll Foundation; and Bayt ar-Rahmah, which helps coordinate the global expansion of NU operations.

The World Evangelical Alliance (WEA) was founded in 1846 by Anglican, Baptist, Scottish Presbyterian, Methodist and Congregationalist leaders from the British Isles, as well as by prominent representatives of American and European Protestants, the latter especially from Germany. It is the largest international organization of evangelical churches, representing over 600 million Protestants and national evangelical alliances in 140 countries. WEA seeks to strengthen local churches through national alliances, supporting and coordinating grassroots leadership and seeking practical ways of showing the unity of the body of Christ.

Evangelicals are recognized by their high regard for the Bible as the Word of God that guides their daily lives; the conviction that salvation is only received by faith through Jesus Christ who died on the cross and was resurrected to life; that God is triune as Father, Son and Holy Spirit; and a few other core beliefs as found in WEA's Statement of Faith. Evangelicals want to share the Good News (in Greek εὐαγγέλιον *evangelion*) of Jesus Christ with others, serve those who are in need and speak up for the marginalized. Their highest commandment is to love God, and to love their neighbor as themselves.

In April of 2020 leaders of the World Evangelical Alliance and Nahdlatul Ulama — including Dr. Thomas Schirrmacher, Dr. Christine Schirrmacher, Dr. Thomas K. Johnson, Kyai Haji Yahya Cholil Staquf and C. Holland Taylor — established the Humanitarian Islam/WEA Joint Working Group. This volume is a product of the Joint Working Group's Subcommittee on Jurisprudence, Human Rights and Ethics.

God Needs No Defense

Reimagining Muslim–Christian Relations in the 21st Century

A Festschrift in Honor of Dr. Thomas Schirrmacher

Secretary General & CEO of the World Evangelical Alliance

**Thomas K. Johnson &
C. Holland Taylor
(Editors)**

WIPF & STOCK · Eugene, Oregon

Wipf and Stock Publishers
199 W 8th Ave, Suite 3
Eugene, OR 97401

God Needs No Defense
Reimagining Muslim-Christian Relations in the 21st Century:
A Festschrift in Honor of Dr. Thomas Schirrmacher
By Johnson, Thomas K. and Taylor, C. Holland
Copyright © 2021 Verlag für Kultur und Wissenschaft Culture and Science Publ.
All rights reserved.
Softcover ISBN-13: 978-1-6667-4432-3
Hardcover ISBN-13: 978-1-6667-4433-0
Publication date 4/4/2022
Previously published by Verlag für Kultur und Wissenschaft Culture and Science Publ., 2021

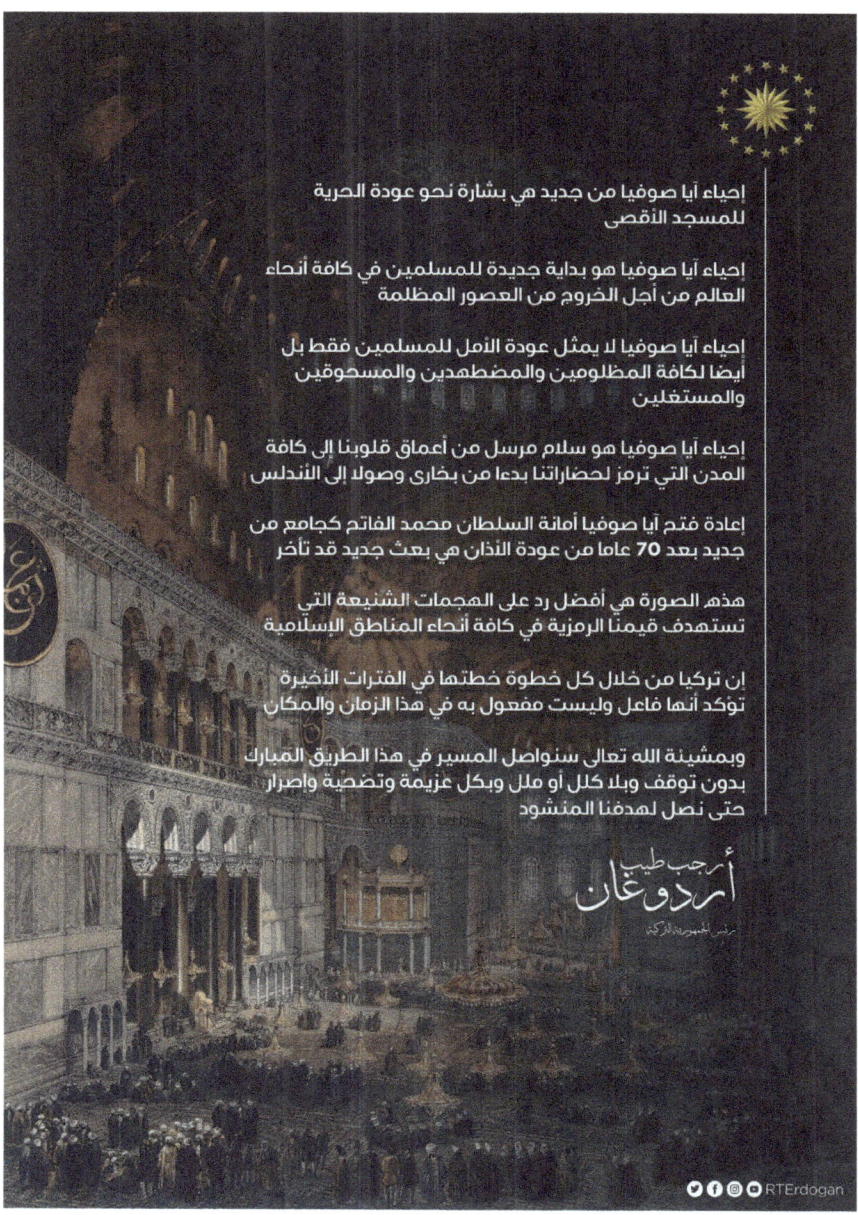

Statement by President Erdogan of Turkey superimposed on a painting that depicts Hagia Sophia's interior during the late Ottoman era

Remarks by President Recep Tayyip Erdogan of Turkey about the conversion of Hagia Sophia into a mosque, tweeted on Mr. Erdogan's official Arabic-language Twitter account on July 10, 2020

Restoring life to Hagia Sophia [by converting it from a museum to a mosque] is an auspicious portent that foreshadows the liberation of al-Aqsa Mosque [in Jerusalem].

Restoring life to Hagia Sophia represents a new beginning for Muslims in every corner of the earth, [a step that we have taken] in order to precipitate our exit from the dark ages [of Islamic decline and domination by the West].

Restoring life to Hagia Sophia symbolizes the restoration of hope not only to Muslims, but also to all the maltreated, oppressed, crushed, and exploited [peoples of the world].

Restoring life to Hagia Sophia constitutes a salutation of peace sent by us, from the depths of our hearts, to all the cities that symbolize [the former heights of] our civilization, from Bukhara [in Central Asia] to *al-Andalus* [Spain].

By re-conquering/re-opening [*i'ādat fatḥ*] Hagia Sophia — a sacred trust bestowed by God upon Sultan Mehmet the Conqueror/Opener [*al-Fātiḥ*] of Constantinople — as a mosque, after 70 years (sic), the return of the Muslim call to prayer constitutes a long-overdue re-awakening [of the Islamic nation, or *ummah, which was largely united under the political and military leadership of a Caliph from the 7th century CE until the dissolution of the Ottoman Caliphate in 1924*].

This painting [of Hagia Sophia, when the former Christian cathedral served as an Ottoman mosque] constitutes the best reply [by Muslims] to the heinous assaults targeting our core [Islamic] values wherever Muslims dwell throughout the earth.

By taking this step, at this time and in this place, Turkey affirms that she is a powerful actor [who imposes her will and values upon others], and not the object of others' domination.

As the will of God Most High is with us, we shall continue our journey on this blessed path without cease, without fatigue or complaint, and with steely determination, resolve and readiness to sacrifice, until we arrive at our desired objective. [NOTE: the language in this final sentence is calculated to echo the terminology of offensive *jihad*. It implies that the speaker will lead the global Muslim community to further "openings/conquests," in a process that results in the continued expansion and ultimate triumph of Islam].

Recep Tayyip Erdogan
President of the Republic of Turkey

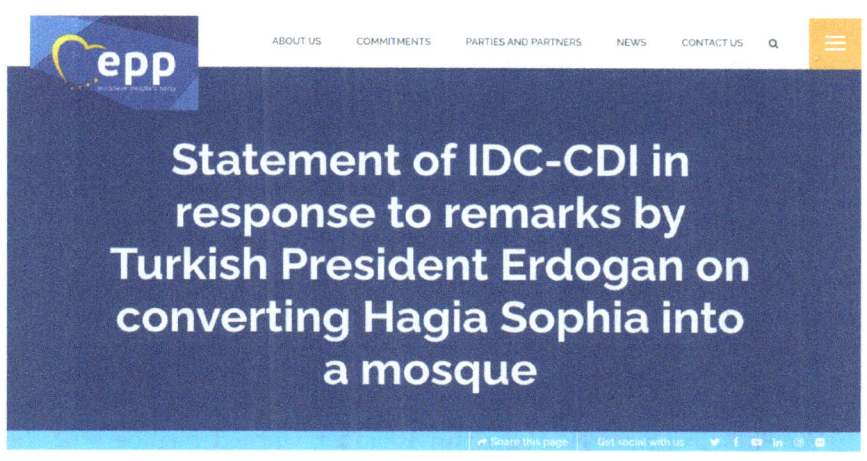

Statement by Indonesia's National Awakening Party

in response to remarks by President Recep Tayyip Erdogan of Turkey regarding the conversion of Hagia Sophia into a mosque

JAKARTA, Indonesia:

On 21 July 2020, Indonesia's largest Islamic political party issued an appeal to Muslims and people of good will of every faith and nation, to prevent the weaponization of religion for political purposes. Responding to inflammatory remarks by President Erdogan of Turkey, the National Awakening Party (PKB) warned that "the rules-based international order is under severe stress, challenged by the emergence of authoritarian, civilizationist states that do not accept this order, whether in terms of human rights, rule of law, democracy or respect for international borders and the sovereignty of other nations."

The PKB statement comes in response to an Arabic-language tweet, in which President Erdogan summoned Muslims "in every corner of the earth" to follow Turkey's lead in reawakening the Islamic nation, or *ummah*, which was largely united under the political and military leadership of a caliph from the 7th century CE until the dissolution of the Ottoman Caliphate in 1924.

As PKB Chairman H. Muhaimin Iskandar warned members of the world's largest political network, Centrist Democrat International (CDI), in January of 2020 at the CDI Eurasia Forum in Yogyakarta, Indonesia: "When religions are deliberately placed upon a collision course, it becomes extremely difficult to prevent universal conflict, for every religion claims to espouse a universal mission. When various religious groups live side by side, closely intermixed, religious conflict will inevitably provoke social unrest and violence, which in turn will lead to widespread enmity or even the expulsion of minorities unable to defend themselves, something that we can clearly see happening in various parts of the world today."

President Erdogan has defended the conversion of Hagia Sophia into a mosque by citing Turkey's right, as a sovereign nation state, to do as it pleases with the former Orthodox Christian cathedral. However, Erdogan's statements to the Muslim world belie this argument. His remarks, in Arabic, are attacking the rules-based international order; inflaming emotions "wherever Muslims dwell throughout the earth"; and threaten to rekindle a clash of civilizations that afflicted humanity for nearly 1300 years, along a fault line stretching "from Bukhara (in Central Asia) to *al-Andalus* (Spain)." The effects of President Erdogan's words and actions thus extend far beyond Turkey's borders and threaten both Muslim-majority and non-Muslim nations worldwide.

This may be clearly seen by the fact that Erdogan's statements were swiftly endorsed by the Muslim Brotherhood, Iran and a wide range of Islamic supremacists worldwide, including Indonesian Muslims who seek to transform the multi-religious and pluralistic Republic of Indonesia into an Islamic State or caliphate.

Erdogan's remarks also threaten peace and security in Europe, the Middle East and Africa, where similar narratives employed by al-Qaeda, ISIS, al-Shabab and Boko Haram have led to countless terrorist attacks and produced millions of refugees. In February of 2019, at a gathering of some 20,000 Muslim religious scholars, Nahdlatul Ulama (NU) — the world's largest Muslim organization, with over 90 million followers — endorsed the 2017 *Gerakan Pemuda Ansor Declaration on Humantarian Islam*, which states:

> The Islamic world is in the midst of a rapidly metastasizing crisis, with no apparent sign of remission. Among the most obvious manifestations of this crisis are the brutal conflicts now raging across a huge swath of territory inhabited by Muslims, from Africa and the Middle East to the borders of India; rampant social turbulence throughout the Islamic world; the unchecked spread of religious extremism and terror; and a rising tide of Islamophobia among non-Muslim populations, in direct response to these developments.
>
> Most of the political and military actors engaged in these conflicts pursue their competing agendas without regard to the cost in human lives and misery. This has led to an immense humanitarian crisis, while heightening the appeal and dramatically accelerating the spread of a de facto Islamist revolutionary movement that threatens the stability and security of the entire world, by summoning Muslims to join a global insurrection against the current world order.

In the midst of these circumstances, it is the height of irresponsibility for Recep Erdogan to further inflame Muslim emotions in pursuit of his domestic political agenda and to serve as a cover for his violation of international norms — by drilling for natural gas within the territorial waters of Cyprus and Greece; supporting al-Nusra (an affiliate of al-Qaeda) in Syria; and intervening in the Libyan conflict on behalf of the Islamist-dominated interim government — in an effort to enhance Turkish regional power and assert maritime rights in the eastern Mediterranean.

As Indonesia knows from its colonial history — and from recent efforts by China to claim "traditional fishing rights" within Indonesia's territorial waters near the island of Natuna — President Erdogan's actions and statements threaten to return human relations to a Hobbesian state of nature, in which the law of the jungle prevails. For if international law is no longer the yardstick for governing disputes between nations, any country that is sufficiently powerful may seize lands or waters internationally recognized as belonging to a smaller nation, and defy the weaker power to assert its claim by force.

In the Name Of

Some, in the name of God, debase and defile religion.
Some, in the name of "patriotism," rob their nation blind.
Some, in the name of "the people," oppress and exploit others.
Some, in the name of "humanity," prey upon their fellow man.
Some, in the name of "justice," demolish the very pillars of justice.
Some, in the name of "unity," rend the fabric of social harmony.
Some, in the name of "peace," harass and torment others.
Some, in the name of "freedom," destroy its very foundations.
So, in the name of whatever or whomever you wish,
Let your curses fly.
Or...
Acting in My Name,
Battle the ignorant with love and compassion.

~ KH. A. Mustofa Bisri

*In honor of Dr. Thomas Schirrmacher
and his vision for the future of
Muslim-Christian relations*

Table of Contents

Epigraph: In the Name Of
    KH. A. Mustofa Bisri

Introduction: "We Wish to Submit to the Dictates of Conscience" 1
    Thomas K. Johnson and C. Holland Taylor

Part I 19

    1. God Needs No Defense 21
        KH. Abdurrahman Wahid

    2. A Case for Ethical Cooperation Between Protestants and
       Humanitarian Muslims 29
        Thomas K. Johnson

    3. *Rahmah* (Universal Love and Compassion) 49
        KH. Abdurrahman Wahid

    4. God's Universal Grace in Protestant Theology 61
        Thomas K. Johnson

Part II 73

    5. Introduction to the Fundamental Principles of Nahdlatul
       Ulama (*Mukaddimah Qanun Asasi*) 75
        KH. Hasyim Asy'ari

    6. Christianity and the Essential Characteristics of Democracy 81
        Christine Schirrmacher

    7. Indonesian Islam and a Tradition of Pluralism 89
        Kyle Wisdom

    8. How Islam Learned to Adapt in 'Nusantara' 105
        KH. Yahya Cholil Staquf

9. The Primary Message of Islam: *Rahmah* (Universal Love and
   Compassion) 115
   KH. Hodri Ariev

Part III 117

10. Theology Matters: The Case of Jihadi Islam 119
    Rüdiger Lohlker

11. Responding to a Fundamental Crisis Within Islam Itself 139
    KH. Yahya Cholil Staquf

12. Gerakan Pemuda Ansor Declaration on Humanitarian Islam 149

13. The Battle for the Soul of Islam 157
    James M. Dorsey

14. Humanitarian Islam: Fostering Shared Civilizational Values to
    Revitalize a Rules-Based International Order 179
    Timothy S. Shah and Thomas G. Dinham

15. "Positive Deviance" Within the Indosphere & the Muslim
    World 191
    Timothy Samuel Shah

16. The Universal Values of Indonesian Islamic Civilization 201
    KH. A. Mustofa Bisri

Invitation 211
   KH. Yahya Cholil Staquf and Rev. Dr. Frank Hinkelmann

Appendix 213

   Biographies 215
   Permissions and Credits 227

Introduction

"We Wish to Submit to the Dictates of Conscience"

Thomas K. Johnson and C. Holland Taylor

In August of 2014, leaders of the world's largest Muslim organization, Indonesia's Nahdlatul Ulama (NU), watched in stunned silence as members of ISIS marched Iraqi Shiites one by one to the edge of a dock, shot them in the head and toppled their lifeless bodies into the Tigris River. Rather than avert their gaze, for nearly two hours these spiritual leaders watched — with mounting shock, moral revulsion and sorrow — a series of ISIS videos that employed classical Islamic law to justify the brutal slaughter and destruction they depicted.

In a front-page story titled, "From Indonesia, a Muslim Response to the Ideology of the Islamic State," *The New York Times* reported on what these NU leaders did next.

> JAKARTA, Indonesia — The scene is horrifyingly familiar. Islamic State soldiers march a line of prisoners to a riverbank, shoot them one by one and dump their bodies over a blood-soaked dock into the water.
>
> But instead of the celebratory music and words of praise expected in a jihadi video, the soundtrack features the former Indonesian president, Abdurrahman Wahid, singing a Javanese mystical poem: "Many who memorize the Quran and Hadith love to condemn others as infidels while ignoring their own infidelity to God, their hearts and minds still mired in filth."
>
> That powerful scene is one of many in a 90-minute film that amounts to a relentless, religious repudiation of the Islamic State and the opening salvo in a global campaign by the world's largest Muslim group to challenge its ideology head-on.
>
> The challenge, perhaps surprisingly, comes from Indonesia, which has the world's largest Muslim population but which lies thousands of miles away from the Islamic State's base in the Middle East.
>
> "The spread of a shallow understanding of Islam renders this situation critical, as highly vocal elements within the Muslim population at large — extremist groups — justify their harsh and often savage behavior by claiming to act in accord with God's commands, although they are grievously mistaken," said A. Mustofa Bisri, the spiritual leader of the group, Nahdlatul Ulama...

"According to the Sunni view of Islam," he said, "every aspect and expression of religion should be imbued with love and compassion, and foster the perfection of human nature."

While NU leaders were systematically examining the methods (*minhaj*) whereby the Islamic State conducted warfare and governance — including its revival of crucifixion, slavery, tossing homosexuals from tall buildings and the execution of polytheists — the jihadi terror group launched a genocidal campaign against Yazidis on Mount Sinjar in northwestern Iraq. This attack came just weeks after the stunning conquest of Mosul and ISIS leader Abu Bakr al-Baghdadi's proclamation of an Islamic caliphate from the *mimbar* of that city's historic al-Nuri mosque. The Sinjar campaign — which entailed the execution of adult men and the mass enslavement of Yazidi women and children — shocked the conscience of the world. In a televised address on August 7, 2014, President Barack Obama announced that the United States would launch airstrikes in an attempt to stop the massacre:

> In recent days, Yazidi women, men and children from the area of Sinjar have fled for their lives. And thousands — perhaps tens of thousands — are now hiding high up on the mountain, with little but the clothes on their backs. They're without food, they're without water. People are starving. And children are dying of thirst. Meanwhile, ISIL forces below have called for the systematic destruction of the entire Yazidi people, which would constitute genocide. So these innocent families are faced with a horrible choice: descend the mountain and be slaughtered, or stay and slowly die of thirst and hunger.

A Systematic and Institutional Response to Crimes Against Humanity

NU leaders' profound concern about the weaponization of obsolete and problematic tenets of Islamic orthodoxy — not only by ISIS, but also by a wide range of state and non-state actors throughout the Muslim world — led them to establish the *Islam Nusantara* (East Indies Islam) movement in 2014; Humanitarian Islam in 2017; and the Movement for Shared Civilizational Values in 2020.

Not long after watching the ISIS videos, Kyai Haji Yahya Cholil Staquf — then-Secretary of the Nahdlatul Ulama Supreme Council — addressed hundreds of NU theologians in Magelang, Central Java, in November of 2014. He was accompanied by KH. A. Mustofa Bisri, Chairman of the NU Supreme

Council, and by KH. Abdul Ghofur Maemun, the head of Bahtsul Masa'il, a division of the NU Supreme Council. Members of Bahtsul Masa'il are prominent scholars whose knowledge and mastery of *fiqh* (classical Islamic law) qualifies them to issue authoritative rulings on matters related to Islamic jurisprudence.

This event in Magelang was captured in the NU-produced film profiled by *The New York Times*, called *Rahmat Islam Nusantara* (*The Divine Grace of East Indies Islam*). His voice filled with emotion, Mr. Staquf asked the Nahdlatul Ulama scholars who attended the historic gathering:

> How many mosques have they [ISIS] blown up? Think about how they destroyed the shrine of the Prophet Job [in Mosul]! And we keep hearing news about the destruction of tombs in Egypt and Libya where Companions of the Prophet were buried.
>
> Perhaps we have not yet witnessed, with our own eyes, our friends and neighbors being slaughtered. We have not yet witnessed, with our own eyes, our mosques being destroyed. We have not yet witnessed, with our own eyes, the graves of our saints and religious scholars being desecrated and destroyed by those people, but it's obvious, obvious! that they're working nonstop to reach us...
>
> What justifies their behavior? According to the rules of *fiqh* [classical Islamic law], their *imam* [political leader] has the right to choose: he may execute, he may ransom, he may enslave prisoners. This provision exists within *fiqh*.
>
> And if we may implement without questioning (*taqlid*) any provision of *fiqh* endorsed by [the authoritative, classical] *ulama*, then we may implement this provision also, and slaughter people like that, according to the rules of *fiqh* that still exist today. This is a problem. (See chapters 10 and 11 of this book.)

As NU leaders recognized, the actions and behavior of ISIS were reminiscent of the Wahhabi conquest of the Hejaz (Mecca and Medina) in 1924 – 1925. In fact, that earlier explosion of Islamist brutality spurred their ancestors to establish Nahdlatul Ulama — which means "Awakening of the Scholars" in Arabic — on January 31, 1926. The speech delivered by NU co-founder KH. Hasyim Asy'ari on that occasion was subsequently adopted by the NU as a statement of its fundamental principles (see chapter 5). In that speech, Kyai Asy'ari described

> a class of people who fall into the depths of strife (*fitnah*), choosing to embrace innovation rather than the Prophet's teachings (saw.), while the majority of believers are simply stunned into silence. And so the heretics and thieves run rampant. They pervert the truth in order to suit themselves, enjoining evil as if it were good and forbidding good as if it were evil. They call

others to follow their interpretation of God's book, even though their actions are not in the least bit guided by the teachings of the Qur'an.

On May 9 and 10, 2016, Nahdlatul Ulama held an International Summit of Moderate Islamic Leaders (ISOMIL) in Jakarta, Indonesia, attended by approximately 400 Muslim scholars from 30 nations. At the Summit's conclusion, the NU Central Board promulgated a 16-point declaration that identified the salient factors driving Islamist extremism and terror worldwide; called upon "people of good will of every faith and nation to join in building a global consensus not to politicize Islam"; and explicitly affirmed that the NU will "strive to consolidate the global *ahlussunnah wal jamaah* (Sunni Muslim) community, in order to bring about a world in which Islam, and Muslims, are truly beneficent and contribute to the well-being of all humanity" (*ISOMIL Nahdlatul Ulama Declaration*, points 15 and 16).

On May 12, 2016, Gerakan Pemuda Ansor (NU's five-million-member young adults movement) and Bayt ar-Rahmah (which helps coordinate the global expansion of NU activities) jointly sponsored the First Global Unity Forum, which was attended by Muslim, Catholic, Protestant, Hindu, Buddhist, and Jewish leaders. At the conclusion of the Forum, the Central Board of GP Ansor issued a three-page statement that called for "an end to conflict in the name of religion, and for qualified *'ulamā'* [Muslim religious scholars] to carefully examine and address those elements of *fiqh* [classical Islamic law] that encourage segregation, discrimination and/or violence towards those perceived to be 'non-Muslim.'"

On March 30, 2017, Gerakan Pemuda Ansor and Bayt ar-Rahmah announced the launch of a concerted effort to promote Humanitarian Islam (*al-islām lil-insānīyah*), by developing and operationalizing a global strategy to recontextualize the teachings of orthodox, authoritative Islam and thereby reconcile certain problematic elements of classical Islamic law (*fiqh*, sometimes conflated with *sharī'ah*, or "Divine Guidance") with the reality of contemporary civilization, whose context and conditions differ significantly from those in which classical Islamic law emerged.

On April 18, 2017, the 21st National Conference of GP Ansor issued a formal decree (Number 04/KONBES-XXI/IV/2017) entitled *Gerakan Pemuda Ansor's View Regarding the Republic of Indonesia's Strategic Interests and National Security Agenda within the Cauldron of Current Geopolitical Dynamics*. This decree states, in part, "the crisis that engulfs the Islamic world is not limited to armed conflicts raging in various and sundry regions. Whether conscious or not, willing or not, the world's 1.6 billion Muslims find themselves in the midst of a profound *religious* crisis. How they respond will determine the future not only of Muslims worldwide, but also of human civilization itself."

Ansor identified four key "areas of concern" that lie at the heart of the complex religious crisis afflicting the Muslim world, which qualified Islamic scholars need to address:

- Normative practices governing relations between Muslims and non-Muslims, including the rights, responsibilities and role of non-Muslims who live in Muslim-majority societies, and vice versa;
- Relations between the Muslim and non-Muslim world, including the proper aims and conduct of warfare;
- The existence of modern nation states and their validity — or lack thereof — as political systems that govern the lives of Muslims; and
- State constitutions and statutory laws/legal systems that emerged from modern political processes, and their relationship to *sharī'ah*.

On May 22, 2017, Gerakan Pemuda Ansor and Bayt ar-Rahmah hosted an international gathering of nearly 300 Muslim scholars at PP (*Madrasah*) Bahrul 'Ulum in Jombang, East Java, in order to "Develop a Strategy to Manifest Islam as a Genuine Blessing for Global Civilization." At the conclusion of this event, GP Ansor issued the *Gerakan Pemuda Ansor Declaration on Humanitarian Islam*, an 8,000-word document that examined the nature and purpose of religious norms (*maqāṣid al-sharī'ah*); analyzed the manner in which state and non-state actors "cynically manipulate religious sentiment in their struggle to maintain or acquire political, economic and military power... by drawing upon key elements of classical Islamic law (*fiqh*), to which they ascribe divine authority, in order to mobilize support for their worldly goals"; called for "the emergence of a truly just and harmonious world order, founded upon respect for the equal rights and dignity of every human being"; and laid out a detailed road map to address "obsolete tenets of classical Islamic law, which are premised upon perpetual conflict with those who do not embrace or submit to Islam."

On October 25, 2018, a coalition of international religious and political figures joined Nahdlatul Ulama leaders at the Second Global Unity Forum (GUF II) in Yogyakarta, Indonesia. The chairmen of Gerakan Pemuda Ansor and Bayt ar-Rahmah signed a joint resolution and decree adopting the *Nusantara Manifesto*, a 40-page document that provides a framework for the renewal of Islamic discourse and the development of *fiqh al-hadarah al-'alamiyah al-mutasahirah* — new tenets of Islamic law suited to the emergence of a single, interfused global civilization, based on cooperation rather than conflict. Explaining the significance of the *Manifesto*, GP Ansor Chairman H. Yaqut Qoumas said:

By adopting the *Nusantara Manifesto*, Ansor and Bayt ar-Rahmah are moving systematically, and institutionally, to address obsolete and problematic elements within Islamic orthodoxy that lend themselves to tyranny, while positioning these efforts within a much broader initiative to reject any and all forms of tyranny, and foster the emergence of a global civilization endowed with nobility of character. This call to nobility reflects the primary message of Islam, and of President Wahid, as demonstrated by the *Manifesto*.

GUF II participants of all faiths joined NU spiritual leaders in co-signing the *Nusantara Statement*, which contains the essence of the *Nusantara Manifesto* and reads:

> *We call upon people of goodwill*
> *of every faith and nation*
> *to join in building a global consensus*
> *to prevent the political weaponization of Islam,*
> *whether by Muslims or non-Muslims,*
> *and to curtail the spread of communal hatred*
> *by fostering the emergence of*
> *a truly just and harmonious world order,*
> *founded upon respect for the equal rights and dignity*
> *of every human being.*

On November 22, 2018, Mr. Qoumas announced the adoption of the *Statement* at a mass rally of over 100,000 Ansor members, and presented a commemorative steel plaque engraved with the *Nusantara Statement* to Indonesian President Joko Widodo, who raised it aloft for all to see. Addressing the multitude — who had gathered in commemoration of the birth of the Prophet Muhammad and National Heroes' Day — Indonesia's head of state urged Muslims to reflect more deeply upon the significance of the key Islamic teaching that God sent the Prophet Muhammad to be a source of universal love and compassion:

> As the people of the Prophet Muhammad, it is fitting that we follow his example. This includes developing noble character, fulfilling the mission of *rahmatan lil 'alamin* ("a blessing for all creation") and safeguarding the spirit of brotherhood among all elements of society — a fellowship that does not discriminate on the basis of religion, social status or political views.

In February of 2019, over 20,000 NU scholars and their followers from all 34 of Indonesia's provinces were joined by President Jokowi, members of his cabinet and prominent Islamic theologians from the Middle East at the

2019 National Conference of Nahdlatul Ulama Religious Scholars ("2019 Munas") held in Banjar, West Java. In a major break with Islamic conservatism, Nahdlatul Ulama abolished the legal category of infidels — those who do not adhere to Islam — which has long cast a shadow over the faith's relationships with other religions.

Furthermore, the 2019 Munas explicitly decreed that:

- The modern nation state is theologically legitimate.
- All citizens, irrespective of religion, ethnicity or creed, have equal rights and obligations.
- If it is concluded that any element of positive (i.e., statutory and/or regulatory) law contravenes the highest principles and purposes of religion, this should be — and may only be — corrected by constitutional means. The existence of such laws and regulations may not be employed as a justification for defying a legitimate government.
- Muslims have a religious obligation to foster peace rather than wage war on behalf of their co-religionists, whenever conflict erupts between Muslim and non-Muslim populations anywhere in the world.

These formal rulings, issued by Nahdlatul Ulama, have enormous potential consequences for Muslim and non-Muslim communities worldwide. They directly undermine the theological framework employed by ISIS, al-Qaeda and other Islamist movements to foster enmity and perpetrate violence against those perceived to be non-Muslim. Moreover, this extraordinary corpus of Islamic jurisprudence has emerged from a systematic and institutional process that constitutes the first wide-ranging, concerted and explicit act of theological renewal (i.e., reform) undertaken by a large body of Sunni Muslim authorities since the Middle Ages. (See chapters 12 through 16.)

HUMANITARIAN ISLAM AND THE WORLD EVANGELICAL ALLIANCE

This process of theological renewal has attracted attention and praise from journalists, academicians, policymakers, religious leaders and statesmen worldwide. Significant global actors who have established relationships with Humanitarian Islam include the world's largest political network, Centrist Democrat International (CDI), and its affiliate, the European

People's Party (EPP), whose member parties include 16 European heads of state and government; U.S. Secretary of State Michael Pompeo, who traveled to Jakarta in October 2020 to address the Humanitarian Islam movement; and both lay and clerical leaders within the Roman Catholic Church, including Pope Francis.

However, among the most striking — and perhaps, to some, most surprising — religious leaders who have sought to engage and partner with the Humanitarian Islam movement is the Right Reverend Dr. Thomas Schirrmacher, Secretary General & CEO of the World Evangelical Alliance (WEA). Founded in 1846, WEA is the largest international organization of evangelical churches, representing over 600 million Protestants and national evangelical alliances in 140 countries.

Dr. Schirrmacher's decision to engage with the Humanitarian Islam movement may prove to be singularly consequential, and perhaps even historic, in its ramifications for the relationship between Christians and Muslims, the world's two largest religious communities, and for world affairs more generally.

Bishop Schirrmacher is descended from Huguenots who fled religious persecution in France, and was raised in a family with a strong commitment to global Christian witness and mission. He has spent much of his life defending oppressed Christians around the world — an experience that both shaped his spirituality and brought him into contact with the WEA. During the Cold War, Dr. Schirrmacher secretly trained pastors in Communist East Germany. A long-time friend of Pope Francis, he is an ordained Bishop of Communio Messianica, an Anglican network of approximately one million "Muslim Background Believers" in 75 nations.

Prior to his inauguration as WEA's new Secretary General & CEO, Bishop Schirrmacher chaired the WEA's Theological Commission. He was deeply involved in producing *Christian Witness in a Multi-Religious World: Recommendations for Conduct,* a major statement jointly published by the World Council of Churches, the World Evangelical Alliance and the Vatican's Pontifical Council for Interreligious Dialogue, which together represent more than 90 percent of global Christianity. As reported by the *Huffington Post*:

> Recognizing the long and troubled history of conversion efforts, the statement called upon Christian missionaries to "reject all forms of violence... including the violation or destruction of places of worship, sacred symbols or texts." In addition, Christians need to "acknowledge and appreciate what is true and good" in other religions; any criticisms of another religion must be made "in a spirit of mutual respect."

In November of 2019, Dr. Schirrmacher led a delegation of senior WEA figures to meet with the leadership of Humanitarian Islam in Jakarta. This meeting resulted in the appointment of Rev. Dr. Thomas K. Johnson as WEA's Special Envoy for Engaging Humanitarian Islam and, at the suggestion of Dr. Schirrmacher, the establishment of a Humanitarian Islam/WEA Joint Working Group (JWG).

In a public statement announcing the formation of the JWG, released on April 10, 2020, Dr. Johnson and C. Holland Taylor, co-chairs of the Working Group, said:

> Many thoughtful observers have expressed concern about a renewed clash between Christian and Muslim civilizations and view every act of aggression between Muslims and Christians as another step in this direction. In these circumstances, the world needs to know that a major Christian body and a major Muslim body are not only at peace with one another, but they have pledged to actively cooperate for the betterment of humanity. Rather than being on opposing sides in a potential clash, Evangelical Christians and Humanitarian Muslims are committing to help protect each other's religious communities, guided by a moral compass that is rooted in universal ethics and values. This is not the peace of shared religious beliefs; it is the peace of compatible approaches to life in society.
>
> Though we may always understand God and relate to God in very different ways, Humanitarian Muslims and Evangelical Christians agree that human life, family, faith, reason and property are fundamental human goods essential to comprehensive well-being in this world. We know these human goods are vulnerable and require protection from various threats, including both religious extremism and forms of secular extremism that seek to marginalize or even eradicate the presence of religion in social and public life. We therefore pledge to work together to strengthen and advance those social and legal norms, including basic human rights and liberties, that are essential to safeguard these fundamental human goods. We also believe in the existence of universal ethical standards, which will inform and inspire our collaboration in the realms of theology, politics, conflict resolution and education, and in the pursuit of shared humanitarian goals.

In the same announcement, Dr. Schirrmacher stated:

> Even though the WEA has a large dialogue program with top Muslim leaders worldwide, we especially seek a close cooperation with those Muslim leaders and theologians who join us in fighting for human rights and against racism, religious extremism outside Islam, and religious extremism inside Islam, and any way to subordinate the State under any religious group. We have studied in depth the reasons why Indonesia takes a different and positive road in its

relation to religious minorities and are convinced that it would be helpful if Indonesia could present its experience to as many other states as possible.

Kyai Haji Yahya Cholil Staquf, General Secretary of the Nahdlatul Ulama Supreme Council and also a co-founder of the Joint Working Group, added his perspective on the emerging partnership between Humanitarian Islam and the WEA:

> We seek to lay the foundation for a peaceful and stable global civilization, and look forward to working with our friends from the World Evangelical Alliance to help bring this about. Certain obsolete and problematic tenets do indeed exist within Islamic orthodoxy and continue to shape the mindset of many Muslims. These problematic elements are the legacy of a past civilizational reality, which was characterized by persistent religious conflict. They are no longer relevant nor compatible with the geopolitical and demographic realities of the 21st century. Hence, we need to develop a new normative platform of religious orthodoxy, which does not legitimize hatred, supremacy and violence.

On February 27, 2021, Bishop Schirrmacher formally assumed leadership of the World Evangelical Alliance from outgoing WEA Secretary General Efraim Tendero of the Philippines. At a leadership handover ceremony broadcast live from Germany to evangelical Christians across the globe, Dr. Schirrmacher delivered his inaugural address as WEA Secretary General & CEO, emphasizing the fact that religious freedom is central to both the history of the World Evangelical Alliance and to evangelical theology itself. He stressed that, while the proper relationship between church and state remains a contested issue for evangelicals to this day, religious freedom and concern for persecuted believers has been integral to the WEA since its foundation.

From the WEA's theological perspective, noted Schirrmacher, religious freedom is not merely a political principle. Rather, it is integral to a proper understanding of God's love and His desire to be in a relationship with His creation. "God Himself wants to be loved, wants us to trust Him, wants our life," Schirrmacher said. "He does not want us to pray to Him because we are forced or because someone paid us or somebody cheated us. He wants our very trust, our very heart and our very love, and love is something that cannot be forced."

WEA was founded in 1846 by Anglican, Baptist, Methodist, and Congregationalist leaders from the British Isles, as well as by prominent European and American Protestant figures. From its founding, the WEA has promoted cooperation among Protestants in preaching the gospel, as well as in fostering religious tolerance, especially for members of minority religions. The WEA's origins may be traced to the "Second Great Awakening," which combined evangelical proclamation with sustained efforts to address social problems such as slavery, alcoholism, and prostitution. British citizens who joined in establishing the WEA emerged from the religious circles that promoted Britain's abolition of the slave trade in 1808 and the banning of slavery in much of the British Empire in 1833. As Queen Victoria's husband, Prince Albert, told 4,500 Christian abolitionists gathered for the Great Anti-slavery Meeting held at London's Exeter Hall in 1840:

> I deeply regret that the benevolent and persevering exertions of England to abolish the atrocious traffic in human beings have not led to a satisfactory conclusion. I sincerely trust that this great county will not relax in its efforts until it has finally and forever put an end to that state of things so repugnant to the principles of Christianity and to the best feelings of our nature. (*The Liberator*, June 26, 1840)

Like the WEA, Nahdlatul Ulama emerged from a unique tradition of religious freedom and tolerance. During the 16th century, the predecessors of Humanitarian Islam deftly employed soft and hard power to defeat Muslim extremists and restore freedom of religion for all Javanese, two centuries before the Virginia Statute of Religious Freedom and the Bill of Rights guaranteed the free exercise of religion in the United States.

On March 5, 2021, the Theological Commission of the WEA published a book by Dr. Thomas K. Johnson, called *Humanitarian Islam, Evangelical Christianity, and the Clash of Civilizations: A New Partnership for Peace and Religious Freedom*. The author's point of departure consists of urgent questions, whose answers underscore the significance of this unprecedented alliance between evangelical Christians and Humanitarian Islam. As stated on the book's back cover:

> Are Muslims and Christians locked in mortal combat forever? Will ever-continuing jihads and crusades continue to cost the lives of millions and destroy once-beautiful cities? Must the Muslim-Christian clash of civilizations, which started almost 1,500 years ago, continue into the future?
>
> Not necessarily, argues Dr. Johnson. Within Islam, a serious reconsideration is underway, broadly parallel to the reconsideration of church-state relations that happened during the early and mid-twentieth century within Christianity. This is leading to a new form of orthodox Islam that is fully compatible with multi-religious global society and that can move beyond conflict toward real cooperation with Christians and adherents of other religions. But this reconsideration, called "Humanitarian Islam," is still mostly found in Indonesia and is not yet well known in the rest of the

world. It is time for Christians to develop extensive interaction and cooperation with Humanitarian Islam. (See Part I of this book.)

As Paul Marshall, Wilson Distinguished Professor of Religious Freedom at Baylor University, observed in his endorsement of *Humanitarian Islam, Evangelical Christianity, and the Clash of Civilizations*:

> Indonesia has the largest Muslim population in the world, yet the country and its forms of Islam, especially Humanitarian Islam, are too little known. This is especially tragic since this may be the most important movement in the Islamic world, and it is engaged in active alliance with Christians and others. Here, Thomas K. Johnson gives us a clear, cogent, and crisp overview of its meaning and importance.

SHARED PRINCIPLES FOR HUMAN FLOURISHING

We believe that there is order to God's creation and that certain fundamental principles are woven into the very fabric of nature. Divinely ordained, these principles — which Muslims associate with the "Beautiful Names of God"; Western philosophers and theologians (both Roman Catholic and Protestant) have termed "natural law" or "universal moral law"; and C. S. Lewis described as "the Tao" — reflect God's infinite love, compassion, wisdom and justice. (See chapters 3 and 4.)

FIRST PRINCIPLES OF CONSCIENCE

When apprehended by human conscience, these "first principles" give rise to universal values that have long been articulated and embraced by the world's great cultural, religious and ethical traditions.

By understanding and acting in accord with these principles, one may develop noble character, or virtue, which the *Catechism of the Catholic Church* defines as "a habitual and firm disposition to do the good." This includes a duty to:

- Seek truth;
- Develop the self-discipline, and summon the courage, required to obey the dictates of conscience; and
- Choose to act justly and with compassion towards others.

"A new heart also will I give you, and a new spirit will I put within you: and I will take away the stony part out of your flesh and I will give you a heart of flesh."

~ Ezekiel 36:26

"Who shall ascend into the hill of the Lord? Or who shall stand in His holy place? He that hath clean hands, and a pure heart: who hath not lifted up his soul unto vanity, nor sworn deceitfully."

~ Psalm 24:3-4

"Thou shalt love the Lord thy God with all thy heart, and with all thy soul, and with all thy mind. This is the first and great commandment. And the second is like unto it, Thou shalt love thy neighbor as thyself. On these two commandments hang all the law and the prophets."

~ Matthew 22:37-40

"Do unto others as you would have them do unto you."

~ Mark 12:30

"My love and compassion embrace all things."

~ Qur'an, 7:156

"I have been sent only to perfect the moral framework of humanity."

~ Hadith, *Sahih Muslim*

"*Agama ageming aji* — (True) religion is a garment, worn by souls endowed with nobility."

~ Javanese proverb from *Serat Wédatama*, 1:1

"We wish to submit to the dictates of conscience."

~ Kyai Haji A. Mustofa Bisri

FIRST PRINCIPLES OF MORAL REASONING

The process of moral reasoning consists of intellectual deliberation informed by an alert and sensitive conscience, which conveys a sense of right and wrong and urges one to act accordingly.

Moral reasoning also requires a proper formation in the disciplines necessary thereto, which are imparted through a complex web of social institutions including the family, community, education and religion. These institutions give concrete form and vitality to the first principles of conscience, and are thus essential both to their application in particular contexts and to their being passed on from one generation to the next, in the form of moral codes.

The human rights project that emerged in the wake of World War II and the Holocaust — including the Universal Declaration of Human Rights, or UDHR — was founded upon these principles. As the Preamble of UDHR and its first article state:

> *Whereas recognition of the inherent dignity and of the equal and inalienable rights of all members of the human family is the foundation of freedom, justice and peace in the world,*
>
> *Whereas disregard and contempt for human rights have resulted in barbarous acts which have outraged the conscience of mankind, and the advent of a world in which human beings shall enjoy freedom of speech and belief and freedom from fear and want has been proclaimed as the highest aspiration of the common people,*
>
> *Whereas it is essential, if man is not to be compelled to have recourse, as a last resort, to rebellion against tyranny and oppression, that human rights should be protected by the rule of law,*
>
> *Whereas it is essential to promote the development of friendly relations between nations...*
>
> *Now, therefore,*
> *The General Assembly*
> *proclaims*
> *this Universal Declaration of Human Rights...*
>
> *Article 1: All human beings are born free and equal in dignity and rights. They are endowed with reason and conscience and should act towards one another in a spirit of brotherhood.*

The Universal Declaration of Human Rights is explicitly rooted in fundamental principles of conscience, reason and human dignity and thus embodies the accumulated wisdom of diverse cultures, civilizations, and religions throughout history.

The world's great ethical and religious traditions teach that human flourishing, both individual and collective, requires that reason obey the dictates of conscience and express itself in principled action.

To engage in sound moral reasoning and principled action, it is essential that human beings:

1. Discern the existence and nature of universal moral law (i.e., the principles of conscience);
2. Develop virtue, or noble character, which entails living in accord with the principles of conscience;
3. Respect one's own inherent dignity and that of others; and
4. Protect the fundamental goods and values essential to human flourishing.

Shared Values in Action

On October 1, 2020, the Executive Committee of the world's largest political network, Centrist Democrat International (formerly Christian Democrat International), unanimously adopted a resolution submitted by leaders of Indonesia's Humanitarian Islam movement. The resolution, explicitly premised upon the existence of "universal ethics and humanitarian values" (i.e., first principles), acknowledged that "virtue and noble character represent the only secure foundation upon which to build a peaceful and prosperous global civilization."

The text of the resolution merits quoting in full:

Resolution on promoting solidarity and respect among the diverse people, cultures and nations of the world

- Recognizing the widespread social isolation, economic hardship, despair, fear and anger triggered by the COVID-19 crisis in societies across the globe;
- Humbled by an awareness of our collective responsibility to this and future generations, and realizing that our actions today will shape the future, for good or ill;
- Realizing that some of the most profound advances in the human condition emerged in response to severe crises, including the horrors of pandemic, war and grave historical injustices, such as genocide and slavery, whose consequences continue to haunt us to the present day;
- Affirming that the Universal Declaration of Human Rights (UDHR) represents a significant contribution to the development of shared civilizational values that may unite the diverse people, nations and cultures of the world;

- Recalling that Western humanism and Christian democracy played a vital role in rebuilding Europe after the Second World War and in establishing the European Community;
- Lauding the historic role of St. Pope John XXIII, Jules Isaac, Jacques Maritain, John Courtney Murray and other spiritual and intellectual luminaries in shaping the Second Vatican Council, including its teaching on religious freedom (*Dignitatis humanae*) and on relations between different religious communities (*Nostrae aetate*);
- Acknowledging the U.S. Department of State's *Report of the Commission on Unalienable Rights* and its re-affirmation of the spirit and substance of fundamental human rights, including those articulated by UDHR;
- Recognizing that the universal values and aspirations expressed in these documents have long been articulated and embraced by the world's great cultural, religious and ethical traditions;
- Noting that the 6th-century BCE *Tao Te Ching* conveys a profound apprehension of the "Way" and how it is expressed through virtue, including humility, mercy and justice;
- Acknowledging that Ashoka's Edicts, created in 3rd-century BCE India, sprang from the aspiration to develop a society characterized by *dharma*, including universal compassion, justice and respect for the inherent dignity of all human beings;
- Recognizing that the foundational texts of the Humanitarian Islam movement represent a comprehensive affirmation of these universal values from within the Islamic tradition, including the principle of *rahmah* (universal love and compassion);
- Recalling the *Document on Human Fraternity*, signed by Pope Francis and Shaykh Ahmed el-Tayyeb of al-Azhar, which urges human beings to live a dignified and virtuous life by embracing a spirit of universal brotherhood and treating others with love and respect;
- Considering that these teachings originated among diverse cultures over thousands of years; embody the collective wisdom of humanity; reflect its aspiration to live in dignity and freedom; and underscore the need for societies to embrace universal ethics and humanitarian values if they are to avoid repeating the cataclysms of the past;
- Discerning that hatred of others — whether based upon ethnic, religious or ideological "tribalism" — is inimical to virtue and noble character, which represent the only secure foundation upon which to build a peaceful and prosperous global civilization;

- Realizing that scientific, technological and economic progress have brought civilization to our present cross-roads, with greater opportunity for advancement — or mass destruction — than ever before;
- Anticipating that the 21st century may witness the emergence of a truly global civilization, which offers an unprecedented opportunity for people of every faith and nation to cooperate in building a better life for themselves and their children;
- Concluding that in order to fulfill the promise of a just and noble civilization, we must promote solidarity and respect among the diverse people, cultures and nations of the world, so that the innate human will to dominate others — and the threat of tyranny posed by the nexus of dogmatism, political and economic power, and technology — do not lead, instead, to the dystopian future anticipated by George Orwell in his novel *1984*, with its memorable image of "a boot stamping on a human face — forever".

The CDI states the following:

- We call upon governments and civil society institutions to join in promoting solidarity and respect among the diverse people, cultures and nations of the world;
- We note that political and ideological polarization tends to create a false dichotomy between "conserving" and "progressing," when in fact these principles are intrinsically symbiotic by nature and essential to human flourishing;
- We urge opinion leaders in the fields of religion, education, popular culture, government, business and the media to advocate and promote the spirit of cooperation rather than conflict, within and between civilizations;
- We recommend that dialogue among the world's diverse peoples, cultures and religions employ the principle of "the highest common denominator," founded upon the noblest aspirations of every civilization;
- We resolve to build and bequeath to future generations a global civilization whose constituent elements retain their distinctive characteristics. To emerge and flourish, such a civilization must respect the equal rights and dignity of every human being and embody the principle of "harmony and unity amid diversity," as expressed in the mottos of the European Union (*In varietate concordia*) and the Republic of Indonesia (*Bhinneka Tunggal Ika*).

PART I

I

God Needs No Defense

KH. Abdurrahman Wahid

SUMMARY

In a 2007 *Wall Street Journal* article titled "The Last King of Java," Pulitzer Prize-winning American journalist Bret Stephens described Abdurrahman Wahid as "the single most influential religious leader in the Muslim world" and "easily the most important ally the West has in the ideological struggle against Islamic radicalism." Popularly known as "Gus Dur," Abdurrahman Wahid (1940 – 2009) was and remains one of the most influential religious and political figures in modern Indonesian history. In 1926 his paternal and maternal grandfathers established Nahdlatul Ulama — the world's largest Muslim organization — in direct response to the Wahhabi conquest of Mecca and Medina.

While serving as General Chairman of the Nahdlatul Ulama Executive Board, from 1984 to 1999, Gus Dur strove to renew (i.e., reform) Islamic discourse and thereby ensure that Islamic teachings and practice embody what he and Nahdlatul Ulama regard as the primary message of Islam: namely, *rahmah* (universal love and compassion). In the words of his *New York Times* obituary, Abdurrahman Wahid was "the single most important figure not merely in Indonesia's transition from Suharto's centralized autocracy to a decentralized democracy but in ensuring that the new democracy was committed to religious and ethnic pluralism."

The following article first appeared as the foreword to the book *Silenced: How Apostasy and Blasphemy Codes are Choking Freedom Worldwide* (Oxford University Press, 2011), by Nina Shea and Paul Marshall. President Wahid often employed the phrase "God needs no defense" to discredit Islamist extremism and rouse Indonesian Muslims to preserve their ancient traditions of religious pluralism and tolerance.

❖❖❖❖❖

As KH. A. Mustofa Bisri[1] wrote in his poem *Allahu Akbar*: "If all of the 6 billion human inhabitants of this earth, which is no greater than a speck of dust, were blasphemous... or pious... it would not have the slightest effect upon His greatness."

Omnipotent, and existing as absolute and eternal Truth, nothing could possibly threaten God. And as *ar-Rahman* (the Merciful) and *ar-Rahim* (the Compassionate), God has no enemies. Those who claim to defend God, Islam or the Prophet are thus either deluding themselves, or manipulating religion for their own mundane and political purposes, as we witnessed in the carefully manufactured outrage that swept the Muslim world several years ago, claiming hundreds of lives, in response to cartoons published in Denmark. Those who presume to fully grasp God's will, and dare to impose their own limited understanding of this upon others, are essentially equating themselves with God, and unwittingly engaged in blasphemy.

As Muslims, rather than harshly condemn others' speech or beliefs, and employing threats or violence to constrain these, we should ask: why is there so little freedom of expression, and religion, in the so-called Muslim world? Exactly whose interests are served by laws such as Section 295-C of the Pakistani legal code, "Defiling the Name of Muhammad," which mandates the death penalty for "blasphemy," which Pakistan's Federal Shari'a Court has effectively defined as:

> reviling or insulting the Prophet in writing or speech; speaking profanely or contemptuously about him or his family; attacking the Prophet's dignity and honor in an abusive manner; vilifying him or making an ugly face when his name is mentioned; showing enmity or hatred towards him, his family, his companions, and the Muslims; accusing, or slandering the Prophet and his family, including spreading evil reports about him or his family; defaming the Prophet; refusing the Prophet's jurisdiction or judgment in any manner; rejecting the Sunnah; showing disrespect, contempt for or rejection of the rights of Allah and His Prophet or rebelling against Allah and His Prophet.[2]

---

[1] Descended from a long line of charismatic religious leaders, Kyai Haji Mustofa Bisri heads the Raudlatuth Tholibin Islamic boarding school in Rembang, Central Java. Widely revered as a religious scholar, poet, novelist, painter and Muslim intellectual, K.H. Mustofa Bisri has strongly influenced the Nahdlatul Ulama's social, educational and religious development over the past thirty years.

[2] Mohammad Asrar Madani, *Verdict of Islamic Law on Blasphemy and Apostasy* (Lahore, Pakistan: Idara-e-Islamiat, 1994)

Rather than serve to protect God, Islam or Muhammad, such deliberately vague and repressive laws merely empower those with a worldly (i.e., political) agenda, and act as a "sword of Damocles" threatening not only religious minorities, but the right of mainstream Muslims to speak freely about their own religion without being threatened by the wrath of fundamentalists — exercised through the power of government or mobs — whose claims of "defending religion" are little more than a pretext for self-aggrandizement.

No objective observer can deny that Pakistani society — like so many others in the Muslim world — has undergone a process of coarsening under the influence of such laws, in tandem with the rise of religious extremism and the loss of true spirituality, without which the profound meaning and purpose of Islam remain veiled from human understanding.

The renowned Qur'anic injunction, "Let there be no compulsion in religion" (2:256), anticipated Article 18 of the Universal Declaration of Human Rights[3] by over 13 centuries, and should serve as an inspiration to Muslim societies today, guiding them on the path to religious freedom and tolerance.

In its original Qur'anic sense, the word *shari'a* refers to "the way," the path to God, and not to formally codified Islamic law, which only emerged in the centuries following Muhammad's death. In examining the issue of blasphemy and apostasy laws, it is thus vital that we differentiate between the Qur'an — from which much of the raw material for producing Islamic law is derived — and the law itself. For while its revelatory inspiration is divine, Islamic law is man-made and thus subject to human interpretation and revision.

For example, punishment for apostasy is merely the legacy of historical circumstances and political calculations stretching back to the early days of Islam, when apostasy generally coincided with desertion from the Caliph's army and/or rejection of his authority, and thus constituted treason or rebellion. The embedding (i.e., codification) of harsh punishments for apostasy into Islamic law must be recognized as an historical and political by-product of these circumstances framed in accordance with human calculations and expediency, rather than assuming that Islam, and *shari'a*, must forever dictate punishment for changing one's religion.

---

[3] "Everyone has the right to freedom of thought, conscience and religion; this right includes freedom to change his religion or belief, and freedom, either alone or in community with others and in public or private, to manifest his religion or belief in teaching, practice, worship and observance."

The historical development and use of the term *shari'a* to refer to Islamic law often leads those unfamiliar with this history to conflate man-made law with its revelatory inspiration, and to thereby elevate the products of human understanding — which are necessarily conditioned by space and time — to the status of divine.

Shari'a, properly understood, expresses and embodies perennial values. Islamic law, on the other hand, is the product of *ijtihad* (interpretation) which depends on circumstances (*al-hukm yadur ma'a al-'illah wujudan wa 'adaman*) and needs to be continuously reviewed in accordance with ever-changing circumstances, to prevent Islamic law from becoming out of date, rigid and non-correlative — not only with Muslims' contemporary lives and conditions, but also with the underlying perennial values of *shari'a* itself.

Throughout Islamic history, many of the greatest *fiqh* (Islamic jurisprudence) scholars have also been deeply grounded in the traditions of *tassawuf*, or Islamic mysticism, and recognized the need to balance the letter with the spirit of the law. The profoundly humanistic and spiritual nature of Sufi Islam facilitated the accommodation of different social and cultural practices as Islam spread from its birthplace in the Arabian Peninsula to the Levant, North Africa, the Sahel and Sub-Saharan Africa, Persia, Central and South Asia, and the East Indies archipelago. By many estimates, a majority of the Muslim population in most of these regions still practice a form of religious piety either directly or indirectly derived from Sufism. And the greatness of traditional Islamic art and architecture — from the wonders of Fes and Grenada, to Istanbul, Isfahan, Samarkand and Agra — bears testimony to the long line of Sufi masters, guilds and individual artists who strove to ennoble matter, so as to transform our man-made environment into "the veritable counterpart of nature, a mosaic of 'Divine portents' revealing everywhere the handiwork of man as God's vice-regent."[4]

Indeed, the greatness of classical Islamic civilization — which incorporated a humane and cosmopolitan universalism — stemmed largely from the intellectual and spiritual maturity that grew from the amalgamation of Arab, Greek, Jewish, Christian and Persian influences. That is why I wept upon seeing Ibn Rushd's commentary on the *Nicomachean Ethics* lovingly preserved and displayed, during a visit some years ago to Fes, Morocco. For if not for Aristotle and his great treatise, I might have become a Muslim fundamentalist myself.

---

[4] Seyyed Hossein Nasr in *Persia, Bridge of Turquoise* (New York: New York Graphic Society, 1975).

Among the various factors which have contributed to the long decline of Arab and Muslim civilizations in general, and greatly hindered their participation in the development of the modern world, was the triumph of normative religious constraints, which ultimately defeated the classical tradition of Islamic humanism. Absorption of "alien" influences — particularly in the realm of speculative thought, and the creation of individual, rational and independent sciences not constrained by religious scholasticism — was defeated by internal control mechanisms exercised by religious and governmental authorities, thus paralyzing Muslim societies.

These same tendencies are still on display in our contemporary world, not least in the form of severe blasphemy and apostasy laws that narrow the bounds of acceptable discourse in the Islamic world, and prevent most Muslims from thinking "outside the box" not only about religion, but about vast spheres of life, literature, science and culture in general.

RELIGIOUS UNDERSTANDING IS A PROCESS

Anyone who is sincere in understanding his or her faith necessarily undergoes a process of constant evolution in that understanding, as experience and insights give rise to new perceptions of the truth. For as God states in the Qur'an: "We will display Our Signs upon the horizon, and within themselves (humanity), until it is clear to them that God is the Truth (*al-Haqq*) (41:53).

Nothing that exists is self-sufficient, other than God. All living things are interdependent, and owe their very existence to God. Yet because God's creatures exist within time and space, their perceptions of truth and reality differ from one to the next, conditioned by their personal knowledge and experience.

As referenced above, Islam views the world and whatever information we may obtain from it, as signs leading to knowledge of God. Muslim scholars traditionally classify three stages of knowledge: *first*, the science of certainty (*'ilm al-yaqin*), which is inferential and concerns knowledge commonly held to be true, whether by scientists, intellectuals or *ulama* themselves. *Second*, the vision of certainty (*'ain al-yaqin*) represents a higher level of truth than the first. At this stage, one directly witnesses that information about an objective phenomenon is indeed true and accurate. *Third* is the truth or reality of certainty (*haqq al-yaqin*), i.e., truth which reaches the level of perfection through direct personal experience, as exemplified by a saint's mystical communion with God.

The fact that the Qur'an refers to God as "the Truth" is highly significant. If human knowledge is to attain this level of Truth, religious freedom is vital. Indeed, the search for Truth (i.e., the search for God) — whether employing the intellect, emotions or various forms of spiritual practice — should be allowed a free and broad range. For without freedom, the individual soul cannot attain absolute Truth... which is, by Its very nature, unconditional Freedom itself.

Intellectual and emotional efforts are mere preludes in the search for Truth. One's goal as a Muslim should be to completely surrender oneself (*islâm*) to the absolute Truth and Reality of God, rather than to mere intellectual or emotional concepts regarding the ultimate Truth. Without freedom, humans can only attain a self-satisfied and illusory grasp of the truth, rather than genuine Truth Itself (*haqq al-haqiqi*).

The spiritual aptitude of any given individual necessarily plays a key role in his or her ability to attain the Truth, while the particular expression of Truth apprehended by one person may differ from that of the next. Islam honors and values these differences, and religious freedom itself, recognizing that each human being comprehends God in accord with his or her own native abilities and propensities, as expressed in the *Hadith Qudsi*[5] "*Ana 'inda zann 'abdi bi,*" — "I am as my servant thinks I am." Of course, one's efforts to know God (*mujahadah*, from the same root as *jihad*) should be genuine and sincere (*ikhlas*), leading to a state of self-transcendence. In such a state, humans experience God's ineffable Presence and their own annihilation. Muslim fundamentalists often reject this notion, because of their shallow grasp of religion and lack of spiritual experience. For them, God must be understood as completely transcendent (*tanzih*) and far beyond the reach of humanity, with no hope for anyone to experience God's Presence. Such views are mistaken, for as the Qur'an itself states: "Whichever way you turn, there is the face of God" (2:115).

Nothing can restrict the Absolute Truth. Sufism — whose purpose is to bring Muslims to the third stage of knowledge, i.e., the truth and reality of certainty (*haqq al-yaqin*) — emphasizes the value of freedom and diversity, both as reflections of God's will and purpose, and to prevent the inadvertent or deliberate conflation of human understanding (which is inherently limited and subject to error) with the Divine. Faith (*îmân*) and surrender to God (*islâm*) on a purely intellectual level are not enough. Rather, a Muslim should continuously strive (*mujahadah*) to experience the actual Presence

---

[5] Muslims regard *Hadith Qudsi* as the words of God, repeated by Muhammad and recorded on the condition of an *isnad* (chain of verification by witness(es) who heard Muhammad say the hadith).

of God (*ihsan*). For without experiencing God's Presence, a Muslim's religious practice remains on a purely theoretical level; *islâm* has not yet become an experiential reality.

Sanctions against freedom of religious inquiry and expression act to halt the developmental process of religious understanding dead in its tracks — conflating the sanctioning authority's current, limited grasp of the truth with ultimate Truth itself, and thereby transforming religion from a path to the Divine into a "divinized" goal, whose features and confines are generally dictated by those with an all-too-human agenda of earthly power and control.

We can see this process at work in attempts by the Organization of Islamic Conferences (OIC), the United Nations General Assembly and the UN Council on Human Rights to restrict freedom of expression and institute a legally-binding global ban on any perceived criticism of Islam, to prevent so-called "defamation of religion." Whether motivated by sincere concern for humanity, or political calculation, such efforts are woefully misguided and play directly into the hands of fundamentalists, who wish to avoid all criticism of their attempts to narrow the scope of discourse regarding Islam, and to inter 1.3 billion Muslims in a narrow, suffocating chamber of dogmatism.

While hostility towards Islam and Muslims is a legitimate and vital concern, we must recognize that a major cause of such hostility is the behavior of certain Muslims themselves, who propagate a harsh, repressive, supremacist and often violent understanding of Islam, which tends to aggravate and confirm non-Muslims' worst fears and prejudices about Islam and Muslims in general.

Rather than legally stifle criticism and debate — which will only encourage Muslim fundamentalists in their efforts to impose a spiritually void, harsh and monolithic understanding of Islam upon all the world — Western authorities should instead firmly defend freedom of expression, not only in their own nations, but globally, as enshrined in Article 19 of the Universal Declaration of Human Rights.[6]

Those who are humble and strive to live in genuine submission to God (i.e., *islâm*), do not claim to be perfect in their understanding of the Truth. Rather, they are content to live in peace with others, whose paths and views may differ.

---

[6] "Everyone has the right to freedom of opinion and expression; this right includes freedom to hold opinions without interference and to seek, receive and impart information and ideas through any media and regardless of frontiers."

Defending freedom of expression is by no means synonymous with *personally* countenancing or encouraging disrespect towards others' religious beliefs, but it does imply greater faith in the judgment of God, than of man. Beyond the daily headlines of chaos and violence, the vast majority of the world's Muslims continue to express their admiration of Muhammad by seeking to emulate the peaceful and tolerant example of his life which they have been taught, without behaving violently in response to those who despise the Prophet, or proclaim the supremacy of their own limited understanding of the Truth. Such Muslims live in accordance with the Qur'anic verse which states, "And the servants of (Allah) the Most Gracious are those who walk in humility, and when the ignorant address them, they say 'Peace'" (25:63).

2

A Case for Ethical Cooperation Between Protestants and Humanitarian Muslims

Thomas K. Johnson

SUMMARY

In August of 2020, Dr. Thomas K. Johnson, the World Evangelical Alliance (WEA) Special Envoy to the Vatican and Special Envoy for Engaging Humanitarian Islam, published a seminal essay in WEA's flagship journal, *Evangelical Review of Theology*. His article described Humanitarian Islam as "a philosophically sophisticated response to some of the crucial questions of our era," which "fully accepts the existence of multiple religious communities within one country, with the hope that those communities and their members can flourish together." What follows is an extended version of that essay, which expands upon and further develops the original paper's key ideas.

On April 19, 2007, as I was preparing to teach a theology class for a low-visibility evangelical seminary in Turkey, I read an email and felt as if I had been kicked in the stomach. Terrorists had slit the throats of three men — two Turkish converts from Islam to Christianity, one German missionary. One of them had enrolled in my class. The motives of their murderers were a sinister mix of nationalist ideology and the desire to enforce an inhumane version of sharia, or Muslim law.

One could, if one wished, place this attack in the broader context of fourteen centuries of conflict between Muslims and Christians.[1] To me, such an assessment would be one-sided. The typical Muslim today, like the typical Christian, is sickened to see religion used to justify violence. But across history, both Islam and Christianity have often included notions of religiously defined empires, kingdoms, lands, and nations within their systems of ethics. This has contributed to involving religions in the conflicts among empires, as well as to countless instances of genocide, terrorism, and persecution.

We would be much better off if, on issues of social and political relations, Islam and Christianity were on the same side, offering a universal ethical compass enabling peace for all. I believe that such a radical step is achievable via a partnership between evangelical Christianity and an impressive intellectual movement known as Humanitarian Islam.

In this paper, I first discuss the inadequacy of some Muslim responses to Islamic extremism, followed by an explanation of why Humanitarian Islam is a preferable alternative. I then draw some comparisons to Christian ethics and close by suggesting how we can work together effectively — including one promising new collaboration.

WHY SOME MUSLIM RESPONSES TO EXTREMISM DO NOT GO FAR ENOUGH

In recent years, many Muslim theologians and jurists have been working hard to convince extremists to turn from their violent ways while explaining to the watching world why violence does not represent Islam. Three prominent responses have been the "Open Letter to Dr. Ibrahim Awwad Al-Badri, alias 'Abu Bakr Al-Baghdadi,' and to the fighters and followers of the self-declared 'Islamic State'" published by 126 Sunni leaders in September 2014; the Marrakesh Declaration of 2016; and the 2019 Document on Human Fraternity (DHF) signed in Abu Dhabi by Pope Francis and the Grand Imam of Al-Azhar.

These documents directly confront and condemn violence in the name of Islam; if these principles were followed, our world would be far less violent. This is significant. However, these recent Muslim statements also perpetuate some convictions that undermine their potential to reduce global conflict and local tragedies. For example, the Open Letter of 2014 (in

---

[1] Raymond Ibrahim, *Sword and Scimitar: Fourteen Centuries of War between Islam and the West* (Hachette Books: Kindle Edition, 2018).

2. A Case for Ethical Cooperation

paragraph 22) directly affirms the obligation of Muslims to form a new caliphate, even while rejecting ISIS's use of morally repugnant means to establish a caliphate. Such a perceived obligation, a central cause of conflict among Muslims as well as between Islam and others, has been perpetuated, not resolved, by the Open Letter.

Likewise, the Marrakesh Declaration of 2016, though rejecting violence in the name of Islam and calling for the development of a Muslim doctrine of citizenship that applies to people of other religions, clearly affirms the notion of "Muslim countries." In a Muslim country, minorities may be tolerated, and citizenship may increase their level of toleration, but non-Muslims will always be regarded and treated as something less than full stakeholders in a country that officially describes itself as Muslim. It seems as if the Marrakesh doctrine of a Muslim country is a smaller version of the same Muslim doctrine of which the Caliphate is the larger version. It does not affirm true freedom of religion.

The 2019 DHF blends important themes in Roman Catholic and Sunni Muslim ethical teaching in a manner that is designed to be understood by followers of either religion or of no religion. It begins to address the problems related to minority religions and citizenship which were identified in the Marrakesh Declaration. The DHF could be a valuable tool for moral instruction in some circumstances; it has the added value of clarifying international and interfaith ethical standards for many areas of public life, though some will suspect that this text implies an ultimate equivalence of religious beliefs.[2] Despite these significant steps forward, the DHF does not explicitly address the problem of the religiously defined state, whether one has a Christian country or a Muslim country in view. By ignoring this topic, the text may unintentionally perpetuate second-class citizenship for adherents of minority religions. And the DHF does not address the explosive issue of how to treat people who convert from one religion to another.

Some recent Muslim statements on public life, such as those just discussed, make passing reference to the 1948 United Nations Universal Declaration of Human Rights (UDHR). However, UDHR article 18, which is painfully explicit about the freedom to convert to a different religion, is seldom quoted. It states, "Everyone has the right to freedom of thought,

---

[2] For example, the DHF claims, "The pluralism and the diversity of religions, color, sex, race and language are willed by God in His wisdom, through which He created human beings." Many Christians would feel unable to say without qualification that "God willed the diversity of religions." Recognition of the similarities of ethical teaching across faith traditions should be balanced by a recognition of the ultimate incompatibility of some claims of those traditions.

conscience and religion; this right includes freedom to change his religion or belief, and freedom, either alone or in community with others and in public or private, to manifest his religion or belief in teaching, practice, worship and observance." If UDHR 18 were fully understood, affirmed, and practiced, it would not only end the persecution of converts; it would also mean the gradual end of religiously defined countries (whether Muslim, Christian, Hindu, Jewish, or Buddhist). No country that consistently protects the freedom to change religions, including freedom to develop the institutions of the newly adopted religions, can expect to consistently affirm its long-term identity as a state belonging to one religion.

HUMANITARIAN ISLAM

One exceptionally large Muslim movement is quite different from those discussed above. It robustly affirms the UDHR (including article 18) and rejects the notion of a Muslim country or caliphate. Its theory of ethics directly and constructively addresses the reality of religiously pluralistic societies. The main voices in this movement are leaders in the world's largest Muslim organization, the Indonesia-based Nahdlatul Ulama (NU). Their perspective, called "Humanitarian Islam," has spawned many publications in English for the international community, especially since ISIS declared its caliphate in 2014.

A careful examination of the ethics of Humanitarian Islam finds that Muslims of this type, when following their own principles, support religious freedom and human rights for Christians and people of other faiths. But their ethic goes much further. Though presented largely as a Muslim alternative to extremist violence, Humanitarian Islam contains a serious assessment of universal moral norms, the relation between faith and reason, fundamental human goods, the laws (both civil and religious) needed to protect those human goods, and the role of religions in societies.

Within the spectrum of varieties of Islam, the Indonesian Humanitarians represent the opposite end from the violent extremists. They present themselves as fully orthodox Muslims, not secularized half-Muslims. Precisely as such, they fully endorse classical human rights, religious freedom for other religions, and constitutional democracy, while openly naming and repudiating "obsolete and problematic tenets" of Muslim orthodoxy which, they claim, have been misused to promote extremism.[3]

---

[3] For example, in February 2019, NU leaders decreed that the term "infidel" no longer be used to describe people who are not Muslims, suggesting that the term "citizen" be used as a replacement. For the political context, see "NU Calls for End

2. A Case for Ethical Cooperation 33

The representatives of Humanitarian Islam believe that Islamic extremists — from ISIS to the Wahhabis of Saudi Arabia — have been misusing Islam for their own purposes and that this misuse of religion has been supported by versions of Muslim doctrine which were contextualized many centuries ago in a radically different situation. In their May 2017 *Declaration on Humanitarian Islam*[4] they write, "Various actors — including but not limited to Iran, Saudi Arabia, ISIS, al-Qaeda, Hezbollah, Qatar, the Muslim Brotherhood, the Taliban and Pakistan — cynically manipulate religious sentiment in their struggle to maintain or acquire political, economic and military power, and to destroy their enemies. They do so by drawing upon key elements of classical Islamic law (*fiqh*), to which they ascribe divine authority, in order to mobilize support for their worldly goals" (para 28).

Therefore, the *Declaration on Humanitarian Islam* says, "If Muslims do not address the key tenets of Islamic orthodoxy that authorize and explicitly enjoin such violence, anyone — at any time — may harness the orthodox teachings of Islam to defy what they claim to be the illegitimate laws and authority of an infidel state and butcher their fellow citizens, regardless of whether they live in the Islamic world or the West." As an alternative, NU seeks to establish a new Islamic orthodoxy that addresses the problematic tenets of medieval Islamic teaching which extremists claim to be orthodox.

Precisely as Muslims, the Humanitarians claim that the extremists do not reflect the best of Islam. The core of their argument is that Islam has a tradition of developing the application of Muslim ethics and law by means of interaction with changing cultures, but that this process stopped several centuries ago, leaving many Muslims bound to an ossified and conflict-producing version of Sharia that is not tenable in a global, pluralistic society. In contrast, truly orthodox Islam contains within itself its own proper theological and legal method that leads to a humanitarian, pro-democracy position, including promoting religious freedom for all and signaling the end of religiously defined countries. Humanitarian Islam seeks to reactivate this authentically Muslim theological method to develop a truly new and more fully orthodox Islam, thereby displacing

---

to Word 'Infidels' to Describe Non-Muslims," *Jakarta Post*, March 1, 2019, https://www.thejakartapost.com/news/2019/03/01/nu-calls-for-end-to-word-infidels-to-describe-non-muslims.html

[4] *Gerakan Pemuda Ansor Declaration on Humanitarian Islam: Towards the Recontextualization of Islamic Teachings, for the Sake of World Peace and Harmony Between Civilizations* (Bayt ar-Rahmah, May 2017), https://baytarrahmah.org/2017_05_22_ansor-declaration-on-humanitarian-islam/

the outdated version of Islam that is fueling many conflicts and possibly a global clash of civilizations.

As Humanitarian Islam explains, "Islamic orthodoxy contains internal mechanisms, including the science of *uṣūl al-fiqh* — the methodology of independent legal reasoning employed to create Islamic law, or *fiqh* (often conflated with *sharī'ah*) — that allow Muslim scholars to adjust the temporal elements of religious orthodoxy in response to the ever-changing circumstances of life. These internal mechanisms entail a process of independent legal reasoning known as *ijtihād*, which fell into disuse among Sunni Muslim scholars approximately five centuries ago" (*Nusantara Manifesto* para 106).[5] As they see it, for some 500 years the proper Muslim theological method, the "internal mechanism" for the unfolding of Muslim orthodoxy, has not been properly implemented, leading to the debacle of the role of Islam on the global stage and leaving their thought leaders with a lot of unfinished homework.

THE THEOLOGICAL METHOD OF HUMANITARIAN ISLAM

Four themes characterize the distinctive theological method used by Humanitarian Islam in its systematic effort to define a new Islamic ethics and theory of law. Each is discussed below.

1. Humanitarian Islam sharply distinguishes eternal, unchanging ethical and legal norms from contingent norms that are limited in their relevance to a particular time and situation.

The *Declaration on Humanitarian Islam* says, "Religious norms may be universal and unchanging — e.g., the imperative that one strive to attain moral and spiritual perfection — or they may be 'contingent,' if they address a specific issue that arises within the ever-changing circumstances of time and place. As reality changes, contingent — as opposed to universal — religious norms should also change to reflect the constantly shifting circumstances of life on earth" (paras 3 and 4). Humanitarian Islam claims that the current crisis of Islam arises from taking contingent norms from previous centuries, whether the seventh century or the Middle Ages, and applying them in the twenty-first century as if they were eternal, unchanging norms. This leads to a horrendous misperception of Islamic religious rules, both by Islamist extremists and by the enemies of Islam.

---

[5] *Nusantara Manifesto* (Bayt ar-Rahmah, October 2018), https://baytarrahmah.org/2018_10_25_nusantara-manifesto/

The eternal norms cited by Humanitarian Islam are general principles of morally sensitive behavior. For example, they emphasize the need "to revitalize the understanding and practice of religion as *rahmah* (universal love and compassion)" in contrast with hatred and violence (*Manifesto* para 7). They continue, "Noble behavior entails acting with compassion and treating others with respect" (para 61). As a dimension of respect for others, they repeatedly mention the UDHR (for example, para 132).

2. This hermeneutic for properly applying religious norms is related to a transcendental definition of the sharia, not a concrete or specific definition of the sharia.

Because of the complex origin of sharia in the Koran, in the early Muslim tradition, and in the interpretations of classical Muslim theology, sharia does not have an historically given source or definition found in one particular text. Nevertheless, among several strands of Islam, the perception of a single, firmly established form of sharia is great enough that several countries have attempted to fully implement a specific set of laws that they call "the sharia," even if the historical claim, that this is the true sharia, is questionable. For example, in recent years Sudan, Pakistan, Libya, parts of Nigeria, the Aceh province of Indonesia, some regions in the Philippines, and Yemen have implemented sharia law to strictly enforce such matters as women's dress, punishment for blasphemy or apostasy, corporal punishment, stoning for adultery, and even cutting off limbs.[6]

Humanitarian Islam decries this practice as the false application of contingent religious norms from a previous era to the current situation. Instead, the term "sharia," which the Humanitarians use sparingly, is applied to eternal principles that exist outside time and space. They see sharia as transcendent moral values leading to God (and protecting creation) that have to be applied anew in every situation, not as specific laws that can be enforced by a police officer.

The *Nusantara Manifesto* (2018) includes an essay by Abdurrahman Wahid (1940 – 2009), president of Indonesia from 1999 to 2001, called "God Needs No Defense," as an official appendix. Wahid writes, "Shari'a, properly understood, expresses and embodies perennial values. Islamic law, on the other hand, is the product of *ijtihad* (interpretation) which depends on circumstances and needs to be continuously reviewed in accordance with ever-changing circumstances, to prevent Islamic law from becoming out of date, rigid and non-correlative — not only with Muslims'

---

[6] Christine Schirrmacher, *The Sharia: Law and Order in Islam*, trans. Richard McClary, ed. Thomas K. Johnson (Bonn: World Evangelical Alliance, 2013), p. 24; https://iirf.eu/journal-books/global-issues-series/the-sharia-law-and-order-in-islam/

contemporary lives and conditions, but also with the underlying perennial values of shari'a itself." In other words, Islam cannot merely copy a law code from a previous era; perennial and eternal values have to be applied in every generation, for which a clear theological and legal method is needed.

Wahid assumes that in some instances, religious law as taught today, based on contingent interpretations from a previous era, would contradict a proper contingent interpretation or application of the perennial values of the eternal, higher sharia to our era. For example, anti-blasphemy or anti-apostasy laws, which may have been proper applications of the eternal sharia in a previous socio-political situation, might themselves become blasphemous in our era because they attempt to defend God in ways that are inappropriate in a multi-religious society.

Such a definition of sharia, if followed by the global Muslim movement, would undermine many reasons for Islamophobia, since it would shift the discussion of the religious ethics of public life away from, for example, the proper way to execute blasphemers and toward a principled discussion of what constitutes human goods and what types of religious and civil laws would serve to protect the primary human goods. People from different religious communities and cultures might have different opinions, but the discussion of human goods and the proper ways to protect human goods would constitute civil public discourse, not an endless war.

3. In its social doctrine, Humanitarian Islam has appropriated and approved selected principles of Indonesian civilization which it views as predating the arrival of Islam.

The Humanitarian Islam movement believes that important moral and political principles that have long existed in Nusantara culture (the historical culture of the Malay Archipelago) merit new application today. In fact, for them, Nusantara culture provides the filter (hermeneutic) through which Islam and other religions can be understood, evaluated, and applied. Clearly, anyone who takes such a stance is already committed to accepting religious pluralism, because he or she has consciously utilized cultural norms and values related to multiple religious traditions.

The *Nusantara Manifesto* concludes with a ringing endorsement of the Indonesian constitutional principle of Pancasila (which affirms humanitarian unity despite diversity), including officially recognizing several religions, which is a specific rejection of Muslim theocratic visions. Humanitarian Muslims are not shy about recommending Nusantara culture to the world. Indeed, in the *Declaration of Humanitarian Islam*, they even suggest that their experience can serve as a "pilot project" for a multi-religious nation-state (para 19).

4. Humanitarian Islam accepts the moral legitimacy of selected socio-political developments of the last two centuries.

The *Nusantara Manifesto* identifies four key social and political developments which make our world different from that of previous centuries: "(1) A complete transformation of the global political order; (2) fundamental changes in demography; (3) evolving societal norms; and (4) globalization, driven by scientific and technological developments that enable mass communications, travel and the emergence of a tightly integrated world economy" (para 108).

Until 200 years ago, and to a large extent even 100 years ago, much of the world's population lived in kingdoms or empires in which there was a supposed unity of a majority religion and the ruling power, though minority religions may have been tolerated. Within Europe, this was described as the "unity of throne and altar." Today most empires have passed away, having been replaced by nation-states that contain millions of immigrants of all religions and cultures, with those populations and states connected by intergovernmental organizations (such as the UN) and international businesses. The age of religiously defined empires, whether in Asia, Europe, Turkey, or the Middle East, is long gone.

Therefore, for Humanitarian Islam, any desire to return to a caliphate or a religiously defined country, as displayed by Muslim extremism, is an impossible desire to return to a previous era and can lead only to conflict, destruction, and death. Instead, Muslims should fully accept a different relationship between religion and society, including a critical endorsement of some societal transitions such as those mentioned.

Importantly, Humanitarian Islam accepts only *selected* socio-political developments of modern global society. It does not endorse atheism, moral relativism, or hyper-individualism. Though religious pluralism is expected, Humanitarian Islam does not call on governments or schools to ignore religious values, practices, and communities. Rather, it believes that people's lives should be shaped by the teachings of their religious communities. The movement fully accepts the existence of multiple religious communities within one country, with the hope that those communities and their members can flourish together.

A Christian Response to Humanitarian Islam

Our Muslim friends have set a very high goal, that of a new and truly orthodox Islam; I hope they can freely pursue their dreams. It is a philosophically sophisticated response to some of the crucial questions of our era.

Theologically, Christian ethics claims to differ in one crucial way from Islam. As the apostle John said, "For the law was given through Moses; grace and truth came through Jesus Christ" (John 1:17). This relationship between law and grace underlies everything we do as Christians. Law is God's command about what to do or not do; grace is his provision of undeserved acceptance and forgiveness in Jesus Christ as proclaimed in the gospel.[7] In contrast, Islam is generally seen as containing a much heavier emphasis on law than on grace, although hints of the latter occur occasionally, such as in the well-known saying attributed to Muhammad, that God's throne bears the inscription "My mercy precedes my wrath." This is obviously an all-important issue for Christians, who believe that the grace that came through Jesus Christ is our only hope of salvation and that we cannot be saved by any amount of obedience to law.

Despite this central theological difference, a comparison of Humanitarian Islam with Christian social ethics and philosophy of law reveals that, amid today's great global threats, we are ideological allies and should treat each other as such. Even though the theological differences between Christians and Muslims may never be resolved, our level of agreement in the spheres of ethics and law calls for global cooperation in the public square. Rather than taking opposite sides, evangelical Christians and Humanitarian Muslims should help to protect each other's religious communities and to articulate and embody a global moral compass.

Moreover, reflecting on the themes expressed by Humanitarian Islam can help us understand key aspects of Christian ethics and how they relate to Muslim thinking more clearly. I will mention three points.

1. A Christian hermeneutic on the law distinguishes among God's moral, ceremonial, and judicial laws, all of which are found in the Bible. This distinction has both similarities to and differences from the distinction made by Humanitarian Islam between eternal norms and contingent norms.

As the Westminster Confession of 1646 states:

---

[7] For more on the relation between law and gospel in Protestant thought, see Thomas K. Johnson, "Law and Gospel: The Hermeneutical and Homiletical Key to Reformation Theology and Ethics," *Evangelical Review of Theology* 43, no. 1 (2019); https://www.academia.edu/38262994/Law_and_Gospel_Luther_and_Calvin

"Beside this law, commonly called *moral*, God was pleased to give to the people of Israel, as a church under age, *ceremonial laws*, containing several typical ordinances, partly of worship, prefiguring Christ, his graces, actions, sufferings, and benefits; and partly, holding forth divers instructions of moral duties. All which ceremonial laws are now abrogated, under the new testament. To them also, as a body politic, he gave sundry *judicial laws*, which expired together with the State of that people."[8]

A few Christians have questioned this threefold hermeneutic, but it has received widespread support. With slight variations, it was used during the Reformation by John Calvin (1509 – 1564) and in medieval Christian ethics by Thomas Aquinas (1225 – 1274), both of whom regarded it as a common distinction long known to Christians. Calvin and Aquinas assumed the similar distinctions used by Augustine (354 – 430) and Justin Martyr (circa 100 – 165); indeed, one of the earliest Christian books after the New Testament, the Epistle of Barnabas, sharply contrasts the moral and ceremonial laws (compare chapters 2 and 19). Jonathan Bayes argues that this hermeneutic was already used in some Old Testament passages, such as Proverbs 21:3: "To do righteousness and justice is more acceptable to the Lord than sacrifice." For Bayes, righteousness refers to the demands of the moral law, whereas justice refers to the demands of the judicial law, while sacrifices were in the realm of the ceremonial law.[9]

This three-part hermeneutic has guided most Christians to view blasphemy or adultery as against God's moral law but to steer clear of punishing blasphemers or adulterers with death, even though the theocratic nation of Israel sometimes applied capital punishment to these offenders. At times, Christians have indeed enforced anti-blasphemy laws, even to the point of executing those accused. This was wrong and based on an improper hermeneutic. Almost all Christians have repented of this sin, even if not all have consciously adopted a better hermeneutic. There is much to learn from ancient ceremonial and judicial laws, but we do not teach Christians to obey them directly. In contrast, the moral laws remain crucial for Christian living today.

2. The whole undertaking of Humanitarian Islam entails an appeal to a universal moral norm which they expect both Muslims and non-Muslims to recognize, even if the source and nature of this norm are not yet always fully articulated. This is what Christians call the "natural moral law."

---

[8] *Westminster Confession of Faith*, chapter 19, paragraphs 3 and 4; emphasis added.
[9] Jonathan F. Bayes, *The Threefold Division of the Law*, The Christian Institute, 2017, https://www.christian.org.uk/wp-content/uploads/the-threefold-division-of-the-law.pdf

When people argue, they inevitably appeal, perhaps implicitly, to a moral norm by which everyone's actions may be evaluated. When the people involved share the same religion, they may refer to a religious text, such as the Bible or the Koran. If they do not, the norm referenced may be less explicit; nevertheless, it is crucial. Normal people seldom say, "There are no standards, so do what you want." Rather, we are implicitly claiming, "According to the standards which we both know, I am right and you are wrong."[10] This unwritten standard is traditionally called "the natural moral law," or sometimes simply "natural law."

Within Christian theology, the natural moral law has been regarded as a part of creation, with the result that humans can hardly avoid distinguishing between right and wrong and almost necessarily make similar assumptions about right and wrong (even though they sometimes deny this knowledge, as Paul states in Romans 1). Christian theology also regards the natural moral law as a prominent theme in God's ongoing "general revelation," or God's speech to humanity which comes to all people through his creation. (God's general revelation is usually contrasted with God's "special revelation," which was given in Christ and Holy Scripture.)

The natural moral law is so strongly assumed in the Bible that the assumption is rarely clarified. Such clarifications typically arise when believers do something which their pagan neighbors properly regard as wrong, showing that unbelievers sometimes respond to the moral law better than do believers. A painful example is when Pharaoh followed principles protecting marriage and truth-telling and confronted Abram for not following such principles (Genesis 12:10–20).

In the twentieth century, some Protestant theologians mistakenly claimed that we cannot know God's natural law; some said we should not even mention the topic. This fatal mistake threatens the soul of civilization, because it removes any explanation of why people of all religions or no religion can distinguish right from wrong, thus eliminating any conceptual basis for ethical agreement between Christians and non-Christians.[11] To take an extreme example, if there were no universal

---

[10] This analysis of moral discourse is heavily dependent on C. S. Lewis, especially *Mere Christianity* (rev. ed. London and Glasgow: Collins, 1952), pp. 15–26. For an assessment of Lewis on this topic, see Thomas K. Johnson, *Natural Law Ethics: An Evangelical Proposal*, Christian Philosophy Today vol. 6 (Bonn: VKW, 2005), pp. 85–105, https://www.academia.edu/36884239/Natural_Law_Ethics_An_Evangelical_Proposal

[11] See Thomas K. Johnson, "The Rejection of God's Natural Moral Law: Losing the Soul of Western Civilization," *Evangelical Review of Theology* 43, no. 3 (2019),

2. A Case for Ethical Cooperation 41

moral law, and there were only the rules taught by particular religious communities, it would be very difficult conceptually to claim that genocide is wrong, unless one is talking to fellow members of one's religious community.

There is wisdom in the observations of Aristotle, the oft-cited hero of both Humanitarian Islam and of many generations of writers about Christian ethics:

> It will now be well to make a complete classification of just and unjust actions. We may begin by observing that they have been defined relatively to two kinds of law... By the two kinds of law I mean particular law and universal law. Particular law is that which each community lays down and applies to its own members: this is partly written and partly unwritten. Universal law is the law of Nature. For there really is, as everyone to some extent divines, a natural justice and injustice that is binding on all men, even on those who have no association or covenant with each other.[12]

Similar ideas were taught by many classical philosophers, including the Aristotelians, Platonists, and Stoics, in contending against moral relativism, represented in the ancient world by the skeptics, sophists, and Epicureans. All the participants in these ancient discussions knew that different communities have different particular laws and moral rules, which raised the question of whether there is a universal moral law that is binding on all people and communities. The relativists claimed that there are no universal moral rules or legal principles, only ethical rules and civil laws that are established by particular communities. Aristotle argued that there are moral and legal principles which are binding on all people simply because they are human; these laws are binding because of the inherent authority of the laws (the nature of those laws), not because they are authorized by a community. To repeat Aristotle, there is "a natural justice and injustice that is binding on all men, even on those who have no association or covenant with each other."[13] This law is binding on all people because of its

---

https://www.academia.edu/39590583/The_Rejection_of_Gods_Natural_Moral_Law_Losing_the_Soul_of_Western_Civilization

[12] Aristotle, *Rhetoric*, Book 1, chapter 13, trans. W. Rhys Roberts; ed. Lee Honeycutt (Alpine Lakes Design, 2011), https://web.archive.org/web/20150213075009/http:/rhetoric.eserver.org/aristotle/rhet1-13.html

[13] I share the opinion of Richard Tarnas, that much of classical philosophy was a complex attempt to overcome the nihilism that was perceived to arise from religious syncretism (especially polytheism) and moral relativism. See Tarnas, *The Passion of the Western Mind: Understanding the Ideas That Have Shaped Our World View* (Ballantine Books, 1993).

nature as a universal moral law, not because people belong to a particular community (an association or covenant in Aristotle's words).

When the Christian message came into contact with the ideas of the Greco-Roman world, the apostle Paul followed the Hebrew Bible and sided with the natural-law theorists against moral relativism. He wrote, "When Gentiles, who do not have the law, do by nature things required by the law, they are a law for themselves, even though they do not have the law. They show that the requirements of the law are written on their hearts, their consciences also bearing witness, and their thoughts sometimes accusing them and at other times even defending them" (Romans 2:14–15). In this way, early Christianity adopted the moral philosophy of the Old Testament (of which the account of the Pharaoh and Abraham in Genesis is one of many examples) and contextualized it in the terminology of the Roman Empire.

The church fathers of the first four centuries usually summarized the demands of the natural law in the Golden Rule: do unto others as you would have them do to you. For example, Augustine wrote, "There is also a law in the reason of a human being who already uses free choice, a law naturally written in his heart, by which he is warned that he should not do anything to anyone else that he himself does not want to suffer; all are transgressors according to this law, even those who have not received the law given through Moses."[14]

Both Aristotle and Augustine taught the doctrine of natural law, but for different purposes. Aristotle pointed to the universal moral law as a basis for a civilized society, assuming the existence of many communities and cultures with their particular laws, but he did not mention God as its source; Augustine preached that all people are accountable to God, even if they do not yet acknowledge God.[15]

In the centuries after Augustine, within Europe and the Mediterranean basin, Christianity grew from a persecuted minority to become the majority religion, sometimes even the official religion. This prompted a discussion within Christian ethics of the relation between the universal moral law and the civil or human laws of particular countries. Consequently, the perceived threats to a humane religious and social life came not so much from moral relativism and cultural diversity as from the church and the state (or states) alternately seeking absolute power. Two different types of tyranny threatened human flourishing.

---

[14] Augustine, Letter 157, paragraph 15; found in Augustine, *Works*, Part 2, Volume 3, Letters 156–210, trans. Roland John Teske, ed. Boniface Ramsey and John E. Rotelle (New City Press, 1990), p. 25.
[15] Ibid.

2. A Case for Ethical Cooperation

In his "Treatise on Law," the great medieval thinker Thomas Aquinas distinguished four types of law in a manner intended to overcome both moral relativism, on the one hand, and religious and political absolutism on the other hand. The four types are (1) eternal law, which is a universal idea that has always existed in the mind of God and is not distinct from God himself; (2) the natural law, which is the participation of the eternal law within human rationality, communicated to humanity by the creation of the human mind in the image of the divine mind, the light of reason which cannot be fully extinguished even by sin; (3) human law, which is framed by human lawgivers and given to a particular community for the common good; and (4) the divine law, which is the special revelation of God in the Bible.[16]

Revolutionary themes were hidden in this medieval text. Though he was writing during the period of "Christendom" or European church-state unity, Aquinas did not claim that human law should be based on the divine law, the Bible; moreover, he said that neither the state nor the church has ultimate authority to evaluate a human law. In a manner that was remarkably non-theocratic and anti-autocratic, he argued that human law is to be derived from and evaluated primarily by the natural law.[17]

For Aquinas, laws coming from a king or government were to be evaluated by the principles of equity which God has built into human reason, but without giving ultimate authority to the church, which would evaluate human law by interpreting and applying religious texts. This was a principled break with both theocracy and autocracy.

During the Reformation, the new Evangelicals, such as Martin Luther and John Calvin, did not carefully follow the precise terminology of Aquinas. They simply assumed the natural law, as was common in the Bible. But their rediscovery of justification by faith alone (not by obeying the moral law) pushed them to clarify what functions God's moral law carries. Luther taught that God's moral law has two special functions (in addition to guiding the lives of Christians). The first is the civic use of the moral law, which restrains sin enough to make life in society possible; the second is the theological use of the law, which reveals our sin to ourselves.[18]

---

[16] See Johnson, *Natural Law Ethics*, pp. 15–18.
[17] Thomas Aquinas, "Treatise on Law," questions 90–96 of the *Summa Theologica* I-II, trans. Fathers of the English Dominican Province (Benzinger, 1947), question 91, article 3. Republished online in *Classics of Political Philosophy*, http://www.sophia-project.org/uploads/1/3/9/5/13955288/aquinas_law.pdf
[18] Martin Luther, *Luther's Works*, ed. and trans. Jaroslav Pelikan, vol. 26: *Lectures on Galatians*, 1535 (St. Louis: Concordia, 1963) pp. 308, 309.

Calvin did not precisely follow the terminology of Luther, but his teaching was remarkably similar. First, Calvin compared the moral law to a mirror that "warns, informs, convicts, and lastly condemns, every man of his own unrighteousness" so one sees the need for forgiveness.[19] He then added, "The second function of the law is this: at least by fear of punishment to restrain certain men who are untouched by any care for what is just and right," almost a repeat of Luther.[20] In this manner the Reformation more clearly distinguished the dimensions of the biblical-classical synthesis that came through Aristotle from those that came through Augustine. The reasoning of Aristotle formed the basis for the civic use of the moral law; the reasoning of Augustine supported the spiritual use of God's moral law. On the question of how to order life in society, Calvin can be taken as speaking for the main Reformers: "There is nothing more common than for a man to be sufficiently instructed in a right standard of conduct by natural law."[21]

3. *Within Christian ethics, there is a developing discussion of the relation between moral laws and human goods that has significant parallels in the philosophy of Humanitarian Islam.*

In Western civilization, it has been common for 300 years to distinguish between doing those things that are good for people and those things which are seen as duties in an abstract sense — i.e., doing what is "right" regardless of the consequences. In moral theory, this is the contrast between utilitarian ethics (doing good for people) and deontological ethics (doing what is good in itself). But this sharp contrast does not seem reasonable to many people in the theistic religions. In other words, we who believe in one God, creator of all people, see a close link between moral norms (i.e., our abstract duties) and human goods (the results of doing good actions). For example, Moses connected is quoted as saying, "The Lord commanded us to obey all these decrees and to fear the Lord our God, so that we might always prosper and be kept alive," clearly connecting abstract duty to God with human well-being (Deuteronomy 6:24).

In his discussion of this question, Aquinas argued that there are definable human goods that correspond with God-given human inclinations, that the natural moral law commands us to protect these goods, and that good, enforceable human laws give more detail about how to

---

[19] John Calvin, *Institutes of the Christian Religion*, ed. John T. McNeill, trans. Ford Lewis Battles (Philadelphia: Westminster, 1960), II, vii, p. 6.
[20] Calvin, *Institutes*, II, vii, p. 10.
[21] Calvin, *Institutes*, II, ii, p. 22.

protect these human goods. Commentators on Aquinas normally say these primary human goods are "life, procreation, social life, knowledge, and rational conduct."[22] To avoid a secularized misunderstanding of Aquinas, one should note that knowledge, in his definition, includes knowing the truth about God; his definition of social life includes the protection of private property.[23]

There is an astonishing similarity between Aquinas' definition of human goods and the definitions provided by the Sunni Muslim jurists Imam al-Ghazali (1058 – 1111) and Imam al-Shatibi (d. 1388), who are quoted in the 2017 Declaration on Humanitarian Islam. These Sunni jurists described five human goods — faith, life, progeny, reason, and property — which should be protected by moral norms. This similarity reflects extensive interaction between Muslim and Christian scholars in the twelfth through fourteenth centuries, which occurred largely in France and southern Europe. They interacted with each other to the extent that it is now difficult to know who influenced whom and who is quoting whom in many books or essays.[24]

One clarification of human goods that has been articulately argued in the twenty-first century points out that freedom of religion should be described as a basic human good to be protected by moral and civil law.[25] Indeed, we should perhaps place freedom of religion at the top of the list, because it plays such an important role in securing or promoting the other human goods.[26]

---

[22] For example, Mark Murphy, "The Natural Law Tradition in Ethics," *Stanford Encyclopedia of Philosophy* (2002, revised 2019); https://plato.stanford.edu/entries/natural-law-ethics/

[23] See "Treatise on Law," question 94, article 2. The "new natural law" theory offers a longer list of primary human goods, mostly by means of dividing Aquinas' categories into distinct parts. For example, John Finnis, *Natural Rights and Natural Law* (Oxford: Clarendon Press, 1980), pp. 59–99, argues that the basic forms of human good, which he also calls "values," are life, knowledge, play, aesthetic experience, sociability (friendship), practical reasonableness, and religion.

[24] For more background on al-Shatibi, see Ahmad al-Raysuni, *Imam al-Shatibi's Theory of the Higher Objectives and Intents of Islamic Law*, trans. from Arabic by Nancy Roberts; abridged by Alison Lake (International Institute of Islamic Thought, 2013).

[25] Robert P. George, 'Religious Liberty and the Human Good,' *International Journal for Religious Freedom* 5, no. 1 (2012): 35–44; https://www.iirf.eu/site/assets/files/92052/ijrf_vol5-1.pdf

[26] Brian Grim and Roger Finke have used social science research to argue convincingly that freedom of religion contributes to many other indicators of societal flourishing, including economic growth, political freedom, freedom of the press, longevity of democracy, lower levels of armed conflict, and reduction of poverty.

Primary Human Goods in Medieval Philosophies

Christian	Muslim
Life	Faith
Procreation	Life
Social life (including property)	Progeny
Knowledge (including God)	Reason
Rational conduct	Property

These Christian and Muslim scholars referenced higher laws that are not precisely written in a particular text to evaluate human laws, though all these writers spent large parts of their lives interpreting the religious texts of their respective traditions. One side (Muslim) references a transcendent or higher sharia, whereas the other side (Christian) references a natural moral law, imprinted in the human mind that was made in the image of God, which no one can truly claim not to know. Nevertheless, the Muslim and Christian scholars came to astonishingly similar conclusions regarding the primary human goods, which are to be protected by the application of moral and human laws. The representatives of Humanitarian Islam have once again made these claims prominent in their twenty-first-century proclamations.

SO WHAT CAN WE DO?

Though we understand and relate to God in very different ways, Humanitarian Muslims and evangelical Christians see life, family, rationality, a faith community, and an orderly socio-economic life as fundamental human goods that lead to comprehensive well-being in this world. We know that these deep human goods are vulnerable, needing protection from various threats. We have similar convictions regarding universal moral standards that should influence religious and legal norms, all of which should protect basic human goods. This must be demonstrated intellectually, politically, in education, and in shared humanitarian efforts.

When the fundamental principles of Humanitarian Islam are brought into interaction with corresponding principles of Christian ethics, one obtains an ethical-jurisprudential method to respond to religious extremism

---

See, for example, *The Price of Freedom Denied: Religious Persecution and Conflict in the Twenty-First Century* (Cambridge: Cambridge University Press, 2011).

2. A Case for Ethical Cooperation

and to efforts to maintain religiously defined states which require a particular religious identity to be full stakeholders in the society. In other words, Christians and Muslims have a clear way to explain the moral wrongness of both religious extremism and religiously defined states — one that does not depend on a prior commitment to any religious view — on the basis of which we can then engage in principled discourse with those who hold other views and seek to eliminate religious-based terrorism and persecution. Our influence could be much greater if presented by official representatives of two major religious traditions that are widely perceived as in conflict with each other.

How can Christians around the world foster such cooperation?

- We could hold joint events at which scholars or civic leaders from both religious communities discuss how we talk about each other and how we address questions regarding religion's role in society.
- We could produce joint publications.
- We could bring political leaders from both faith communities together to talk about how they can develop civil laws, based on their shared understanding of the universal moral law, that will protect all people's basic human goods.
- We could work together to provide information for the business, government, and education sectors on how to promote harmonious interaction among people from multiple cultures and religions.
- We could cooperate in delivering humanitarian aid or in addressing other problems that government alone cannot readily solve, such as homelessness, human trafficking, drug addiction, and environmental problems.

The World Evangelical Alliance is currently taking on this challenge at a global level. In November 2019, while in Indonesia for the WEA's General Assembly, several of us spent most of a day with leaders of Nahdlatul Ulama. After further correspondence and discussion, in April 2020 we announced a joint project to respond to threats to religious freedom arising from both religious extremism and secular extremism. In our June meeting, we decided to pursue cooperative efforts in three main areas: opposing "tyranny" (i.e., governments and movements that threaten basic human rights and freedoms); articulating shared messages in the areas of jurisprudence, ethics, and human rights; and public communications.

The expansion of secularism, atheism, and moral relativism in the modern West have been partly fueled by the widespread, though generally false, perception that organized religions are a cause of war and oppression. The level of philosophical agreement between evangelical Christians and Humanitarian Islam demonstrated in this paper justifies a concerted joint effort to build a world in which religious faith can flourish for the benefit of humanity.

3

Rahmah
(Universal Love and Compassion)

KH. Abdurrahman Wahid

SUMMARY

Abdurrahman Wahid's life and teachings inspired the birth of the Humanitarian Islam movement, which seeks to restore *rahmah* (universal love and compassion) to its rightful place as the primary message of Islam. The movement, established by close friends and disciples of President Wahid, does so by addressing obsolete and problematic elements within Islamic orthodoxy that lend themselves to tyranny, while positioning these efforts within a much broader initiative to reject any and all forms of tyranny worldwide. Major vehicles for accomplishing these objectives include the Institute for Humanitarian Islam, the Center for Shared Civilizational Values, and *Bayt ar-Rahmah li ad-Daʻwa al-Islamiyyah Rahmatan li al-ʻAlamin*, which help coordinate the global expansion of Nahdlatul Ulama activities.

President Wahid is widely regarded as a saint by Nahdlatul Ulama followers, and each year millions of pilgrims visit his grave in Jombang, East Java. The inscription on his tombstone — "Here Rests a Humanist" — is written in Indonesian, Arabic, English, and Chinese.

Never before published, the following article was written prior to Abdurrahman Wahid's death on December 30, 2009. President Wahid frequently collaborated with C. Holland Taylor and Kyai Haji Hodri Ariev in drafting books (*The Illusion of an Islamic State*) and articles published by Western media, including the *Wall Street Journal*, *Washington Post*, and Oxford University Press. "Rahmah (Universal Love and Compassion)" — whose final text, in English, was completed by Mr. Taylor after President Wahid's death — expresses Abdurrahman Wahid's conviction that "Islam should always and everywhere constitute a manifestation of love, mercy and compassion in the widest possible sense."

❖❖❖❖❖

In the 21ˢᵗ chapter of the Qur'an, God — Pure and Exalted is He![1] — proclaims that He sent the Prophet Muhammad (saw.) as His emissary, for no purpose other than to serve as *rahmah* — that is, a manifestation of God's infinite love, mercy and compassion for all creation (*"wa mâ arsalnâka illâ rahmatan lil 'âlamîn,"* Qur'an 21:107). It is significant to note that Muslim theologians have consistently and correctly defined the term *'âlam*, as used in this context, to mean "all that exists, other than God." Thus, far from being restricted to humanity or any "privileged" subset thereof, God's infinite love and compassion envelops, and nourishes, all of creation.

As the religion conveyed by the Prophet Muhammad (saw.), Islam should always and everywhere constitute a manifestation of love, mercy and compassion in the widest possible sense, whose teachings inspire human beings to love others and to strive to create a truly safe and tranquil world. By the same token, every thought, word or deed that undermines or negates the peace and well-being of others should be regarded as a violation of Islam's primary message, and of its essential teachings. Given current circumstances in the world — by which I mean the horrific acts committed daily in the name of Islam, and the consequent rise of Islamophobia in the West — it is vital that Muslims and non-Muslims alike understand the meaning and significance of the term *rahmah*, both within the context of the Qur'anic verses in which it appears, and in the context of human relationships, including the constellation of contemporary society, politics and culture.

Rahman is a noun, which in its superlative subject form (*fâ'il*) represents one of "the most perfect names" (*al-asmâ al-husnâ*) of God (swt.), and appears as such in the *basmalah* formula (*Bism Allâh al-Rahmân al-Rahîm* — "*In the name of God, the Compassionate, the Merciful*"), with which Muslims often initiate actions or discussions of religion and other serious topics. Both words in this formula, *al-Rahmân* (the Loving; the Compassionate; the All-Gracious) and *al-Rahîm* (the Merciful), are derived from same root, *r-h-m*, whose literal meaning is "love" or "compassion." The word *al-Rahmân* is so uniquely precious that one Qur'anic verse not only permits, but even

---

[1] Translator's note: When Muslims speak or write the name of God, they usually follow this with the phrase *subhanahu wa-ta'ala* (Arabic: سبحانه وتعالى), which means, "Pure and Exalted is He (Allah)." The phrase is often abbreviated as "swt." Similarly, when they say or write the name of Muhammad, they usually follow his name with the phrase *sall Allahu 'alayhi wa sallam* (Arabic: صلى الله عليه وسلم), which means, "May God bless him and grant him peace." This is often abbreviated as "SAW." or "saw."

3. Rahmah (Universal Love and Compassion)

suggests, that His creatures address Him using either the name Allah or *al-Rahmân*, for both refer to Him as the One and Only God (*qul ud' Allâh aw ad' al-Rahmân, fa ayya mâ tad'û falillâh al-asmâ' al-husnâ*, Q. 17:110). "Say (unto mankind): 'Call upon God, or call upon the Loving One; by whichever name you invoke Him, His are all the attributes of perfection.'"

In a different Qur'anic verse, *al-Rahmân* is used to accompany a symbolic expression which affirms that "The Loving One is established on the throne (of His Omnipotence)" (*al-Rahmân 'alâ al-'arsy-istawâ*, Q. 20:5). Many theologians have interpreted this verse as a reference to God's justice. On one hand, the throne (*'arsy*) symbolizes God's omnipotent Power, which none can resist. On the other hand, by stating that *al-Rahmân* sits upon the throne (of omnipotent power), the Qur'an conveys the image of Infinite Love (*al-Rahmân*) serving to balance Absolute Power in such a way as to establish Divine Justice. This interpretation is in accordance with a *hadith qudsi*[2] which states that God's love and compassion supersede His anger.[3]

---

[2] *Hadith qudsi* are sayings of the Prophet Muhammad whose meaning and authority are believed to originate directly with God.

[3] "The Prophet (saw.) mentioned that Allah said: 'I create mankind and disembodied spirits, then they worship other gods that they make for themselves. I bless them with My bounties, then they thank someone else for what I sent them. My mercy descends to them while their evil deeds ascend to me. I bestow countless gifts upon them, even though I have no need of them, while they alienate themselves from Me with their sins, even though they are desperate for My help.

"Whoever returns to Me, I accept him no matter how far he has wandered; and whoever turns away from Me, I approach him and call on him. Whoever abandons a sin for my sake, I reward him with many gifts and whoever seeks to please Me, I seek to please him.

"Whoever acknowledges My will and power in whatever he does, I make the iron bend for his sake. My dearly beloved are those who [have opened their hearts to] experience My presence.

"Whoever thanks Me, I grant him further blessings. Whoever obeys Me, I elevate and ennoble him further. Whoever disobeys Me, I keep the doors of My mercy open for him. If he returns to Me, I bestow him with My love, since I love those who repent and purify themselves for My sake. If he does not repent, I continue to nurture and purify his soul, by subjecting him to hardship. Whoever prioritizes Me over worldly things, I will favor over others. I reward every good deed ten times over; seven hundred times over; countless times over. I view every single bad deed as but one, unless the person repents and asks for My forgiveness, in which case I forgive even that one.

"I take into account any small good deed and I forgive even major sins. My mercy supersedes My wrath. My tolerance supersedes my blame. My forgiveness supersedes My punishment, as I am more merciful with My slaves than a mother with her child." (*Hadith qudsi* narrated by al-Bukhari).

Thus, *rahmah* (love, compassion and divine grace) constitutes the principal message of Islam, and in turn serves as the animating spirit and applicable standard of reference for the three pillars of Islamic teaching, i.e., *îmân* (faith), *islâm* (self-transcendent awareness of, and surrender to, Divine Will), and *ihsân* (good deeds arising from a state of pure devotion).

The Qur'an's proclamation that God (swt.) sent the Prophet Muhammad (saw.) for no purpose other than to serve as a blessing (*rahmah*) for all creation, and its revelation that the Loving One (*al-Rahmân*) sits upon the throne of power, represent theological imperatives that should be accepted and embraced by every Muslim and form the well-spring of individual and collective action within Muslim communities at large.

On an intellectual and epistemological level, every interpretation of Islam should be conducted within the context of a sincere and continuous effort to manifest, establish and preserve the flow of love and compassion (*rahmah*) for the benefit of all of creation. Any interpretation of the Qur'an that disrupts — or even worse, negates — this flow of love and compassion (*rahmah*) should be viewed, by Muslims, as threatening the very existence of Islam as the dynamic expression of God's infinite love and compassion towards all His creatures.

This primary teaching of Islam reflects the spiritual imperative for humanity to *feel and experience* God's infinite love and compassion, and not simply contemplate or acknowledge these Divine qualities in a dry and reflexive manner. To feel genuine love and compassion assumes the existence of those who are beloved, and towards whom one feels compassion, for the experience and flow of love must have an object. This accords with God's declaration, via the tongue of His Prophet, that He is Beauty and loves that which is beautiful. Thus beauty, and every form of goodness, are the clearest manifestations of the Loving One (*al-Rahmân*), for it is impossible that He would love or embrace that which is neither good nor beautiful in its essence.

By the same token, there is no human being who does not love and appreciate beauty in some form. The rich textures of nature, melodious sounds and stirring poetry are all partial aspects of beauty. Other artistic activities, such as painting, music and dance, also represent partial manifestations of true Beauty. Indeed, only those who are extremely close to God can truly understand, value or express the various manifestations of partial beauty. For God's loved ones perceive His Face "whichever way they turn" (Qur'an 2:115) — and through all they see, hear or touch — because every aspect of God's creation is beautiful in essence.

3. Rahmah (Universal Love and Compassion)

Beauty will always bring joy and serve to attract humanity. Yet it is important to emphasize that the beauty of which we speak is not physical beauty per se, grounded in carnal desire. Rather, it is beauty as the manifestation of God's infinite love and compassion, which assumes the form of *spiritual* beauty — a beauty which leads those who appreciate its subtleties to ultimately feel and experience true Beauty and Greatness itself. Partial beauty such as that expressed in painting, music and the rich textures of nature can serve as a stairway leading human beings to the cognition of Divine Beauty itself. Yet unlike the beauty of this world, Supreme Beauty can be experienced only through self-transcendent apprehension of, and surrender to, Divine Will — the state of *islâm*, which all His Messengers have taught — which is to say: through awareness of, and whole-hearted devotion to, God Himself.

Thus the condemnation or rejection of art constitutes a rejection of the partial beauty derived from genuine, or Divine, Beauty itself. Such condemnation is generally voiced — and, in the case of the Buddhist statues in Bamiyan, Afghanistan — conducted by those who are incapable of discerning God's spiritual messages: messages that lie concealed behind the formal structure of letters, words and sentences that constitute holy scripture. Yet it is precisely within this context of spiritual messages that we must view Islamic law (*sharî'ah*), which should always be interpreted, and implemented, in such a way as to ensure the flow of universal love and compassion (*rahmah*). For to act in any other manner leads to the betrayal of Islam itself.

This acknowledgment of universal love and compassion (*rahmah*) as the animating spirit of Islam should be established as a guiding principle, thoroughly and inextricably embedded within every aspect of the Muslim community's religious life. Specifically, this entails inspiring Muslims to act with genuine love and compassion not merely toward those whom they regard as fellow Muslims, but toward all human beings, and indeed, *all of creation*. Several examples may serve to illustrate this point.

Art is often described as "a language without boundaries," through which one may express a wide range of personal thoughts and views, as well as emotional and/or spiritual experiences. For example, Ruzbihan Baqli (d. 1209) is often called Islam's *fideli de'amor* — a poet of love whose verses tempted listeners, and subsequent generations of readers, to immerse themselves in the presence of He Who is All-Beautiful (*al-Jamîl*). Jalâluddîn Rûmî (d. 1273) was another great Sufi master who expressed his understanding and vision of Divine Beauty through the melodious language of his *Mathnâwî*, sometimes referred to as "the Qur'an in Pahlavi (Farsi)." Ibn 'Arabî (d. 1240), the author of *Turjumân al-Ashwâq (The Translator of Desires)* and numerous other works, is widely admired for having revealed mysteries of Divine love rarely vouchsafed to others. Through his voluminous writings, Ibn 'Arabi called upon humanity not to rest content with the enjoyment of physical beauty, but to soar beyond the outer dimension of life to its inner, spiritual essence.

Other remarkable examples of this artistic/spiritual phenomenon include the Egyptian and Lebanese singers Umm Kulthum (1904 – 1975) and Fairuz (b. 1935). Both so enchanted audiences that feuding Arab heads of state were known to temporarily abandon their political rivalries in the presence of such overwhelming beauty. Umm Kulthum used the language of art to communicate not only with spiritual and intellectual elites but also with a mass audience, while Fairuz emphasized literary aesthetics in every poem she sang, which included many crafted by the Lebanese-born Christian poet Khalil Gibran. In Indonesia, Ahmad Dhani of the legendary group Dewa has followed in the footsteps of Umm Kulthum and Fairuz — composing and performing love songs imbued with profound spirituality, such as *Laskar Cinta (Warriors of Love)*, *Pangeran Cinta (The Prince of Love)*, *Satu (Oneness)* and many others, in order to disseminate God's love and compassion (*rahmah*) through the vehicle of music.

Even within the field of Islamic law, the spirit of love and compassion (*rahmah*) should never be forgotten or neglected. One of the pioneers of this approach was Abû Hâmid al-Ghazalî (d. 1111), who described the purposes of Islamic law (*maqâshid al-sharî'ah*) as falling into three categories, i.e., primary (*dlarûriyyât*), secondary (*hâjiyyât*), and tertiary (*tahsîniyyât*). The first category pertains to human beings' primary interests, such as the right to freely practice one's religion, the right to life and property, freedom of thought, and rights of inheritance. The second category involves aspects of life that are necessary to help ensure fulfillment of the first. The third category concerns various human desires that are lawful according to the standards of religious teaching.

With regard to Islam's primary objective — i.e., to serve as a blessing (*rahmah*) for all creation — it is evident that certain Qur'anic verses have been, and continue to be, interpreted outside the corridor of universal love and compassion (*rahmah*). Such interpretations generally result from a selective, literal and non-contextual reading of the Qur'an — divorced from the context of the specific time and place these verses (such as 9:5; 9:29, etc.)[4] were revealed, as well as the present context in which these same verses are cited as scriptural references, in order to justify a specific response or proposed "solution" to various contemporary problems faced by the Muslim community.

Al-Ghazalî's method of reading the Qur'an is well-suited to addressing this problem, by re-establishing universal love and compassion (*rahmah*) as the primary message of Islam. From this perspective, imposing the death penalty for murder — or severing a thief's hand — is not the law's primary, or even secondary, objective. The execution of murderers and the amputation of thieves' hands are specific sanctions, rather than goals. The actual purpose of Islamic law, in these two cases, is the protection of life and property, respectively. The distinctive feature of Islamic law — viewed from the perspective of *rahmah* — is thus its focus upon the objectives to be accomplished, rather than the application of specific sanctions. In the cases cited above, legal sanctions need not assume the form of execution or amputation, despite the fact that the Qur'anic text — when read literally and without reference to its context and primary objectives — is often interpreted to require precisely that.

Reading the Qur'an in such a way as to grasp its true message, as did al-Ghazalî, requires a methodological approach that combines rational insight with heightened spiritual awareness — in other words, an approach designed to unveil the true meaning and spirit of Islam. For this reason, scriptural interpretation should be conducted as part of an ongoing attempt to link the text (scripture) with context, and to harmonize Divine revelations with social reality. Such an interpretive approach requires combining and utilizing both classical and contemporary exegetical methodologies, with the intention of preserving those traditions that remain suitable to our present age, while augmenting these with contemporary methodologies that are both useful and responsive to the requirements of Qur'anic interpretation (*al-muhâfazhah 'alâ al-qadîm al-shâlih wa al-akhdz bil-jadîd al-ashlah*).[5]

As an historical precedent, we may note that the second caliph, 'Umar ibn al-Khaththab, replaced the amputation of hands with an alternative

---

[4] "And so, when the sacred months are over, slay those who ascribe divinity to aught beside God wherever you may come upon them, and take them captive, and besiege them, and lie in wait for them in every conceivable place" (Qur'an 9:5). "And fight against those who — despite having been vouchsafed revelation [aforetime] — do not [truly] believe either in God or the Last Day, and do not consider forbidden that which God and His Apostle have forbidden, and do not follow the religion of truth [which God has enjoined upon them], till they [agree to] pay the head tax (*jizya*) with a willing hand, after having been humbled [in war]" (9:29).

[5] Translator's note: In March of 2008, President Wahid co-founded the International Institute of Qur'anic Studies (www.iiqs.org) to help accomplish this objective.

legal sanction to punish theft. 'Umar was clearly motivated by his conviction that Islam is a religion of love and compassion (*rahmah*), and that while responsible to protect society from criminal acts, Muslim authorities should also treat criminals with an eye to rehabilitation, in the hope that they may become normal and productive members of society at large. This positive approach to criminal justice, exemplified by 'Umar, differs dramatically from the view expounded by contemporary literalists, who insist that Islamic law must apply precise and invariable sanctions — such as caning, stoning or beheading — rather than focusing on how to achieve the various purposes of the law, as described by al-Ghazalî.

As part of our effort to establish Islam as a source of universal love and compassion (*rahmah*), we need to reassert the views of al-Ghazalî and other like-minded theologians and jurists regarding the purposes of the law (*maqâshid al-sharî'ah*), to serve as an effective counterpoint and refutation of literalist streams of thought, which tend to be exclusivist. Of course, the struggle to affirm universal love and compassion (*rahmah*) as the primary message of Islam should not be narrowly confined to the field of Islamic law. Rather, it is essential that we re-enliven Islam in its entirety (not merely Islamic jurisprudence) as a source of infinite love and compassion (*rahmah*) for all sentient and non-sentient beings. Indeed, this primary message of Islam should become *the living soul* of every reading, discussion, interpretation and application of Islamic teaching. For to disregard *rahmah* — which constitutes the vital spirit of Islam — is to transform the religion from a vital organism into a soulless machine that is neither appreciative of nor responsive to the ever-changing needs and circumstances of God's creatures.

This point has grown increasingly vital in recent years, precisely because the social constellation of contemporary Islam has become severely distorted by the behavior of those who advocate and/or commit destructive acts in the name of Islam, which have absolutely nothing to do with its true nature or purpose.

Countless horrific acts — such as the attack on the World Trade Center in New York; the kidnapping and beheading of journalists, diplomats and various other figures; and an endless parade of suicide bombings — have stained the image of Islam in recent years. In virtually every case, those who instigated and/or committed these acts employed verses from the Qur'an or hadith to justify their behavior. The use of Islamic texts to legitimize and even sanctify these gruesome acts is and can only be accomplished through a literal reading of scripture that rips the verses in question from their original context, and/or relies upon a heavily politicized and obsolete understanding of Islamic law to accomplish the same objective.

Indeed, the advocates of such violence proclaim that their interpretation of the verses in question constitutes the sole legitimate understanding thereof, and often threaten to wreak "God's vengeance" on any who dare to challenge their presumptions. This attitude leaves no room for the discussion of alternate interpretations with those who disagree. Such an approach to the Qur'an may be described as a form of "textual violence," for those who commit destructive acts in the name of Islam (whether in a figurative or a literal sense) have amputated the verses they use to justify such acts from Islam's primary message of *rahmah*, thus denying and opposing the true spirit of Islam, even as they claim to uphold it.

Muslims and non-Muslims alike need to recognize, acknowledge and confront the reality that this "textual violence" is intimately linked with — and, indeed, inseparable from — the countless violent acts committed in the name of Islam in recent years. Without denying the contributory influence of various social, political and/or economic factors, this ideologically motivated "textual violence" has clearly played a crucial role in encouraging and facilitating the commission of countless brutal and inhumane acts in the name of religion itself. Hence, the struggle to eliminate Islamist violence, including terrorism, cannot be divorced from efforts to prevent the commission of "textual violence" — i.e., a hateful, brutal and supremacist interpretation of scripture — by transforming Muslims' understanding of Islam and their religious obligations thereunder.

People of good will of every faith and nation should join hands and work in close cooperation, to help ensure that Islamic teachings are universally understood and applied in accord with its primary message of *rahmah*, and thus serve as a conduit through which God's infinite love and compassion may flow to all sentient beings. Given the current dynamics in the Muslim world — and the institutional paralysis of the West, in the face of Muslim extremism — this is admittedly an ambitious or even daunting endeavor. Yet for that very reason, it is a task worthy of anyone who feels the stirring of God's love in their breast, and the whispering of a conscience that refuses to yield all that is most precious in life to the forces of hatred, intimidation and violence.

A profound understanding and conviction, on the part of Muslims, that Islam summons us to the practice of universal love and compassion (*rahmah*) will help stimulate the sincere, widespread and systematic efforts necessary to overcome the ideology of religious hatred and violence, and establish *rahmah* as the "lived reality" of Muslim communities worldwide, as opposed to an imaginary blessing confined to dogma, theory and/or wishful thinking, as propagated by extremists themselves. Of course, this inner conviction must be accompanied by practical and systematic action on the part of Muslims who realize that the primary message of Islam is *rahmah*, and who have the strength and courage required to act upon this knowledge amid the whirling chaos of our deeply troubled world. The spiritual awareness and inner certainty of which I speak represents the "basic capital" that stands at our disposal in the struggle against inhumane acts of violence and the ideology that justifies them — including every destructive act committed in the name of Islam.

This effort to ensure that Islam manifests as a blessing for all creation (*rahmah*), rather than a curse, is built upon scriptural references and irrefutable theological foundations. *First*, when God — Pure and Exalted is He! — proclaimed that His Messenger (saw.) was sent to be nothing but a source of universal love and compassion (*rahmah*) for all creation (Qur'an 21:107), this signified that the true purpose of the Prophet Muhammad's (saw.) struggle was to establish God's infinite love and compassion upon the face of the earth. This struggle (*jihad*) constitutes a sacred duty that must be fulfilled by all who claim to belong to the Prophet Muhammad's community.

Second, when God — Pure and Exalted is He! — proclaimed that His love and compassion (*rahmah*) supersedes His wrath (*ghadab*), this was in fact meant to serve as a guidance for humanity, reminding us to habitually refrain from directing hatred or anger towards anyone.

Third, the revelation that *al-Rahmân* (the Infinitely Loving and Compassionate One) sits on the Throne (*'arasy*) of His Omnipotence (Qur'an 20:5) constitutes an affirmative and profoundly enlightening command: instructing His creatures to use their God-given abilities to rise above their egotistical impulses and realize their potential — as creatures ennobled by God (Qur'an 17:70) — to share His love and compassion with all who dwell upon the face of the earth. For anger, no matter how small or inconsequential the form it appears to take, contains a seed of destruction that threatens to annihilate love and compassion.

By restoring love and compassion to Islam, we will simultaneously help to re-enliven the central role that love plays in her sister religions. For that which Muslims call *rahmah* is, in fact, the primary message of all religions, and of the 124,000 prophets whom God is said to have dispatched to every nation on earth, "for there was never any community but a herald has [lived and] passed away in its midst" (Q. 35:24).

Thus we would invite all those who feel the pulse of love within their hearts to join in the struggle to establish and perpetuate the dynamic flow of universal love and compassion (*rahmah*). This is the *true* jihad, known in Arabic as the great jihad (*jihad al-akbar*), waged against one's lower self (*hawâ nafs*), and thus against every form of egotism, arrogance and selfishness that may lead us to harm others and thereby frustrate the very purpose of religion itself.

4

God's Universal Grace in Protestant Theology

Thomas K. Johnson

Summary

The doctrine that God is the supreme embodiment of unconditional love, or *agape*, is central to Christian theology. As the apostle John states in his First Epistle, "God is love." In some respects, this core theological doctrine resembles the Islamic concept of *rahmah* (universal love and compassion), which lies at the heart of the Humanitarian Islam movement. In the following essay, Thomas K. Johnson explores "eight biblical themes related to God's universal grace, themes which Christian theology has often related to knowing God the Father and his work of creation. All of these are themes to which Muslims can probably relate more easily than they can grasp the mysteries of a Trinity with which they are unfamiliar."

The amazing growth of Christianity from obscurity toward becoming a global faith began when the first apostles spread out from Jerusalem to proclaim the novel message that God was reconciling the world to himself through a crucified but resurrected Savior. But most people overlook the fact that in their preaching, the early apostles repeatedly referred to the universal grace of God, especially when addressing people from a non-Jewish background. They seemed to believe that understanding the experience of God's universal grace provided the necessary background for their hearers to appreciate the special things that God had done in Christ. In our modern, globalized multi-religious context, we would do well to pay more attention to this feature of Christianity.[1]

---

[1] What I am calling God's universal grace has also been called common grace or general grace within Protestant theology. As background, see Jochem Douma,

When Paul addressed a Gentile audience in Lystra (a Roman colony in today's southern Turkey) he claimed that God "has not left himself without testimony: He has shown kindness by giving you rain from heaven and crops in their seasons; he provides you with plenty of food and fills your hearts with joy" (Acts 14:17). In a speech to learned people in Athens, he made a similar appeal to their ingrained perception of the existence of a Creator:

> The God who made the world and everything in it is the Lord of heaven and earth and does not live in temples built by human hands. And he is not served by human hands, as if he needed anything. Rather, he himself gives everyone life and breath and everything else. From one man he made all the nations, that they should inhabit the whole earth; and he marked out their appointed times in history and the boundaries of their lands. God did this so that they would seek him and perhaps reach out for him and find him, though he is not far from any one of us. "For in him we live and move and have our being." As some of your own poets have said, "We are his offspring." (Acts 17:24–28)

With these words, the apostle interpreted the life experience of his hearers in light of his knowledge of God learned from the Hebrew Bible. They had experienced their Creator's kindness, including rain, food, and joy. They received the gift of life and the destiny of inhabiting the earth as God's sub-creators and developing civilizations. In the deepest level of their minds and souls, they should have perceived a call to seek God, a call from the Creator that echoed through Greek poetry and philosophy, that God is near because we are his offspring. This God, whose universal grace had made their lives possible, had now come to humanity in Jesus the Christ, whom Paul proclaimed. The universal grace of God provides the background for the nations to appreciate the Christian message.

Today, Christians are less likely to encounter Athenian philosophers, but they are very likely to interact with Muslims. There are more than a billion Muslims and close to two billion Christians in our world. Thanks to globalization, the extent of interaction among people of different backgrounds and beliefs continues to increase. As a result, there will be

---

Common Grace in Kuyper, Schilder, and Calvin: Exposition, Comparison, and Evaluation, ed. William Helder, trans. Albert H. Oosterhoff (Lucerna: Canadian Reformed Theological Seminary Publications, 2017; originally published in Dutch in 1967), and Richard J. Mouw, *All That God Cares About* (Brazos Press, 2020).

countless conversations every year between Christians and Muslims. And among those who view their faith as the central defining feature of their lives, those discussions are not likely to be limited to medicine or technology.

When Christians and Muslims talk with each other about their faith, Christians tend to mention the themes that are most dear to them: the incarnation, death, and resurrection of Jesus, themes that seem strange to Muslims. It would seem wise for them instead to follow the example of the apostle Paul and talk about the universal grace of God as a long preamble before making a link to the particularities of Christianity. By doing so, they might facilitate a higher quality of Muslim-Christian interaction and a higher level of desirable cooperation in public life.

In this essay, I explore eight biblical themes related to God's universal grace, themes which Christian theology has often related to knowing God the Father and his work of creation. All of these are themes to which Muslims can probably relate more easily than they can grasp the mysteries of a Trinity with which they are unfamiliar.[2]

I. GOD THE FATHER AND THE GOODNESS OF CREATION

God made the world *good*. Genesis 1 tells us this several times. "God saw all that he had made, and it was very good" (Genesis 1:31). This theme is emphasized repeatedly, as if people might have a tendency to forget that the earth and the heavens were made by God, belong to God, and are therefore both real and good. Of course, people have indeed forgotten this truth. In ancient Greece, various types of Hellenistic religion and philosophy doubted the goodness of the physical world. Many Hindus similarly doubt the reality of the physical world, treating it as an illusion. And these ways of thinking appear even among Christians, who often think that to find authentic spirituality they must flee from the physical world into an unseen spiritual world. But if the creation is good, we should seek to serve God and find authentic spirituality within the everyday world of creation. We can also accept the everyday gifts of God — family, friends, work, relaxation — as truly good gifts for which we can give thanks and which we can enjoy for the glory of God.

---

[2] The following section is adapted from a chapter in Thomas K. Johnson, *What Difference Does the Trinity Make? A Complete Faith, Life, and Worldview* (Bonn: VKW, 2009).

2. GOD THE FATHER AND THE CREATION OF MANKIND

"God said, 'Let us make man in our image'" (Genesis 1:26). Believing that God is our creating Father answers one of the deepest questions in the human heart: "Who and what are we?" The answer is that we are his creations, made for a relationship with himself, and therefore our human reason, will, and emotions should be a created reflection of his own. What a magnificent destiny we have been given! How awesome it is to interact daily with other creatures who have the same temporal and eternal destiny! How monumentally tragic it is when people are described and treated as mere creatures of dust and descendants of animals! This is not only an affront to the pinnacle of creation; it is a personal insult to the Creator.

Believing that God is our Father profoundly changes how we think and feel about ourselves and others. It satisfies both our own longing for significance and our intuitions that our neighbors and relatives are somehow worthy of respect and care. As the Psalmist reflected, "When I consider your heavens, the work of your fingers, the moon, and stars, which you have set in place, what is man that you are mindful of him, the son of man that you care for him? You made him a little lower than the heavenly beings and crowned him with glory and honor" (Psalm 8:3-5).

When God created us in his image, he did not leave us with empty hearts and minds, like a computer with no software. We might say that God created us with a lot of software already built in, ready to be activated by life experience. This includes not only the ability to understand God's world, but also the ability to understand love, justice, loyalty, honesty, and the other unseen realities that make life interesting and either frustrating or meaningful. For this reason, we long to experience such moral/spiritual realities, even while we sense that we never experience them totally in this world. Yet our partial experiences of these realities on the human level point us toward God, in whom these realities are fully present and from whom the cries of our hearts receive their answers. God created us with the ability and need to get to know him as our Creator and Redeemer.

3. GOD THE FATHER AND THE DEVELOPMENT MANDATE

"God blessed them and said to them, 'Be fruitful and increase in number; fill the earth and subdue it. Rule over the fish of the sea and the birds of the air and over every living creature that moves on the ground'" (Genesis 1:28). "The Lord God took the man and put him in the Garden of Eden to work it and take care of it" (Genesis 2:15). Everywhere we look, people are very busy and working hard. Through their hard work they create careers and families, businesses and schools, cultural institutions and communities. Seldom do we stop and ask, "Why?" Maybe we do not want to recognize that all our work and activity are not only a human necessity for our own well-being and fulfillment but part of a divine mandate — how God created us. In all this intense activity, we overlook that God created us to be active in his world. This does not mean that we must never rest. It does mean that our everyday activity is our primary place of service to God, who has given us a "development mandate" to build families, societies, and cultures that honor him as our Creator.

It is possible to divide this mandate into multiple parts. God has given us a mandate and drive to work, to marry, to have children and raise families, to worship, and to create communities. We see these parts of the development mandate lived out across the biblical record and in society today. They are usually expressed through social institutions: marriage, family, work, church, education, science. For this reason, we can talk about such institutions as "creation orders," recognizing that God has ordered our lives by how he created us. The creation orders are part of God's means of developing and preserving human life and culture from one generation to the next. They delineate the primary places where we serve God and love our neighbors.

Closely related to our work in the world as God's sub-creators is the rapid growth of scientific and technological knowledge. Twenty-first-century society is increasingly built on information and technology, though people seldom pause to wonder how it is possible for people to truly understand the physical world of nature. A proper answer to this question has two components. On one hand, God created the world with a certain order built into it; the orderly days of creation hint in this direction. What we often call the "laws of nature" are descriptions of certain laws God has built into his creation, part of the creation order. On the other hand, God has created our minds and sensory abilities so that we can perceive and understand his world. Furthermore, God has created a correspondence between the world he made and our perception of it, so that — with much hard work and many mistakes — we can gain such an amazing knowledge of the physical world as to build computers, perform delicate surgeries, or send communication satellites into orbit.

This increasing knowledge plays a massive role in the societal changes of our time. But without acknowledging the orderly creating work of our heavenly Father, we would have great difficulty explaining why such progress in scientific and technical knowledge is possible. Once we recognize that God makes the growth of knowledge possible, we can accept our better computers and improved medical care as gifts from our Father's hand. God certainly deserves far more gratitude than we give him, but this may be especially true in the realm of the growth of knowledge and practical wisdom.

4. God the Father and Practical Wisdom

"When a farmer plows for planting, does he plow continually? Does he keep on breaking up and harrowing the soil? When he has leveled the surface, does he not sow caraway and scatter cummin? Does he not plant wheat in its place, barley in its plot, and spelt in its field? His God instructs him and teaches him the right way. Caraway is not threshed with a sledge, nor is a cartwheel rolled over cummin; caraway is beaten out with a rod, and cummin with a stick. Grain must be ground to make bread; so one does not go on threshing it forever. Though he drives the wheels of his threshing cart over it, his horses do not grind it. All this also comes from the Lord Almighty, wonderful in counsel and magnificent in wisdom" (Isaiah 28:24–29).

In this passage, Isaiah describes the farming techniques used in his country from around 700 BC. They required practical wisdom, accumulated through trial and error and passed on from one generation to the next. To be a successful farmer, one had to learn these things from one's relatives and neighbors. And Isaiah adds the surprising comment about such a wise and successful farmer, "His God instructs him and teaches him the right way." Isaiah clearly saw such practical wisdom as coming from God, even though it might be learned directly from fellow humans. God is the ultimate source of the practical wisdom that people need to live in his creation.

The Bible strongly exhorts people to pursue and seek wisdom. "Get wisdom, get understanding; do not forget my words or swerve from them. Do not forsake wisdom, and she will protect you; love her, and she will watch over you" (Proverbs 4:5–6). This wisdom may be about farming techniques, relationships, avoiding adultery and other sins, fearing God, working diligently, raising children, or controlling one's tongue. It may come to us through various means: tradition, personal observation and experience, the Scriptures, or even the sayings of various peoples. Such wisdom tends to make life flourish, and people are commanded to seek wisdom because God the Creator is the source of this wisdom.

Believers have generally recognized that there is also a problem in this realm: unbelief leads to false claims to wisdom. The command to seek wisdom must be understood in light of warnings like this one given by the apostle Paul: "You must no longer live as the Gentiles do, in the futility of their thinking. They are darkened in their understanding and separated from the life of God because of the ignorance that is in them due to the hardening of their hearts" (Ephesians 4:17-18). Darkened hearts produce false claims to wisdom that must be avoided. If we believe in God the Father, we will recognize him as the source of practical wisdom and seek it in the ways he directs.

5. GOD THE FATHER AND CREATIONAL REVELATION

"The heavens declare the glory of God; the skies proclaim the work of his hands. Day after day they pour forth speech; night after night they display knowledge" (Psalm 19:1-2). Everything that people make, whether buildings, chairs, paintings, or books, is a statement from those people that tells us something about them. Similarly, God's creation tells us about him. God continues to speak through his creation — including our accountability to him, not only about his glory, majesty, and beauty. As Paul wrote, "The wrath of God is being revealed from heaven against all the godlessness and wickedness of men who suppress the truth by their wickedness, since what may be known about God is plain to them, because God has made it plain to them. For since the creation of the world God's invisible qualities — his eternal power and divine nature — have been clearly seen from what has been made" (Romans 1:18-20).

This speech of God through creation has been given different names: "natural revelation," meaning God's revelation through nature; "general revelation," meaning God's revelation that goes generally to all people everywhere; or "creational revelation," meaning God's self-revelation through creation. It is different from God's special or saving revelation of himself in Christ and Scripture, which should lead to faith and to participating in the believing community, the church. God's creational revelation impacts each person and every community, even those who may not want to believe or accept God's revelation. People often suppress the truth about himself that God makes known through creation, and this suppression leads to a deep tension within the mind and heart of the unbeliever, who knows that everything good, wise, beautiful, or just comes from God but who does not want to acknowledge God as the source of all these tremendous gifts. But all who believe in "God the Father Almighty" should recognize that God is speaking through his world and is the source of all truth in this world.

6. God the Father and the Universal Moral Law

At the end of Romans 1, Paul makes a startling statement. After giving a rather repulsive list of the sins that characterize the lives of people who reject God, he claims, "Although they know God's righteous decree that those who do such things deserve death, they not only continue to do these very things but also approve of those who practice them" (Romans 1:32). What is so remarkable about this statement is Paul's claim that people know the demands of God's law and even know that God punishes evildoers. Sin is not primarily the result of a lack of knowing right and wrong; it is a result of not wanting to do what is right. And all people have at least a substantial knowledge of God's universal moral law.

The older, more traditional terms for how people without the Bible came to know right and wrong were "the natural moral law" or simply "the natural law." These terms were really abbreviations for a longer phrase, something like "God's moral law as it is revealed through nature." The assumption is that there is a God-given moral rationality that forms the fabric of creation. It is a part of God's general revelation, a means of his universal grace. Acknowledging the natural moral law is part of believing that our Father is the Creator of heaven and earth, who speaks to us through his world, which he also maintains and sustains.

We should never suggest that God's natural moral law makes his commandments in the Bible less important; after all, we truly need more specific commands that confront us in our sinfulness and arouse us to repentance and faith. But the natural moral law has great value. It means that God's moral principles are built into human reason, emotions, and relationships so deeply that his written law finds a profound echo in our hearts and minds, making clear and specific those things we might otherwise neglect or question. It means that his written law fits our human nature and relationships in such a way that both his law written in creation and his law written in Scripture guide us in a direction that makes life flourish. It also means that people are partly prepared for the gospel; when people hear the gospel, they already have at least some experience of God's natural moral law condemning them for their sins and making them partly aware of their need for forgiveness and reconciliation. For this we can be grateful.

God's law, both in creation and in Scripture, always has multiple functions and uses in our lives. Three of these functions of God's law are especially important. First, it confronts us with our sin, making us aware of our sinfulness; this is the "theological," condemning or converting use of God's law. Second, God's law also tends to restrain sin, even if people do not fully acknowledge or understand it; this is the civil or political (meaning "community-oriented," based on the Greek word πόλις *polis* or community) use that makes life in society possible, so that we do not usually practice a war of all against all. Third, God's law shows us how to live lives of gratitude to God for his gifts of creation and redemption. This third use (as a guide for the life of gratitude) is active only in believers, whereas the theological and civil uses of the law are active in both believers and unbelievers. If people do not trust in God's forgiveness, they may often have very negative thoughts and feelings about God's law as it comes to them in creation and Scripture, but this does mean that God's law has no role in their lives. They may be partly aware of their need for the gospel, and they are often reasonably good neighbors and citizens (displaying what used to be called "civic righteousness"), because no one can totally avoid God's law.

7. GOD THE FATHER AND THE UNIVERSAL QUESTIONS

When God came to Adam and Eve after they had revolted in the Garden of Eden, he greeted them with a question. "Then the man and his wife heard the sound of the Lord God as he was walking in the garden in the cool of the day and they hid from the Lord God among the trees of the garden. But the Lord God called to the man, 'Where are you?'" (Genesis 2:8-9). The all-knowing God does not ask questions to gain new information; he already knew that Adam and Eve were playing a silly game, trying to hide from God in the trees. So why did he ask this question? It was a way of starting the dialog with Adam and Eve that would lead to a renewed relationship between them and God.

This new relationship did not immediately overcome the wide-ranging effects of their revolt against God. The subsequent discussion shows signs of a comprehensive alienation — a permanent brokenness in their relation to God, each other, themselves, and even the physical world. But at least Adam and Eve are talking with God, and God makes a vague but profound promise that the offspring of the woman would crush the head of the serpent (3:15). This whole dialog started with God asking a probing question that revealed something deeply wrong within Adam and Eve.

Our Creator continues to be a questioning God, and these questions go out to all people by means of God's general revelation. Certain questions seem to come to all people's minds, all over the world and in every generation. We might call these universal questions. What is a human being? What is wrong with the world? What is the meaning of life? Where did everything come from? What has always existed? What is death? Why do we feel guilt? How can we find forgiveness? Is there any real hope? These questions are not mere mind games; often they express deep anxieties that people ponder through philosophy, culture, and religion. These questions are much like God's question to Adam and Eve, "Where are you?" These questions can torment people deeply because deep within they retain some suppressed knowledge of the Creator, whose moral law they know and whose wrath they fear. By means of these questions, God seeks to chase the sons and daughters of Adam and Eve out from their hiding places to begin an honest dialog with God.

The answers to these deepest questions of religions, culture, and philosophy are found in the Bible; human experience is the question and faith provides the answer. Or we could say that life is the question and Christ is the answer. When we say we believe in "God the Father Almighty, Creator of heaven and earth," we are claiming that our Father is still the questioning God who raises questions for all people — questions that prepare the way for his answer, which is Christ, the Savior.

8. God's Universal Grace and the Teaching of Jesus

Jesus taught us, "Love your enemies and pray for those who persecute you, that you may be sons of your Father in heaven. He causes his sun to rise on the evil and the good, and sends rain on the righteous and the unrighteous" (Matthew 5:44–45). Our Creator gives his rain and sun to all people, even his enemies; in this statement of Jesus, sun and rain probably represent all the things people need to live in this world. This means that all the good things we receive in the political, economic, social, personal, and medical realms come from our Father's hand.

God deserves our continued gratitude for his good gifts that come to us in so many ways. Maybe we owe God an even greater debt of gratitude than did our ancestors of a century ago, as God's common grace seems even more bountiful and generous than it was in the past, especially for those who live in the developed world.

If God's universal grace to us today seems even greater than it was to our ancestors in previous centuries, the need to love our enemies is also greater. Enmity among races, religions, parties, and communities is the human heritage which we have received. God's universal grace, in which he gives the sun and the rain to his enemies, stands above us in condemnation and inspiration. All who believe in such a God must devote themselves to loving those who are called their enemies, regardless of the cause of the conflict.

4. God's Universal Grace in Protestant Theology

We must not overlook that the universal grace of God is one way in which God calls us to repentance and faith. In Paul's sermon to the unbelievers in Lystra, he claimed that God "has not left himself without testimony: He has shown kindness by giving you rain from heaven and crops in their seasons; he provides you with plenty of food and fills your hearts with joy" (Acts 14:17). And in Romans 2:4 Paul seems to complete the thought: "Do you show contempt for the riches of his kindness, tolerance, and patience, not realizing that God's kindness leads you toward repentance?"

Rather than letting the comfort, safety, peace, and affluence of life in the developed world make us forget God, we need to remind ourselves that all these gifts come from God's universal grace. And we need to say very loudly and clearly that the bounty of God's common grace calls all the sons and daughters of Adam and Eve to repentance and faith. Life in a world of plenty should lead us to gratitude toward God, not toward thinking that God is now somehow irrelevant.

CONCLUSION

It is overwhelming to think about these works of God the Father Almighty, Creator of heaven and earth. We should stand in awe and amazement, recognizing that he is worthy of all our praise and thanks. All our actions, as well as all our thoughts and feelings, should be part of our worship of our Heavenly Father. If we have not yet considered what it means to believe in the Creator, we must begin to let these truths overwhelm and transform our hearts and minds. Sometimes Christians live almost as if they have not heard that Jesus, the Savior, is the Son of this God and Creator, and this leads to a distorted life and faith. But this problem can be solved!

Surpassing our previous considerations are Christian claims about the trust people can have in the Creator. Jesus said, "Are not two sparrows sold for a penny? Yet not one of them will fall to the ground apart from the will of our Father. And even the very hairs of your head are all numbered. So don't be afraid; you are worth more than many sparrows" (Matthew 10:29–31). This is God's providence, the promise that the infinite Creator not only structures the universe and society, but that he also cares for each person.

Throughout the twenty-first century, Christians and Muslims will surely interact millions of times around the globe. If we Christians talk only about the incarnation, death, and resurrection of Jesus, our Muslim friends will have difficulty understanding us. But if we say a lot about the many dimensions of God's universal grace, following the example of the apostle Paul, we can interpret and draw attention to the experience of God's goodness that makes daily life possible for all human beings. These themes not only make the distinctives of Christian proclamation more comprehensible; they also provide much-needed principles for peaceful and responsible life together in global society.

PART II

5

Introduction to the Fundamental Principles of Nahdlatul Ulama (*Mukaddimah Qanun Asasi*)

KH. Hasyim Asy'ari

Summary

In 1926, preeminent Islamic scholars in the Dutch East Indies established an organization they called "Nahdlatul Ulama" or "Awakening of the Scholars." They were acting in direct response to the recent conquest of Mecca and Medina by Abdulaziz Ibn Saud and his Wahhabi army, which massacred traditional Sunni Muslims and spread terror in its wake. On January 31, 1926, Kyai Haji Hasyim Asy'ari — founding Chairman of the Nahdlatul Ulama Supreme Council and grandfather of Indonesia's fourth president, H.E. KH. Abdurrahman Wahid — addressed the inaugural meeting of the newly formed organization in Surabaya, East Java. Nearly a century after its delivery, this address, which articulates the ethical and theological framework embraced by the world's largest Muslim organization, remains the foundational document of Nahdlatul Ulama.

To the best of our knowledge, this historic speech has never before been translated or published in English. The following text is drawn from the central portion of Kyai Hasyim Asy'ari's address, while omitting extensive quotations from the Qur'an and Hadith (sayings of the Prophet Muhammad), with which Kyai Hasyim Asy'ari opened and concluded his speech. We believe that *Mukaddimah Qanun Asasi* remains as relevant today as when it was first delivered. For the past century, Nahdlatul Ulama has consolidated and preserved traditional Islam within Indonesia, in the face of repeated threats from transnational Islamist movements and their ideology, originating in the Middle East.

As Nahdlatul Ulama approaches its centenary, NU spiritual leaders look to this document as a source of inspiration and guidance in their efforts to project strategic influence worldwide. For its message remains relevant not only to Indonesians but also to the people of North America and Europe, where political divisions threaten to undo the unique achievements of Western civilization, which helped give birth to a rules-based international order founded upon respect for the equal rights and dignity of every human being.

A single nation is like a single body, and its people are like its limbs. Each member has an appropriate task and role, the performance of which the body cannot neglect.

As is universally acknowledged, human beings are inherently social creatures, mingling with others; for no one can fulfill his or her every need by acting alone. Willing or not, every person must interact socially, interaction that should ideally contribute to the well-being of all other members of society while preserving them from danger. The unity of human hearts and minds, as people help one other achieve a common goal, is the most important source of human happiness and the strongest factor inducing human beings to love one another.

Because of this principle, many nations have become prosperous. Slaves have become rulers, fostering widespread development. Nations have become advanced; the rule of law enforced; transportation networks constructed, enabling economic and cultural exchange to flourish. Countless other benefits arise from social unity, for social unity is the highest virtue and most powerful instrument for promoting the common good...

The above affirms the words of the poet who rightly said:

> *Gather together my children if*
> *The moment of crisis strikes*
> *Do not become scattered and alone*
> *Cups are averse to breaking when together*
> *When scattered*
> *One by one they shatter*

Sayyidina Ali (ra.) [601 – 661 CE] said, "God gives nothing good to those who are divided, either in the past or in the future."

The reason for this is that a people whose hearts are divided are ruled by their passions, leaving no place for the common good. Instead of being a unified nation, they are merely individuals gathered together in the physical sense: though one might think that they are unified, their hearts are, in reality, disunited and discordant.

They have become — as some say — like goats scattered in an open field, surrounded by ravenous beasts. If the goats are well for a time, this is merely because predators have yet to reach them, but one day, these predators will surely arrive. It may be that the ravenous beasts fight among themselves and subdue one another, such that the victors become robbers and the losers thieves. Even so, the goats will fall prey to both the robbers and the thieves.

Division has been the cause of weakness, defeat and failure throughout the ages. It is the root of destruction and bankruptcy, the source of collapse and ruination, and the agent of humiliation and chaos.

How many large families have lived — at first — in prosperity and comfort in many houses that made them feel at ease until, one day, the scorpion of divisiveness crawled among them, its creeping poison corrupting their hearts as the devil played his part against them? In the end, the family becomes a chaotic mess, and their houses collapse upon them.

The Prophet's Companion Ali (ra.) eloquently stated, "The cause of Truth can become weak due to strife and internal division; while evil may grow strong through cohesion and unity of purpose."

In short, whoever looks into the mirror of history and turns its many pages about diverse nations and the ebb and flow of time — and sees what happened to these nations up until the point of their extinction — will know that the glory which once enveloped them was nothing other than a blessing attributable to their unity of ideals, thoughts and purpose. This unity was the decisive factor that elevated their dignity and ensured their sovereignty, the impregnable fortress that safeguarded their strength and ensured the preservation of their teachings.

A united people's enemies can do nothing to harm them; rather, they bow their heads in respect for that people's power and dignity. A united people are able to brilliantly accomplish their many goals.

This is the destiny of a people upon which God's sun never sets; rather, the rays of His Light always shine upon them and not upon their enemies.

O *ulama* and God-conscious [enlightened] leaders of the Sunni community, who follow the four schools of jurisprudence: you have all drawn from the well of knowledge of those who came before you; and those who came before you drew knowledge from those who came before them, in an unbroken chain of transmission (*sanad*) that extends [from the Prophet Mohammad saw.] to each of you today. And each of you is continually learning from whoever may impart unto you the wisdom of your religion.

Thus, you are the gatekeepers and the guardians of this precious knowledge. Do not enter a house except through its front door. Whoever enters through a different means will be called a thief.

For there is a class of people [Wahhabis] who fall into the depths of strife (*fitnah*), choosing to embrace innovation rather than the Prophet's teachings (saw.), while the majority of believers are simply stunned into silence. And so the heretics and thieves [including Wahhabis] run rampant. They pervert the truth in order to suit themselves, enjoining evil as if it were good and forbidding good as if it were evil. They call others to follow their interpretation of God's book, even though their actions are not in the least bit guided by the teachings of the Qur'an.

They did not stop at this, but rather, founded organizations to systematically propagate their deviant teachings and amplify their manifest error. The poor flocked to these assemblies and did not hear the words of the Prophet (saw.):

فَانْظُرُوا عَمَّنْ تَأْخُذُونَ دِينَكُمْ

"So look carefully at those from whom you take your religion" (a reliable Hadith narrated by Imam Ahmad and Imam al-Hakim). "Indeed, as the day of Apocalypse approaches, many liars will appear. Do not weep for religion if it is in the hands of those who know the Truth (*ulama*). Rather, weep for this religion (Islam) if it falls into the hands of ignorant charlatans."

Umar bin Khattab (ra.) [584 – 644 CE] was entirely correct when he said, "The religion of Islam disintegrates in the hands of hypocrites who argue, skillfully manipulating the Qur'an."

All of you are upright souls capable of dispelling the falsehoods of those who are expert at propagating evil, the religious interpretation of fools, and the debauchery of those who exceed all bounds, by employing the proofs (*hujjah*) that have been provided to us by God, Lord of the universe, who demonstrates the proof of His Truth through the tongue of whomever He wills.

And all of you are among the community described by the saying of the Prophet (saw.): "There is a group of my people who never waver; who always stand firmly upon the truth; and who always obtain victory. They cannot be harmed by their enemies before the coming of God's Day of Judgement."

Come! All of you, and all your followers among the poor and the wealthy, the weak and the strong. Flock to this blessed community (*jam'iyyah*), which is called "*Jam'iyyah* Nahdlatul Ulama."

Enter [this community] with a spirit overflowing with love, compassion, harmony and unity of purpose. Enter with a bond that unites us, body and soul. This is an upright community (*jam'iyyah*): peaceful, whose nature is to improve character and foster politeness towards others. It tastes sweet in the mouths of those who are devoted to goodness and obstructs the throats of the wicked, choking those [who may be skilled at reciting the Qur'an, but do not apprehend its inner meaning in their hearts]. In this regard, all of you should seek to remind one another to work harmoniously together, employing means that are satisfying and appeal to the heart, along with irrefutable proofs [regarding one's convictions]. Clearly convey what God has commanded you, so that religious fabrications are purged from all people in every direction.

For the Prophet (saw.) said, "Whenever religious fabrications and strife appear, and my companions are reviled, beseech those who know the Truth (*ulama*) to reveal their knowledge. Whoever fails to do this shall be cursed by God, the Angels and all humanity." (Hadith narrated by al-Khaṭīb al-Baghdādī [1002 – 1071 CE] in *al-Jāmi'*.)

God (swt.) has declared:

وَتَعَاوَنُوا عَلَى الْبِرِّ وَالتَّقْوَى

"And assist one another in fostering virtue and developing full awareness of God." (Qur'an 5:2)

Translated by Thomas G. Dinham and C. Holland Taylor

6

Christianity and the Essential Characteristics of Democracy[1]

Christine Schirrmacher

SUMMARY

> Christine Schirrmacher is a Professor of Islamic Studies at the University of Bonn, Germany and the *Evangelische Theologische Faculteit* in Leuven, Belgium. In this article, Dr. Schirrmacher explains why the fundamental principles of Christianity are compatible with and support those of a modern democratic state. She also examines the problematic nature of a so-called "Christian state" and the vital role played by religious communities in preserving the humanitarian underpinnings of a largely secular state. In doing so, she quotes the "Böckenförde Dictum": "'*The liberal, secular state lives on preconditions which it cannot itself guarantee.*' This means that the state can pass laws imposing sanctions against murder and theft, but the state cannot ensure that the majority of the citizens will continue to judge murder and theft to be wrong."

The term "democracy," composed of the words for "people" (Greek δῆμος *demos*) and for "rule" (Greek κράτος *kratos*), stems from ancient Greece and stood for rule that directly went forth from the people and was exercised by the people. The high point of democracy, as it developed there, has primarily been set at the beginning of the fifth century B.C.[2] In the broadest

---

[1] This essay is an excerpt from *Islam and Democracy: Can They Be Reconciled?* (Bonn: VKW, 2020), pp. 11–17.
[2] See Thomas Meyer, *Was ist Demokratie? Eine diskursive Einführung* (Wiesbaden: VS Verlag, 2009), p. 16.

sense, the term "democracy" designates a government put into a position of power according to the will of the majority of the people via free elections. It receives its legitimacy from the conscious expression of the people's will. In a democracy, the people comprise the actual responsible body for the authority of the state, and they charge their elected representatives with the formulation of a constitution (written or unwritten) and the configuration of a political system.

Democracies are characterized by a separation of powers into an executive branch (sometimes called "the government"), a legislative branch (a congress or parliament), and a judicial branch (which is formally independent from the other branches of government). Democracies act within the framework of a constitution that governs the actions of the state and respects the basic rights of citizens as well as the rights of identified groups, especially religious communities. Among these rights are, above all, the rights of freedom of opinion (both political and personal), freedom of the press, freedom of religion, and the freedom to organize. Democracies protect the right of minority political parties to exist and maneuver, as well as the opportunity to freely voice their opinions and to peacefully change the balance of power.

What is expected of a democracy is that it embodies the rule of law, with the certainty that legal rights will be protected, in such a manner that representatives of the state are legally accountable for their actions. Furthermore, it is expected that these representatives will adhere to prevailing law. In particular, true democracies grant their citizens the opportunity to peacefully dissolve government by a majority decision and to replace it with another via just, free, and general elections conducted via secret ballot.

Although there are diverging democratic theories within political science, there is a broad consensus that one of the most important preconditions for democracy is the equality and freedom of all citizens. The fundamental equality of all people means, consequently, that all people are to be treated equally before the law. It also means that the same measure of rights and freedoms will be granted to them within the constitutional state. Citizens' freedom encompasses their freedom of self-determination, the freedom to form their own personal, political, and religious opinions, and the freedom to act upon their opinions in their participation in the political process. At the same time, it is also a freedom and, more specifically, a right to be protected from arbitrary state action and the violation of their rights. With that said, fundamental democratic rights are implemented, which according to content are closely linked with the principles of freedom and equality. For the most part, these are set down in a constitution and are legally enforceable. Among the inalienable fundamental rights in Germany, for instance, are the protection of human dignity, the right to free development of one's personality, the right to physical integrity, the right to equal treatment for men and women, the freedom of belief, and the freedom of opinion, as well as the right to freely choose one's profession.

DO DEMOCRACIES HAVE CHRISTIAN ROOTS?

A democracy is not a religiously legitimated form of rule or form of state. As a result, it cannot be deemed "Christian" *per se*. However, according to the opinion of many, democracies possess a collection of characteristics which could be designated as the implementation of a number of foundational Christian principles, even if not all democracies — and this applies above all to Indonesia and Turkey — are culturally shaped by Christianity: "Today, of a total of 88 free democracies, 79 of them, thus 90%, are majority Christian. Next to this there is one Jewish democracy and seven democracies which have Far Eastern religions representing the majority, whereby in Mauritius and in South Korea Christians make up the second-largest segments of the population."[3] And yet the following applies: "Christianity fits with democracy like a hand fits in a glove."[4] This is because "liberal democracy," according to the notion of leading representatives of Evangelical and Catholic churches, "corresponds in a special way to the Christian view of humankind."[5] This is the case even if Christians, as the same statement emphasizes, cannot "expect the comprehensive realization of what is good or, as it were, the establishment of a perfect world free from problems" from any form of government or, in other words, from "any human action."[6]

It is a basic Christian assumption that people are fallible and that power, therefore, can lead to the abuse of power. The attempt to limit the power of those who rule within democracy comes through the oppor-

---

[3] Thomas Schirrmacher, "Demokratie und christliche Ethik," in *Aus Politik und Zeitgeschichte* 14/2009. http://www.bpb.de/apuz/32086/demokratie-und-christliche-ethik?p=all (December 18, 2012)

[4] William J. Hoye, *Demokratie und Christentum: Die christliche Verantwortung für demokratische Prinzipien* (Münster: Aschendorff, 1999), p. 366.

[5] *Demokratie braucht Tugenden*. Gemeinsames Wort des Rates der Evangelischen Kirche in Deutschland und der Deutschen Bischofskonferenz zur Zukunft unseres demokratischen Gemeinwesens (Hannover/Bonn: Kirchenamt der EKD/Sekretariat der Deutschen Bischofskonferenz, 2006), p. 12.

[6] Ibid., p. 14.

tunity to vote all democratically elected representatives out of power. It is also expressed in the form of oversight bodies (such as parliaments). The principle of the general and equal right to vote, which allots to every citizen the same number of votes and the same weight to his or her voice, can be viewed as the political application of biblical thinking on the equality of all people before God. The similar principle, that the individual person is free before God in his decisions, and is therefore bound primarily to his own conscience and not to the consciences of other people, requires free elections by secret ballot to prevent manipulation of the individual's voting decision. Therefore, there are prohibitions on one individual voting representatively for another and on deliberating with others in the voting booth.

A number of authors additionally mention the desacralizing of worldly rule, meaning a turning away from the notion that a quasi-divine and uncontested authority is manifested in worldly power. This is possible only if the human fallibility of the ruler is also truly recognized. According to this notion, there are no infallible and unquestionable god-kings who are not to be scrutinized. Rather, they are stewards in high places who may find themselves in need of correction. This corresponds with the biblical insight into the susceptibility of all people to temptations, as well as with the prohibition against placing people in the position of God. In particular, the idea of an emperor as god in Roman times is a cautionary example regarding the dangers for society when unlimited power is placed in the hands of a ruler who exercises authority similar to that of a god and is revered as a god. It is precisely against the emperor god-kings of the Romans that Jesus directs his demand to separate worldly and religious spheres, to give to God and to the emperor separately what properly belongs to each (Matthew 22:21).

The idea that the ruler finds himself in principle on the same plane as that of those who are ruled, such that he is not *per se* above the plane of the ruled, can definitely be viewed as the political implementation of the Christian view of humanity, in which every individual has the same inalienable image of God awarded to him or her. The accountability of those in power, in the sense of responsibility to the community, could be understood as an application of the biblical principle according to which everyone, irrespective of the person, has to give an account of his stewardship before God and humankind (Luke 12:20).[7] The logical consequence of the

---

[7] Hans Maier defends the notion that the establishment of democratic constitutional states would not have been possible without Christianity. Hans Maier,

image of God in humanity, of humanity's dignity and freedom, is humankind's freedom of conscience and freedom of religion. The inalienable dignity of humanity, which springs from humanity's *imago Dei* as a creation, protects individuals from coming under the complete grasp of others, thus protecting them "from the state, society, the people, the consensus"[8] and, with that said, protecting them from comprehensive monopolization and capture under totalitarian demands of thought and action without alternative courses of action.

WOULD DEMOCRACY BE BETTER SERVED WITH A "CHRISTIAN STATE?"

In Germany, the state as an institution is to adhere to neutrality in religious questions, even if the history and culture of Germany have been shaped by Christianity. Though a number of Christians seem to desire a "Christian state" that would represent and embody the Christian faith, it should be noted that such a state would then almost automatically see itself as a representative of the interests of one or both major churches (Catholic and Protestant) and offer them exclusive privileges. This would bring about disadvantages for other Christian denominations, such as Coptic or Greek Orthodox. Even if the state were to make itself the representative of all Christian denominations, there would be the remaining problem of demarcation: Who would define the boundary cases as "Christian" or "non-Christian," to decide which group is a special type of Christian and which is a different religion? If this happened, the state would become a theological authority regarding the contents of the Christian faith. This has never been successful in the past.

For that reason, the state should preserve what could be called "respectful non-identification"[9] by acknowledging the right of all religious communities to development and expression, to a public presence, and to peaceful solicitation for new members.[10] Moreover, the state can enter into

---

Demokratischer Verfassungsstaat ohne Christentum - Was wäre anders? (St. Augustin/Berlin: Konrad-Adenauer-Stiftung, 2006).

[8] As formulated by William J. Hoye, *Demokratie und Christentum. Die christliche Verantwortung für demokratische Prinzipien* (Münster: Aschendorff, 1999), p. 35.

[9] According to Heiner Bielefeldt, *Muslime im säkularen Rechtsstaat: Integrationschancen durch Religionsfreiheit* (Bielefeld: Transcript, 2003), p. 23.

[10] See the comprehensive explanation on the relationship between the religiously neutral state and churches in Maria Pottmeyer, *Religiöse Kleidung in der öffentlichen*

contractual relationships with religious communities that are set up for permanence and with representation as statutory bodies under public law (in German, Körperschaften des öffentlichen Rechts or KdöR), loyal to Germany's Basic Law (constitution) whereby both sides profit. Partisanship on the part of the state for a certain religious community would suspend or severely limit the religious freedom and legal equality of non-Christian religious communities. Such action would not only be irreconcilable with the law; it would also be politically impossible in our country in which one-third of the population does not belong to either of the two major national churches (*Volkskirchen*) and where only a part of the remaining two-thirds of the citizens who are still official church members see themselves as convinced Christians. [Ed: The German word *Volkskirche* refers to the Protestant Church of Germany (EKD) and the Catholic Church of Germany; both have extensive cooperative agreements with the German government, partly resulting from their history, which are designed to serve selected public purposes within Germany today; neither is truly a "state church" in the sense of being state-run or state-endorsed.] Additionally, it remains an open question how a Christian state would judge atheists, especially which privileges it would possibly withdraw from them on the basis of their lack of a faith confession; this would indicate an abrupt end to religious freedom.

A religiously neutral, democratic state does not face religious communities indifferently. Rather, in a multifaceted manner, such a state is dependent upon cooperation with religious communities. The state theorist and expert in constitutional law, Ernst-Wolfgang Böckenförde, in his famous "Böckenförde Dictum," formulated it as follows: "The liberal, secular state lives on preconditions which it cannot itself guarantee."[11] This means that the state can pass laws imposing sanctions against murder and theft, but the state cannot ensure that the majority of the citizens will continue to judge murder and theft to be wrong. That is to say, the state cannot ensure that people will agree with a canon of values upon which state legislation is based. If a large portion of the population no longer agrees with this canon or platform of values and the legislation deriving from it, the democratic state can no longer enforce compliance with these laws. Therefore, the state encourages religious communities, to which it grants statutory corporate rights under certain preconditions, and with which it

---

Schule in Deutschland und England: Staatliche Neutralität und individuelle Rechte im Rechtsvergleich (Tübingen: 2011), especially pp. 34ff; 148ff; 164ff; 178ff.

[11] Ernst-Wolfgang Böckenförde, *Staat, Gesellschaft, Freiheit* (Frankfurt: Suhrkamp, 1976), p. 60.

cooperates. For their part, religious communities support the state in the sense of developing and maintaining a canon of values in which they promote peace, law, and moral values, while acknowledging the state's monopoly on force and punishment. This cooperation between the state and religious communities is expressed in the tax exemption of donations, the giving of religious instruction (allowed in German public schools), or special regulations in labor law and social law.

The mutual relinquishment of power by the church and by the state within German culture was achieved through a tenacious struggle. On the one hand, state goodwill toward religious communities and state neutrality with respect to the content-based assessment of religious beliefs, and on the other hand the foundational acknowledgment of the state monopoly on force and the state realm of control where the commandments of the church do not apply, have had far-reaching ramifications: the separation of powers and the allocation of separate spheres for religion and the state have led to the development of religious freedom, universal human rights, a type of secularism that is not necessarily anti-religious, the freedom to conduct research, and religious pluralism. This is the case even if, for a long time, there was suspicion on the part of churches in regard to democracy with civil rights and liberties. Both mainline churches (Protestant and Catholic) did not finally affirm democracy with full civil rights and liberties until the twentieth century, when they published position papers accepting democracy and religious diversity.

While the church retains only the position of a moral authority in a constitutional state, so that the church is no longer a lawmaking and political authority, the state, on the other hand, preserves neutrality and distance toward religions, so that no citizen of the state is forced to practice a religion or consider a religion to be true. The state, which no longer poses as a judge over religious content, does not force the representatives of religion to abandon their truth claims and take up the position of state neutrality. Reciprocally, representatives of religions can be expected to accept people as citizens of the state even if they think or believe differently and to accept legislation with a secular orientation. In this manner, the self-limitation of the state to the non-religious sphere makes reconciliation between churches and a secular state possible.

7

Indonesian Islam and a Tradition of Pluralism

Kyle Wisdom

SUMMARY

In a companion piece to that of Christine Schirrmacher, Kyle Wisdom discusses the life and writings of the renowned 20th-century Indonesian Muslim scholar Nurcholish Madjid, whose ideas addressed "the inherent tension between state and religion, while inculcating the values of an open, pluralistic, and democratic nation-state." A student of Fazlur Rahman, who taught at the University of Chicago, "Madjid largely succeeded where Fazlur Rahman had failed in Pakistan: i.e., in developing a reform-oriented approach to Islamic teachings that became widely accepted in Indonesian society and helped shape the post-Suharto political order" and the socio-cultural environment from which the global Humanitarian Islam movement emerged.

In the West, discussions regarding the proper role of religion in society often fall prey to mistaken assumptions. For example, those on the political right frequently assume that Islam and democracy are incompatible.[1] This assumption is particularly strong in the United States, where the popular image of Islam is colored by the events of 9/11, ISIS, and a steady drumbeat of Islamist terror attacks perpetrated throughout the world. In light of these circumstances, a flattened perspective of the Islamic

---

[1] A well-known article by Samuel Huntington (1993) articulated this view and prompted extensive public debate, though Huntington's views are more nuanced than some popularizations.

tradition is understandable, albeit lamentable, for those who have not encountered other dimensions of the world's second-largest religion.[2] Scholars have attempted to counter this myopic approach to Islam as a whole (Benard 2003; Salvatore and Eickelman 2004; Tibi 2008; Hashemi 2009; Soroush 2009), but those without specialized knowledge are still susceptible to it.

A second erroneous assumption, prevalent among those on the cultural-political left, presumes that peaceful coexistence between religion and society can only occur by removing religion as far as possible from the state. This view is widely represented among contemporary liberal-secular streams of thought, but its roots predate the modern era and nation-state.[3] In Western nations, religion is often marginalized in the public sphere due to suspicion and its perceived competition with state authority. This second assumption has become dominant among Western intellectual, cultural, and political elites and is partly due to historical perceptions of how poorly things went when Christianity was wedded to power in medieval and Reformation-era Europe. Ironically, those who hold this view often deny any causal relationship between what Humanitarian Islam leaders have termed "obsolete and problematic tenets of Islamic orthodoxy" and the actions of groups such as ISIS, al-Qaeda, and Boko Haram.

Contrary to these assumptions, Islam is not invariably hostile to democracy. Nor is a complete separation between state and religion the only viable means to avoid the abuses of the past. Indonesia, the world's largest Muslim-majority nation and democracy, demonstrates the error of both assumptions. Situated at the eastern edge of the Islamic world, far from the Arabian Peninsula, Indonesia has a long history of religious pluralism and tolerance. Yet the preamble to its constitution posits the existence of God and acknowledges the essential role of religion, and religious values, in ensuring a harmonious and prosperous society.

Although the example of Indonesia conclusively demonstrates that Islam is far from monolithic, this fact — crucial to inform public discourse — is little known in the West. This is partly due to the fact that Indonesia was a Dutch colony, its Muslim intellectuals do not write in English, and their seminal texts have rarely been translated into foreign languages.[4] I believe

---

[2] This stereotype can be categorized as an essentialist image of Islam. Its historical development among notable Western and Islamic scholars was traced by Jung (2011).

[3] Perhaps the best-known contemporary advocate of this view is John Rawls, although the perspective in question dates back to John Locke.

[4] Adeney-Risakotta (2018, p. 1) claims that Indonesia may be legitimately considered the center of contemporary Islamic civilization, as it not only has more

that the writings of a 20th-century Indonesian scholar, Nurcholish Madjid, speak powerfully to these important issues of how religion and society can interact harmoniously in the modern world.⁵ A highly respected Muslim intellectual, Madjid developed sophisticated, reformist ideas within the Islamic tradition that are fully compatible with the modern world of democracy and human rights. As such, his ideas address the inherent tension between state and religion while inculcating the values of an open, pluralistic, and democratic nation state.

In this essay, I provide a biographical summary of Madjid, introduce three key themes in his broader work, and analyze an article he wrote on the issue of democratic pluralism in Indonesia.

BIOGRAPHICAL SUMMARY

Nurcholish Madjid was born on March 17, 1939, between the world wars and before the founding of the modern state of Indonesia in 1945, in the eastern part of the island of Java, in an area called South Jombang. This area is known for its many Islamic boarding schools and was reputed to be a center of Islamic "traditionalism,"⁶ a stronghold of the Nahdlatul Ulama organization. Nahdlatul Ulama (NU) was formed as a response to Wahhabism in Saudi Arabia and the "modernist"⁷ Muhammadiyah movement in Indonesia.

Madjid was raised in a religious environment within the Sunni tradition, as was his father, a notable student under a famous *kyai* (that is, a

---

Muslims than the entire Middle East, but is also at the forefront of innovative developments vital to the future of the Muslim world and humanity at large.

5   Madjid has received some attention from scholars outside Indonesia; see Saeed (1997); Kull (2005); Perlez (2005); Van Bruinessen (2006); Kersten (2009); Rozak, Budimansyah, Sumantri, and Winataputra (2015); and Woodward (2018).

6   The terms "traditional" and "modern" have distinctive uses in Indonesia. "Traditional" generally refers to Nahdlatul Ulama, or NU (established in 1926), because its teachings are aligned with those of traditional Sunni Islam, including the wide array of Islamic sciences, both formal (such as fiqh, or Islamic law) and spiritual (Sufism). NU is also rooted in Indonesia's indigenous cultural environment, embracing its traditions of diversity and inclusion.

7   In contrast to the term "traditional", the term "modern" is often used to describe the Muhammadiyah organization, established in 1912 by Kyai Haji Ahmad Dahlan, who was strongly influenced by the Egyptian Islamic scholars Muhammad Abduh and Rashid Rida, who wished to "purify" Sunni Islam from "innovations" made subsequent to the life of the Prophet and his companions. Nahdlatul Ulama has far more members (a reported 93 million) than its modernist alternative, Muhammadiyah (28 million).

religious teacher also seen as possessing mystical knowledge).[8] Nurcholish, the oldest son in the family, was raised with much love and happiness by his devout father and mother. He attended his parents' religious school during his elementary years, studying the Islamic sciences (the Qur'an, its interpretation, the Arabic language, logic, ethics, mysticism and jurisprudence). He also attended a non-religious elementary school, where he learned the secular sciences. For his secondary education, he was sent to a leading school (Darul Ulum) at Rejoso that taught the Islamic sciences but also incorporated secular subjects such as mathematics and physics.

As Nurcholish was approaching his final years of secondary school, a division occurred within his father's political party. His father chose to stay with the Islamist-dominated Masyumi Party rather than join the emerging NU party. This caused serious problems at school for Nurcholish, as his *pesantren* (an Islamic boarding school) was firmly in the traditionalist camp. After deep discussions between father and son, Nurcholish transferred to a more modernist school (Pondok Modern Darussalam Gontor) in Ponorogo. Living and learning alternately in schools characterized by traditionalist and modernist thought exerted a lasting impact on Nurcholish Madjid. Gontor had a reputation for strict language education, enabling Nurcholish to develop a solid command of both Arabic and English. His school experiences were formative in preparing Nurcholish to become a leading Muslim intellectual and to engage with the modern world.[9]

While attending Syarif Hidayatullah State Islamic Institute in Jakarta, Madjid became president of Indonesia's largest Muslim student association, *Himpunan Mahasiswa Islam* (HMI), where he began his long "career of stirring Muslims to undertake reform and adapt Islam to Indonesian needs" (Fathimah 1999, 4). He held the presidency for two terms and became widely known as someone who could forge links between two Islamic organizations with conflicting ideas about the still-young Indonesian nation-state: HMI (which he led) and the Masyumi political party, with which his father had been affiliated. The primary issue dividing HMI and Masyumi was the question of whether Indonesia should be an Islamic state.

Although Madjid was an effective mediator between these two significant elements within Indonesian society, he developed an unfavorable

---

[8] The kyai in this case was Kyai Hasyim Asy'ari, co-founder of Nahdlatul Ulama. A blessing from a kyai was considered very significant for those who received it. See Lukens-Bull and Dhofier (2000).

[9] Madjid is considered the last great Indonesian philosopher who was also a prominent educator (Van Bruinessen 2006, 2011; Hooker and Hooker 2009). He is referred to as *"guru bangsa"* or "teacher of the nation," employing his affectionate and public nickname "Cak Nur" (Nafis 2014).

view of Masyumi's uncompromising political attitude, believing that "they suffered from inflexibility, dogmatism, and impractical considerations" (Fathimah 1999, 27). In 1960, President Soekarno dissolved Masyumi, after senior Masyumi leaders participated in the CIA-backed PRRI-Permesta rebellion against the central government. This personal experience of Islamic political parties left a bitter taste in Madjid's mouth, which would be expressed in his later writings and most clearly in his renowned slogan, "Islam, Yes; Islamic parties, No."

Madjid traveled to the United States for further study and was awarded a Ph.D., with highest honors, by the University of Chicago in 1984. He completed his dissertation under the tutelage of Fazlur Rahman, a reform-oriented Islamic scholar who was born in the Northwest Frontier Province of British India, in what is now Pakistan.[10] By the time Madjid returned from Chicago, he had become an acknowledged expert in both Islamic and secular sciences, thus positioning him to make major contributions to the development of contemporary Islam in Indonesia (Liddle 1996, 323–356; Barton 1997). Following in his mentor's footsteps, Madjid largely succeeded where Fazlur Rahman had failed in Pakistan, i.e., in developing a reform-oriented approach to Islamic teachings that became widely accepted in Indonesian society and helped shape the post-Suharto political order (Fathimah 1999).

Madjid established a nonprofit organization called the Paramadina Foundation in 1986 and Paramadina University in 1998. During his long career, he published many books, articles and scholarly essays addressing significant issues related to Indonesia's political life. He passed away on August 29, 2005. His major works have been compiled by the Nurcholish Madjid Society (established in 2008), which published an extensive collection of those works in 2019. Nurcholish Madjid's writings are available online at http://nurcholishmadjid.net.

THREE KEY THEMES

A number of major themes within Madjid's collected writings address common assumptions regarding the perceived incompatibility between Islam and democracy. These include (1) the need to contextualize Islam in contemporary time and space; (2) Nurcholish Madjid's respect for how other religions value consciousness of, and obedience to, God

---

[10] Rahman wrote extensively on Islam as a reformer (Abbas 2017; Rahman 1966, 1982, 2010).

(*takwa*); and (3) an alternative to the Western Enlightenment's singular use of reason to ascertain truth, which limits human knowledge to the phenomenological world while neglecting truths revealed through the practice of mysticism.

Both Muslim fundamentalists and many non-Muslims believe that core elements of Islamic teaching — such as the body of Islamic law, or *fiqh*, that emerged in the centuries following Muhammad's death — must be universally applied and may not be re-contextualized due to its being a fixed, unchanging aspect of Islam itself (Jung 2011). However, Madjid pointed out various difficulties inherent in this view of Islam. Many early Muslim scholars were not preoccupied with a fixed or rigid way of interpreting scripture. Mainstream Sunni Islam historically accepted the contextualization of Islamic teachings in different cultures and time periods, such as when Imam Shafi'i, who founded one of the four major schools of Sunni jurisprudence, moved from Mesopotamia to Egypt and adapted his legal rulings to accommodate the pre-existing culture and traditions of the Nile region.

As Abdurrahman Wahid — the former Indonesian president and long-time chairman of Nahdlatul Ulama — points out in his essay "God Needs No Defense":

> [M]any of the greatest *fiqh* (Islamic jurisprudence) scholars have also been deeply grounded in the traditions of *tassawuf*, or Islamic mysticism, and recognized the need to balance the letter with the spirit of the law... Among the various factors which have contributed to the long decline of Arab and Muslim civilizations in general, and greatly hindered their participation in the development of the modern world, was the triumph of normative religious constraints, which ultimately defeated the classical tradition of Islamic humanism. Absorption of "alien" influences — particularly in the realm of speculative thought, and the creation of individual, rational and independent sciences not constrained by religious scholasticism — was defeated by internal control mechanisms exercised by religious and governmental authorities, thus paralyzing Muslim societies.

Like his friend Abdurrahman Wahid, Madjid believed that the flexible mindset characteristic of early Islam allowed Muslims to benefit from the strengths of other civilizations and thereby produced Islam's golden age, which featured openness to learning from other cultures' insights in science and philosophical endeavors. It is precisely this openness to other cultures that has been largely missing in Islam for many centuries, thereby preventing the re-contextualization of Islamic teachings in such a way as to encourage Muslims to live in harmony with the modern world of democracy and human rights.[11]

Nurcholish Madjid acknowledged that since the Enlightenment had produced invaluable scientific and technological breakthroughs, Muslims' embrace of Western science could easily enable the rationalist and materialistic ideology that has come to dominate the West, in conjunction with these advancements, to slip into Muslim societies undetected. Rather than simply "filter out" these harmful elements, Madjid observed, all too many Muslims have adopted a counter-productive and reflexively negative response to the West, perhaps due to feeling inferior and rejecting Western hegemony. This response to Western culture has unnecessarily constrained the development of modern Islam. It needs to free itself, but this need for liberation is not yet widely recognized. Instead, modern Islam has internalized this counter-productive narrative and embedded this rejection of alien influence within its understanding of Islam itself and its interaction with other cultures. This has led to the rigidity so characteristic of Islam today.

According to Madjid, rather than embrace a reactive view of Islam, Muslims should simply relax — recognizing Islam's true superiority, rooted in their faith regarding Allah and the Qur'anic revelation. A Muslim who is confident that his or her religion embodies and conveys ultimate truth can freely learn from other traditions and reap the benefits from doing so, without feeling insecure.

A second theme in Madjid's writings extends this openness and willingness to engage with alien cultural influences toward other religions, while remaining rooted in Islam. The Qur'an communicates absolute moral truths delivered by the prophet Muhammad. This understanding of the Qur'an is fundamental to Islam and encourages Muslims to live in accord with its ethical teachings. The message was revealed to the Prophet, who lived in 7th-century Mecca and Medina. Yet many if not all of the absolute and transcendent moral truths conveyed by the Qur'an have also been perceived and applied by other cultures. Madjid explores the implications of this in his discussion of *takwa*,[12] an Arabic term which, from the perspective of Islamic mysticism, refers to a state of being fully conscious of and surrendered to God. According to Madjid, most humans, whether Muslim or not, are aware of the existence of a divine being. This tends to encourage

---

[11] One example of understanding and interpreting the Qur'an in a contextualized manner may be found in the work of Madjid's doctoral supervisor, Fazlur Rahman, who described a method of interpretation involving a "double move" (Budiarti 2017).

[12] This is the Indonesian spelling of the Arabic word.

those who possess this awareness to adopt an attitude of humility or *takwa*. Muslims know that this state of *takwa* consists of submission to God, as expressed by the term Islam, which literally means "submission." For a Muslim who believes in Allah, this awareness of God's existence can refer only to Allah Himself. Adherents of other religions, who do not accept the Qur'an, may also demonstrate *takwa* in their own ways. This shared perception of God's existence creates "meeting points" between those of different faiths, a concept that Madjid (1995) mentioned frequently.

According to Madjid's perspective, the adherents of other religions can sense the existence of God, even if their understanding of Him differs from that of Islam. They may understand him as Christians, Buddhists, or Hindus, but the reality they are apprehending is Allah. This conviction helped to shape Madjid's understanding of inclusivism and was a critical part of his argument for the compatibility of Islam and democracy.

The final theme relates to Madjid's interest in mysticism as an alternative or complementary means to ascertain truth, rather than relying solely upon human reason (Munawar-Rachman 2008). Traditional Islam teaches a variety of paths through which one may approach and please Allah, and various Islamic terms are associated with these different paths. This implies that there is not a single way of being religious but, rather, many expressions of religiosity which are — or should be — viewed as complementary. Madjid (1995) considered a mystical approach to acquiring knowledge of God (Sufism, or *tassawuf*) as one essential component of Islam, alongside *falsafah* (philosophy or rational thinking), *kalam* (theology), and *fiqh* (Islamic law).

Madjid's theme of mysticism finds historical expression in the Sufi tradition, which is integral to traditional Sunni Islam but anathematized by Wahhabi extremism. This Wahhabi rejection of Sufism explains why ISIS and similar Islamist groups have consistently destroyed the tombs of Sufi masters, from Pakistan, Syria, and Iraq to Libya and Timbuktu. Madjid felt that Sufism highlights the spiritual truth embodied in the Qur'an, but he also emphasized that this spiritual truth must be reinterpreted from time to time in order for Islam and its teachings to align with the context of contemporary civilization. (The established method of interpreting the Qur'an to create Islamic law is known as *ijtihad*.) For instance, modern scientific advancements had not yet occurred at the time when the Qur'an was revealed. Therefore, according to Madjid, Islamic law must be re-examined and re-contextualized to address such developments within Muslim communities worldwide. The validity of spiritual modes of acquiring knowledge and belief in the truth of the Qur'an were foundational to Madjid's faith and his confidence in the vitality of Islam. This faith and confidence inspired Madjid's — and his fellow Islamic scholar and reformer, Abdurrahman Wahid's — passion to help Islam negotiate the modern age and adapt to changing times.

ISLAMIC ROOTS OF MODERN PLURALISM

One of Madjid's most important texts, accessible in English, is an essay written for the launch of the Indonesian journal *Studia Islamika* (Madjid 1994). In it, Madjid grounded his ideas of modern pluralism within the history of Islam as it has historically, and necessarily, been contextualized in Indonesia. He advanced his argument through five main sections of the essay: (1) Indonesia is a modern nation-state with a special commitment to religion and society, as expressed in the preamble to its constitution, which identifies five key principles called *Pancasila*; (2) Indonesian society is dominated by non-Arab expressions of Islam whose differences are important to understand; (3) this distinctive Indonesian context fosters tolerance, which is fully compatible with the Qur'an and the message of the prophet Muhammad; (4) tolerance is a vital component of modern nation states and integral to Indonesia's own cultural heritage; and (5) Indonesia's unique blend of democracy and religion is both theologically legitimate and compatible with Islamic history.

Indonesia, Madjid stressed, is not an Islamic state but, rather, is founded upon the five basic principles known as *Pancasila*: "One Supreme God or Monotheism, Just and Civilized Humanism, the Unity of Indonesia, Democracy, and Social Justice" (Madjid 1994, 57). The first principle, belief in God, was essential to render the nation's constitution acceptable to Muslims and was thus vital to ensure cohesion among diverse religious, ethnic, and social elements within the newly established state. This first principle of *Pancasila*, affirming that Indonesians share a belief in the existence of God, underlies and animates the modern Indonesian nation state. Ever since the founding of Indonesia in 1945, Islamists have contested *Pancasila*, both politically and, at times, through armed rebellion. However, during the course of President Suharto's 32-year rule, nearly all major civil society institutions acknowledged and accepted *Pancasila* as the sole and final "ideological basis for Indonesia as a nation, a state, and a society" (Madjid 1994, 58).

Having established that Indonesia is a profoundly religious nation, and predominantly Muslim in its demographic composition,[13] Madjid next

---

[13] Madjid (1994, pp. 76–77) noted that the Indonesian population was approximately 90% Muslim at that time.

pointed out that Indonesia is "the least Arabized of the major Islamic countries" (1994, 59). This is because Islamization in Indonesia occurred primarily through trade and not by the sword, and this peaceful process allowed for a longer and deeper engagement with those who brought Islam to the archipelago. Some have labeled the result of this process as syncretism, but Madjid contested this view. He acknowledged that Geertz's (1960) seminal work, published as *The Religion of Java*, cast local Islam in this light, but then proceeded to critique this perspective as reflecting a shallow and colonial bias with an overreliance on modernist (i.e., Muhammadiyah) sources.

Madjid buttressed his critique of Geertz by citing other Islamic scholars, including Marshall Hodgson, Robert Hefner and Mark Woodward, who have written extensively about Indonesian Islam. For Madjid, there is a crucial difference between syncretism and contextualization. He argued that Indonesian society is characterized by a contextualized understanding of Islam, expressed through *Melayu* — the predominant language employed by Muslims throughout the vast Malay Archipelago. The decision by Indonesia's founders to position Malay, or "Indonesian," as the nation's official language was a decisive point in modern Indonesian history. In contrast to High Javanese, whose vocabulary is dominated by Sanskrit, Malay is full of Arabic loan words and Islamic terminology. Madjid believed this reflects Indonesia's genuine Islamic heritage while also exhibiting distinct cultural variations from Arab societies in the Middle East.

After arguing that Indonesia is both religious and Islamic in its own right, Madjid proceeded to defend the principles contained in Pancasila by citing the Qur'an. Here he moved into the heart of his argument. Modern pluralism is not only suitable to Indonesia's diverse religious, ethnic, and cultural milieu, but has its very roots in the Qur'an and the rich history of Islamic thought. Madjid wrote, "[F]or many Muslims, *Pancasila* is, from the Qur'anic perspective, a common term between different religious factions that God commands to seek and find" (1994, 65). *Pancasila's* five principles are consistent with the beliefs of "People of the Book"[14] and therefore provide "a firm basis for the development of religious tolerance and pluralism in Indonesia" (1994, 68). Madjid wrote that the key ideas embodied in *Pancasila* were also present within the history of Islam, as evidenced by the Constitution of Madina, which created a unified political community in

---

[14] Madjid quoted here from Surah 3:64: "Say: O People of the Book! Come to common terms as between us and you; that we worship none but God; that we associate not partners with him; that we erect not, from among ourselves, lords and patrons, other than God."

7. Indonesian Islam and a Tradition of Pluralism

which those of other faiths, including Jews, enjoyed the "same rights and duties as Muslims" (1994, 64). Therefore, Muslims who exclude and/or repress other "People of the Book" do so without the support of the Qur'an and without a proper understanding of the Prophet's Charter of Madina.[15]

Madjid cited the concepts of *fitrah* (our natural disposition or inborn, intuitive ability to discern between right and wrong, true and false) and *hanifiyyah* (a natural inclination toward the good, true, and sacred) as further demonstrating that Islam teaches the societal value of tolerance (Madjid 1994, 67). *Fitrah* and *hanifiyyah* are common to all humanity, but weakness often tempts men and women to pursue their short-term interests and/or self-gratification to the exclusion of justice and morality. Herein lie the seeds of tyranny, responsible for many of the world's problems. Yet a robust understanding of human nature, which incorporates the Islamic concepts of *fitrah* and *hanifiyyah*, will naturally encourage Muslims to respect those of noble character, who exhibit pure thoughts, intentions and actions, even if they are non-Muslim. Islamic doctrine itself acknowledges the "original oneness of humanity and the basic equality of all people" (Madjid 1994, 68).

Madjid's argument acquires further momentum by asserting the need to adapt the universal truths of the Qur'an to various contingent, cultural environments, thereby enabling Islam to be a truly universal religion (Madjid 1994, 70). This is possible because the Qur'an — which conveys eternal truths — nevertheless communicated these truths in a particular time and place through the prophet Muhammad. "All human experience in history is subject to the operation of the Sunnat Allah [the Law of God] which is immutable and objective, independent of human wishes. Therefore a certainty of historical relativism is needed here, a value that leads people to a readiness for change in a positive and constructive way" (Madjid 1994, 71). The creation of a tolerant, democratic society may thus be successfully pursued if Islam returns to its Qur'anic roots, if its teachings are properly contextualized, and if Muslims recall their own history.

At this point in his argument, Madjid cited the example of tolerance displayed in 8th-century Iberia, when Christians, Muslims, and Jews lived and worked together under Muslim rulers. While this example of peaceful coexistence is certainly commendable, Madjid acknowledged that the

---

[15] Madjid acknowledged the difficulty Muslims often experience in living up to this high ideal: "It is stated that the fact that one Revelation should name others as authentic is an extraordinary event in the history of religions. However, it is almost too much to ask that a man holds other people's religion as equal to his own" (Madjid 1994, p. 65).

tolerance briefly displayed in Umayyad Spain has not been fully developed in other Muslim communities. Commenting on this point, Madjid quoted Bernard Lewis: "For Christians and Muslims alike, tolerance is a new virtue, and intolerance a new crime" (Lewis 1984, 3–4, quoted in Madjid 1994, 65). Despite the intolerance prevalent in many modern Muslim communities, Islam has experienced various historical periods characterized by pluralism and tolerance. The problem today is not Islam itself, but "how Muslims adapt themselves to the modern age" (Madjid 1994, 67). Indeed, in isolating themselves from other cultures and religious traditions, Muslims in the late 20th century had generally lost the strength and self-confidence widely displayed by Muslims during Islam's golden age.[16]

Madjid concluded that Islam has the innate capacity to adapt to modern culture and that Muslims have an urgent duty to facilitate the "modernization of Islam, that is, its adaptation to the environment of the modern age, [which] should occur without disturbing its genuineness and authenticity as a revealed religion" (1994, 72). Both the Qur'anic view of human nature and Islamic history provide justification for the creation of a pluralistic democracy. Madjid wrote that Indonesia's multi-cultural, multi-religious, multi-linguistic environment positions it to make a unique contribution to the world, for its own heritage parallels the era of Islamic tolerance in Spain. "Being the largest among Muslim nations, Indonesia could offer itself as a laboratory for developing modern religious tolerance and pluralism" (Madjid 1994, 76). The Humanitarian Islam movement, which emerged from this Indonesian laboratory, demonstrates the validity of Nurcholish Madjid's observation.

Conclusion

Madjid's writings provide a strong argument that pluralism and tolerance are legitimate elements within the Islamic tradition. His perspective — along with the experience of Indonesia since the fall of the Suharto regime — undermines assumptions that Islam is incompatible with democracy. There are, in fact, various options for the role of Islam in contemporary society, and a clash with Western civilization is not inevitable. Indonesia

---

[16] "From the positive perspective, it is always possible that the classical Muslims fully internalized such a positive and optimistic conception of humanity, a conception which then made them such a cosmopolitan and universalist community that they were ready to learn and adopt anything valuable from the experiences of other communities. Thus, [we see] the role of early Muslims as one of the first communities to internationalize sciences" (Madjid 1994, p. 68).

also demonstrates that a complete separation of religion and society is not the only, nor — considering the history of anti-religious sentiment in the West — even a viable means to create a peaceful and prosperous nation.

Religious communities have great potential to enrich public discussions regarding both the need for and the effective means to facilitate harmonious coexistence. By its very nature, civil society provides mediating spaces that encourage pluralism. By the same token, wise (as opposed to opportunistic) religious leaders are inherently motivated to support the common good and often possess significant spiritual and cultural resources with which to do so.

Civil society may prove to be of increasing importance as globalization proceeds. The potential for religion to play a positive role in public discourse, as demonstrated by Indonesia, offers a strong counter-argument to those who wish to marginalize religion and ban religious values from the political sphere. Such an agenda is inconceivable to most Indonesians. For it is precisely religion and religious communities that have created and maintain the shared ethical framework embraced by the vast majority of Indonesians, Muslim and non-Muslim alike. This brief presentation of this brief presentation of Nurcholish Madjid's thought — which was rooted in Indonesia's traditions of pluralism — suggests that it is important for Westerners to learn from the experience of nations where democracy has flourished due to the support of religious and cultural traditions largely unknown in Europe and North America.

As Madjid stated in a different article, "We would remind ourselves that in an increasingly interdependent and interpenetrating global community, any human rights and civil orientation that does not genuinely support the widest possible shaping and sharing of all values among all human beings is likely to provoke widespread skepticism" (Madjid 2001, 111). In light of these considerations, religion and religious believers should not be excluded, *a priori*, from participating in and shaping civil and political discourse. For religious organizations and their spiritual leaders — including those of Humanitarian Islam and the World Evangelical Alliance — can provide "genuine support" to Western and non-Western societies alike as we confront the daunting challenges posed by an increasingly globalized, militarized, and polarized world.

REFERENCES

Abbas, M. 2017. "Between Western Academia and Pakistan: Fazlur Rahman and the Fight for Fusionism." *Modern Asian Studies*, 51 (3): 736–768.

Adeney-Risakotta, B. 2018. *Living in a Sacred Cosmos: Indonesia and the Future of Islam.* New Haven: Yale University Southeast Asia Studies.

Barton, G. 1997. "Indonesia's Nurcholish Madjid and Abdurrahman Wahid as Intellectual Ulama: The Meeting of Islamic Traditionalism and Modernism in Neo-Modernist Thought." *Islam and Christian-Muslim Relations,* 8 (3): 323–350.

Benard, C. 2003. *Civil Democratic Islam: Partners, Resources, and Strategies.* Santa Monica, CA: Rand.

Budiarti, B. 2017. "Studi Metode Ijtihad Double Movement Fazlur Rahman terhadap Pembaruan Hukum Islam." *Zawiyah: Jurnal Pemikiran Islam,* 3 (1): 20–35.

Fathimah, S. 1999. *Modernism and the Contextualization of Islamic Doctrines: The Reform of Indonesian Islam Proposed by Nurcholish Madjid.* M.A. thesis, McGill University.

Geertz, C. 1960. *The Religion of Java.* Chicago: University of Chicago Press.

Hashemi, N. 2009. *Islam, Secularism, and Liberal Democracy: Toward a Democratic Theory for Muslim Societies.* Oxford: Oxford University Press.

Hooker, M. B., & Hooker, V. 2009. "Faith and Knowledge: Nurcholish Madjid as Educator and Philosopher." *Review of Indonesian and Malaysian Affairs,* 43 (2): 1–12.

Huntington, S. P. 1993. "The Clash of Civilizations?" *Foreign Affairs,* 72 (3): 22–49.

Jung, D. 2011. *Orientalists, Islamists and the Global Public Sphere: A Genealogy of the Modern Essentialist Image of Islam.* London: Equinox.

Kersten, C. 2009. "Indonesia's New Muslim Intellectuals." *Religion Compass,* 3 (6): 971–985.

Kull, A. 2005. *Piety and Politics: Nurcholish Madjid and His Interpretation of Islam in Modern Indonesia.* Lund: Lund University.

Lewis, B. 1984. *The Jews of Islam.* Princeton: Princeton University Press.

Liddle, W. 1996. "Media Dakwah Scripturalism: One Form of Islamic Political Thought and Action in New Order Indonesia." In *Toward a New Paradigm: Recent Developments in Indonesian Islamic Thought,* edited by Mark R. Woodward. Tempe, AZ: Arizona State University.

Lukens-Bull, R. A. 2000. Review of *The Pesantren Tradition: A Study of the Role of the Kyai in the Maintenance of the Traditional Ideology of Islam in Java* by Zamakhsyari Dhofier. *Journal of Asian Studies,* 59 (4): 1091.

Madjid, N. 1994. "Islamic Roots of Modern Pluralism: Indonesian Experience." *Studia Islamika,* 1 (1): 55-77.

Madjid, N. 1995. *Pintu-Pintu Menuju Tuhan.* Jakarta: Paramadina.

Madjid, N. 2001. "Potential Islamic Doctrinal Resources for the Establishment and Appreciation of the Modern Concept of Civil Society." In *Islam and Civil Society in Southeast Asia*. Singapore: Institute for Southeast Asian Studies.

Munawar-Rachman, B. 2008. *Ensiklopedia Nurcholish Madjid*. Indramayu, Jawa Barat: Yayasan Pesantren Indonesia Al-Zaytun.

Nafis, M. W. 2014. *Cak Nur Sang Guru Bangsa: Biografi Pemikiran Prof. Dr. Nurcholish Madjid*. Jakarta: Buku Kompas dan Nurcholish Madjid Society.

Perlez, J. 2005. "Nurcholish Madjid, 66, Advocate of Moderate Islam, Dies." The New York Times. Accessed August 14, 2017. http://www.nytimes.com/2005/09/01/world/asia/nurcholish-madjid-66-advocate-of-moderate-islam-dies.html.

Pew Forum. "Mapping the Global Muslim Population." *Asia-Pacific Overview*. Accessed April 30, 2018. http://www.pewforum.org/2009/10/07/mapping-the-global-muslim-population9/.

Rahman, F. 1966. *Islam*. London: Weidenfeld and Nicolson.

Rahman, F. 1982. *Islam & Modernity: Transformation of an Intellectual Tradition*. Chicago: University of Chicago Press.

Rahman, F. 2010. *Revival and Reform in Islam: a Study of Islamic Fundamentalism*. Oxford: Oneworld.

Rozak, A. et al. 2015. "Political Thoughts and Socio-cultural Nationalism Ideologies of Nurcholish Madjid on Strengthening Democracy, Civil Societies and Civic Virtues in Indonesia." *Asian Social Science*. 11 (27): 142–154.

Saeed, A. 1997. "Ijtihad and Innovation in Neo-Modernist Islamic Thought in Indonesia." *Islam and Christian-Muslim Relations*." 8 (3): 279–295.

Salvatore, A., & Eickelman, D. F. 2004. *Public Islam and the Common Good*. Leiden: Brill.

Soroush, A. (2009). *The Expansion of Prophetic Experience: Essays on Historicity, Contingency and Plurality in Religion*. Leiden: Brill.

Tibi, B. 2008. *Political Islam, World Politics and Europe: Democratic Peace and Euro-Islam Versus Global Jihad*. London: Routledge.

Van Bruinessen, M. 2006. "Nurcholish Madjid Indonesian Muslim Intellectual." *ISIM Review*. 17: 22–23.

Van Bruinessen, M. 2011. *Indonesian Muslims and Their Place in the Larger World of Islam*. Proceedings from Indonesia Update Conference, Canberra.

Woodward, M. R. 2018. "Nurcholish Madjid." *Oxford Encyclopedia of the Modern Islamic World*. Accessed April 27, 2018. http://www.oxfordislamicstudies.com/article/opr/t236/e0602

8

How Islam Learned to Adapt in 'Nusantara'

KH. Yahya Cholil Staquf

SUMMARY

The following article was originally delivered as a presentation at the Beijing Forum in 2014, in cooperation with the United Nations Alliance of Civilizations. It was subsequently featured as the cover story of the April–June 2015 issue of *Strategic Review: The Indonesian Journal of Leadership, Policy, and World Affairs*. Former Indonesian Foreign Minister Dr. Hassan Wirajuda wrote of this article, "[I]f one looks at the history and teachings of Islam, and the application of the religion today in Indonesia, it's not difficult to see why the country is a model of tolerance and peace, as our lead essay clearly argues. It is that adaptability and acceptance which has enabled Islam to flourish in Indonesia for centuries."

Nusantara is a term used to describe the vast archipelago that stretches across the tropics from Sumatra in the west to Papua in the east: a region characterized by immense geographic, biological, ethnic, linguistic and cultural diversity. The word Nusantara first appeared in Javanese literature in the 14th century CE, and referred to the enormous chain of islands that constituted the Hindu-Buddhist Majapahit Empire.

Nusantara is a compound noun derived from ancient Javanese: *nusa* ("islands") and *antara* ("opposite" or "across from"). In his book *Negarakertagama* (composed ca. 1365 CE), the author and Buddhist monk Mpu Prapanca described the territory that comprised Nusantara, which included most of modern Indonesia (Sumatra, Java, Bali, the Lesser Sunda Islands, Kalimantan, Sulawesi, part of the Malukus and West Papua), plus a substantial portion of the territories that now comprise Malaysia, Singapore, Brunei and the southern Philippines. As of 2010, this region was inhabited by approximately 1,340 distinct ethnic groups, which speak nearly 2,500 different languages and dialects (cf. Indonesia's Central Bureau of Statistics).

Indonesia's national motto — *Bhinneka Tunggal Ika* — was also coined during the so-called "golden age" of Majapahit. *Bhinneka* means "different" or "diverse." The Sanskrit word *neka* (like the Latin term *"genus"*) signifies "kind," and is the etymological antecedent of the commonly used Indonesian word *aneka*, which means "variety." *Tunggal* means "one." *Ika* means "that." Thus, *Bhinneka Tunggal Ika* may be literally translated as "Variative (i.e., Different) Yet One." Within the context of modern Indonesia, this implies that despite enormous ethnic, linguistic, cultural, geographic and religious differences, the people of Indonesia are all citizens of a single, unified nation — the Unitary State of the Republic of Indonesia, or NKRI.

Yet the connotations of this motto are far more profound, and universal in their significance, than may appear at first glance. In fact, the concept, historical precedent and spiritual reality of *bhinneka tunggal ika* may serve as a model for establishing a true alliance of civilizations, capable of addressing a wide array of dangers that threaten contemporary humanity.

The phrase *bhinneka tunggal ika* first appeared in an ancient Javanese *kakawin* (book of poetry), known as *Kakawin Sutasoma*. Composed in the 14th century by Mpu Tantular, this renowned *kakawin* promotes mutual understanding and tolerance between Buddhists and Hindu followers of Shiva. The phrase appears in *pupuh* (chapter) 139, verse 5:

> *Rwāneka dhātu winuwus Buddha Wiswa,*
> *Bhinnêki rakwa ring apan kena parwanosen,*
> *Mangka ng Jinatwa kalawan Śiwatatwa tunggal,*
> *Bhinnêka tunggal ika tan hana dharma mangrwa.*

> It is said that Buddha and Shiva are two distinct substances (or entities).
> They are indeed different,
> yet it is impossible to regard them as *fundamentally* different
> (when one apprehends the underlying Unity of existence).
> For the essence (Truth) of Buddha and the essence (Truth) of Shiva
> is One (tunggal).
> (The diverse forms of the universe) are indeed different,
> yet simultaneously One,
> For Truth is indivisible.

It is important to note that the civilizational greatness attained in the East Indies archipelago (Nusantara) did not begin with the Majapahit dynasty. Archaeological remains and other historical records indicate that complex socio-cultural systems had developed within Nusantara from at least the 3rd century CE. And long before that, intense economic and cultural interchange had occurred, both among local populations within Nusantara and with the outside world, especially India and China. An economic boom stimulated by maritime trade is evident from at least the first century CE, with an abundance of ancient Roman gold coins found in Nusantara attesting to the remarkable scope and extent of such trade.

Given the remarkable ethnic, linguistic and cultural heterogeneity of the region, and the dynamic interactions between members of different groups, Nusantara societies naturally developed a highly pluralistic outlook on life. Cultural and religious influences from abroad were quickly assimilated by Nusantara's highly adaptive and flourishing civilization. Thus, Mpu Tantular's observation regarding *bhinneka tunggal ika* did not emerge from a void. Rather, it expressed the collective wisdom of Nusantara, which had developed over the centuries and was already deeply rooted within the culture of a wide geographic region that lay at the crossroads of many ancient civilizations.

The value of this single quatrain of poetry from *Kakawin Sutasoma* is that it encapsulates — and helps us to comprehend — the worldview embraced by Nusantara civilization as a whole, which underlay its remarkable religious pluralism and tolerance. Namely, that the universe arises from a single source, which constitutes the "spiritual essence" of all things. From this perspective, cultures and religions that appear to be widely divergent, are in fact like colors emerging from a prism, derived from a single source of Light.

This profoundly spiritual worldview emerged spontaneously among the people of Nusantara. Given the enormous cultural and linguistic diversity present within the East Indies archipelago, it was impossible to create, much less enforce, the relatively high degree of cultural, linguistic and/or religious uniformity characteristic of some regions of the world. The people of Nusantara concluded that they must accept the reality of this diversity, which confronted them on a daily basis, and hone their ability to coexist peacefully with others. As a result, they came to view cultural and religious differences as inevitable, and developed a civilization that emphasized attaining a state of harmony, as the most effective way to maintain order within a complex social and cultural environment.

The Arrival of Islam

From the 7th to the 10th centuries CE, Islam established deep roots in the Middle East, from Spain and Morocco to western India — giving birth to a new civilization and countless works of genius. These territories underwent a gradual process of Islamization — and Arabization as well, in the Levant, Mesopotamia, and the northern coast of Africa — as a result of having been conquered and subjugated by Muslim rulers.

In other words, military conquest was the essential prerequisite, and catalyst, for the development of classical Islamic civilization. Islam quickly attained military and political supremacy in the Middle East, which enabled Muslim rulers to enforce order and manage the community at large in accordance with religious doctrine and dogma. It was precisely in this atmosphere that the classical teachings (i.e., *interpretation*) of Islam evolved, including *aqidah* (the system of Islamic doctrine, as related to Divine teachings); *fiqh* (the vast body of classical Islamic jurisprudence); and *tasawwuf* (Islamic mysticism, through which Muslims explored the spiritual dimension of life).

Although Muslims' interpretation of Islamic doctrine, dogma, law and spirituality was inevitably diverse, it was the responsibility of Muslim rulers (i.e., conquerors) to establish order, which in turn created a powerful impetus to establish uniformity of religious doctrine and law, at least within an "acceptable" set of parameters. Thus, for purely political reasons, the question of religious "authenticity" became a central topic in the heated debates that often occurred among various competing schools (i.e., interpretations) of Islam. Given these circumstances, it is no surprise that *fiqh* (often conflated with *shari'ah*) dominated such discourse, due to the central position of law in establishing order and governing the relationship between various members of society.

What about Nusantara?

Given the paucity of contemporaneous historical records, no convincing explanation has been provided, to date, of the precise mechanisms through which Islam penetrated Nusantara. A number of records indicate that Islamic kingdoms were established in Nusantara from the late 13th through the 15th centuries (including Jeumpa, Tambayung and Malacca), prior to the process of Islamization gaining decisive momentum in Java with the establishment of the Demak Kingdom.

Notably, virtually all academicians agree that Islam spread throughout Nusantara through a "diffusive" and "adaptive" process which, for the most part, eschewed military conquest. Like Hinduism and Buddhism before it, Islam "dissolved" and was gradually absorbed into the prevailing local civilization of Nusantara.

In distinct contrast to other regions of the Muslim world (e.g., from Spain to India), there is no record of the application of *fiqh* as a comprehensive legal system within the Islamic kingdoms of Nusantara. The resolution of legal issues (such as crimes and disputes) was generally handled through the application of customary law (*adat*), which differed from region to region. For example, to this day the Minangkabau people of West Sumatra retain a matrilineal system, distinctly opposed to the patrilineal system employed in mainstream *fiqh* interpretation of family law. And yet, this Minangkabau adherence to *adat* is accompanied, smoothly and unselfconsciously, by a strong self-identification with Islam on the part of the Minang people as a whole. Indeed, over time local customs (*adat*) throughout Nusantara have become flavored, or colored, by the influence of Islam. Yet there has never been any systematic and comprehensive application of "Islamic law" in public affairs — i.e., "Islamic law" as defined by the mainstream of classical Islamic discourse.

In other words, Islam was forced to "surrender" to the prevailing local customs, and power, of Nusantara's highly pluralistic civilization. To cite yet another example from West Sumatra, the Islamic law of inheritance, which favors males, was subordinated to — or at least compromised with — Minang customary law, in which land and houses are bequeathed through a matrilineal line. Islam thus experienced a softening of its "original discipline." Likewise in Java, where many traditional rituals have been adopted as a "part of Islam" after being adjusted, to a lesser or greater extent, through a steady process of assimilation.

THE ISLAM THAT LEARNS

Within the regions dominated by 'classical Islam" (i.e., the Middle East, North Africa, the Persian and Turkish cultural basins and much of South Asia), Islam arrived in the form of a "judge": subduing, imposing order and adjudicating disputes. In Nusantara, Islam arrived as a guest and was later adopted into the family. In turn, Nusantara Islam developed a distinct character, which is quite different from that manifested by Islam in other regions of the Muslim world. In the Middle East, for example, Islam is commonly viewed as a socio-religious-political system that is "complete," "final" and authoritative, offering human beings no choice but to comply with the dictates of that final construction. In Nusantara, on the other hand, Islam is in a state of constant learning. For more than six hundred years, its leading practitioners have carefully studied social reality, in order to ascertain the most elegant means to achieve their goals, while maintaining harmony within a diverse and highly pluralistic society.

Although Nusantara Islam is distinct from the Middle East model of Islam, this does not mean that it constitutes any form of heresy. Prominent *ulama* (religious scholars) and other Muslim leaders within the East Indies archipelago have been quite deliberate and prudent in ensuring that the manner in which they practice and promote Islam adheres to the fundamental teachings of the Islamic paradigm; follows its intellectual traditions; and maintains an unseverable bond to the established references of classical Islam, anchored in the teachings of authoritative *mujtahid* (leaders within various schools of Islamic thought) from the earliest generations who lived in the Middle East. In other words, the model of "Nusantara Islam" is an absolutely authentic stream of Sunni Islam, as preserved and taught by authoritative *ulama*.

The task of ensuring the authenticity of Islamic teachings — while maintaining harmony with the prevailing social reality — has never been easy. Nusantara's *ulama* have traditionally utilized two principal strategies in order to accomplish this.

The *first* is to ensure a balanced focus of attention upon the spiritual dimensions of Islam *(tasawwuf)*, so that the animating spirit of religion — as a source of universal love and compassion — is not neglected when issuing judgments *(fatwa)* involving the formal/exoteric norms of Islamic law *(fiqh/shari'ah)*.

Nusantara's *ulama* introduced Islamic mysticism *(tasawwuf)* and a variety of spiritual brotherhoods *(tariqa)* established by their predecessors in the Middle East, to local communities throughout the East Indies archipelago. Their teachings on Islamic mysticism elicited an enthusiastic response from locals and soon became the prevailing image/face of Nusantara Islam. In fact, mysticism became the primary attraction of Islam to local communities throughout the region, for it is compatible with the long-established mystical traditions prevalent throughout Nusantara. In an article entitled "Indonesia's Big Idea: Resolving the Bitter Global Debate on Islam," published in the journal *Strategic* Review, Kyai Haji A. Mustafa Bisri and C. Holland Taylor described the principal elements of Islamic mysticism, which have become integral to the spiritual orientation/cultural heritage of Nusantara, and form its basic character.

8. How Islam Learned to Adapt in 'Nusantara'

Two brief citations may serve to illustrate the manner in which Mpu Tantular's concept of *bhinneka tunggal ika* parallels the worldview held by the renowned Persian poet and mystic Jalal ad-Din Rumi (1207 – 1273):

> The difference among men results from the outward name; when you reach the inner meaning you reach peace. Oh marrow of existence! It is because of the perspective in question that there is a difference between a Muslim, a Zoroastrian and a Jew.... Every prophet and every saint hath a way, but it leads to God; all the ways are really one.

The Spanish-born Sufi Ibn 'Arabi (1165 – 1240) — who is often referred to as "Shaykh al-Akbar," or "The Great Master" — expressed a similar view when he wrote:

> My heart has become capable of every form; it is a pasture for gazelles and a cloister for Christian monks, and a temple for idols, and the pilgrim's Ka'ba, and the tables of the Torah and the book of the Koran. I follow the religion of Love, whichever way his camels take. My religion and my faith is the true religion.

Significantly, Jalal ad-Din Rumi and Ibn 'Arabi are two of the most authoritative figures within the realm of Islamic spirituality and mysticism.

It is clear that these spiritual insights provide "doctrinal legitimacy and protection" which not only authorizes but actively encourages the participation of Muslims in the affairs of a highly pluralistic society. This profoundly spiritual worldview also provides a psychological and emotional safety-valve for Muslims, who might otherwise be disturbed by others' rejection of Islamic proselytism (*da'wa*), or their reluctance to fully adopt the formal teachings and rituals of Islam. Due to their understanding of Islam as an "offer of salvation," Nusantara *ulama* consider proselytism as an attempt to "save" others, which will only succeed if the persons concerned are willing. If not, the proselytizer has no responsibility for others' decision to choose a different path in life.

The *second* strategy referenced above is to position Islam as an equal citizen within a highly pluralistic society, rather than as the beneficiary or carrier of a violent, supremacist ideology. Nusantara *ulama* generally believe that public affairs should be managed with the consent of all parties concerned. In Nusantara, Muslim leaders have rarely been burdened by the expectation or demand to impose Islamic law on others.

Nusantara *ulama* creatively seek "space for maneuver" in regard to *shari'ah*, in order to remain closely involved within the wider social arena, without abandoning their affiliation with or practice of *shari'ah* itself. In the case of the Minangkabau tradition cited above, *ulama* utilize the *shari'ah*-sanctioned practice of allowing the distribution of inheritance in accord with any consensus reached among heirs. Thus, local customs (*adat*) that might otherwise conflict with *fiqh* (Islamic law) are positioned within the "realm of consensus."

This approach to Islamic law has served as the basis for Nusantara *ulama* to accept the *secular state* of the Republic of Indonesia, and to reject the establishment of a so-called "Islamic State" or caliphate. Because Islam arrived in Nusantara as a respected guest and not a conqueror, Muslims generally accept the fact that they are not the only party destined to determine the fate of society as a whole. Nusantara's political systems — and particularly the relationship between state and religion — have traditionally reflected consensus among all the stakeholders concerned. Even Islamic kingdoms such as Jeumpa, Tambayung and Mataram have traditionally been regarded as the product of consensus among adherents of traditional law (*adat*), rather than the embodiment of a formal "Islamic state."

In general, it may be said that the ability of Nusantara *ulama* to adapt to social reality without abandoning their own adherence to *shari'ah* stems from the fact that they have mastered *shari'ah* — not merely in the sense of compilations of Islamic jurisprudence, but as profound *legal theory*. Islam teaches that the law must be based upon Divine guidance. But Islam also teaches that in providing guidance, God's purpose is never the pursuit of His own interests. God provides guidance for the benefit of humanity. Thus, anything beneficial to humanity is in harmony with God's "objective" and the purpose of *shari'ah* itself.

PURIFICATION

Regardless of their ethnic or geographic origin, conquerors generally have similar anxieties and behavioral tendencies, as they seek to promote their own self-interest. The most fundamental of these impulses is to ensure the perpetuation of their rule, in the face of overt or latent resistance from those who have been subjugated. Thus, it is logical that conquerors tend to be repressive. Classical Islamic law (*fiqh*) is replete with such repressive dictates. One of the more dramatic examples may be found in a book entitled *Kifaayat 'l Akhyaar* (*The Satisfying Selections*), written by Taqiyudin Abu Bakr bin Muhammad al-Husaini al-Husni (14th century CE). Among the various dictates of Islamic law cited in this book is an explicit requirement that Muslims discriminate against non-Muslims.

In Nusantara, Islam never had to struggle beneath the burden of such injunctions. In the absence of foreign conquerors, there was no threat of resistance to a so-called "foreign religion." Thus, within the 16th-century Islamic kingdom of Demak, the Sultan's chief religious advisor — Ja'far Sadiq Azmatkhan, popularly known as Sunan Kudus — forbade Muslims to slaughter cows within the territorial limits of Kudus, due to his respect for Hindus' belief in the animals' sanctity.

Another early propagator of Islam in Java — Raden 'Ainul Yaqin, who is popularly known as Sunan Giri — was the main arbiter of disputes among his contemporary *ulama,* in regard to Islamic law, because of his profound expertise in the field of *shari'ah.* Yet the best known of Sunan Giri's teachings, which have become indelibly associated with his memory, are his teachings about universal virtues, which are sculpted upon his tomb in East Java:

> *Wenehana mangan marang wong kang luwe*
> *Wenehana sandangan marang wong kang wuda*
> *Wenehana payung marang wong kang kudanan*
> *Wenehana teken marang wong kang wuta*

> Give food to those who are hungry.
> Give clothes to those who are naked.
> Give shelter to those caught in the rain.
> Give walking sticks to those who are blind.

In general, the Islamic narratives that have long thrived in Nusantara are oriented towards the spirit, rather than the letter, of the law. *Fiqh* (Islamic jurisprudence, as an instrument to maintain order) was not considered to be urgent, because preserving public order was not the most crucial challenge facing local societies or their rulers. A strong cultural disposition to seek harmony served as the primary foundation, and guarantor, of social order. In such circumstances, detailed and sophisticated legal instruments were not required, nor was there any need for coercion to enforce such dictates. These circumstances allowed the proponents of religion to delve deeply and unveil the core of religious teachings: namely, spirituality and ethics.

A HARMONIOUS CIVILIZATION AND COMPASSIONATE RELIGION

For nearly two thousand years, Nusantara's civilization has constituted a unique experiment, and direct experience of, human beings' ability to live peacefully amid diversity. Of prioritizing harmony with others, above one's own self-interest. Of spiritual self-confidence, which allows one to experience and embrace new ideas and teachings. Of seeking nobility of character, rather than purely material achievements. Of knowing that differences of opinion (and religion) are not harmful.

Nearly all of the world's religions have come to Nusantara, without encountering resistance. The people of Nusantara are free to embrace any religion that suits them, and to abandon said religion without harm, if and when they desire to do so. And everyone who becomes a citizen within the communal life we share is part of an indivisible unity, regardless of what superficial differences may exist: *Bhinneka Tunggal Ika.*

Within the civilization of Nusantara, Islam found its "heaven." Islam was not burdened with worldly concerns such as rebellion, or other internal and external threats. Islam was blessedly free of being instrumentalized, to serve as a vehicle for advantage in conflict, because in Nusantara, religion has rarely been regarded as a worthy cause for quarrel. Islam thus enjoyed the widest possible opportunity to engage in relaxed dialogue, with social and historical reality.

Within this non-politicized atmosphere, Islam has proved more successful at grounding its core teachings in public life than in many parts of the world. This is because of Nusantara Islam's willingness to empathize with others and engage in dialogue with reality, rather than seeking to impose one's own understanding of reality upon others by force. The success of Nusantara Islam also stems from its conviction that religion should serve as a path to enlightenment for individual souls, and that *shari'ah* should serve to promote the well-being of humanity, rather than functioning as a tool of repressive authority. In Nusantara, Islam was free to fulfill its Qur'anic mandate: i.e., to become a source of universal love and compassion.

In our present era, both the civilization of Nusantara and the variant of Islam it has long nurtured are in a state of decline. This is due to a wide range of pressures stemming from globalization, including the spread of a highly politicized and supremacist understanding of Islam. The memories I have tried to evoke in this essay — of Nusantara's glorious civilization, and its unique expression of Islam — may be rightly viewed as a civilizational plea for help.

Yet it is simultaneously a reminder and an offer to the world: an invitation to imbue social, cultural, political and religious life with love and spiritual beauty. A profound love and beauty that lies at the heart of our vision of an alliance of civilizations, and stands within our grasp, should we elect to transform this vision into reality.

9

The Primary Message of Islam: *Rahmah* (Universal Love and Compassion)

KH. Hodri Ariev

Islam provides multiple explanations for the emergence of creation. Two of these explanations will be explored here. The first is derived from a *ḥadīth qudsī* (a message from God directly conveyed to the Prophet Muhammad without the archangel Gabriel serving as an intermediary). In this *ḥadīth qudsī*, Allah explains, "I was a hidden treasure, I desired (*aḥbabtu*) to be known. Hence I created sentient beings, that they might know Me." The term "hidden treasure" is commonly understood by Muslim scholars to refer to the 99 Beautiful Names of God (*al-Asmā' al-Ḥusná*).

The second explanation for the emergence of creation appears in a work by the renowned Muhyiddin Ibn 'Arabi (1165 – 1240), who is known in Sufi circles as *al-Shaykh al-Akbar* (the Greatest Master). In *Fuṣūṣ al-Ḥikam* (*Pearls of Wisdom*), which Ibn 'Arabi claimed to have received directly from the Messenger of Allah (saw.), the author explains that God created nature because He wished to perceive His own complete perfection. However, nature is a not a clear mirror and cannot reflect God's absolute perfection. Hence, God created mankind to serve as a clear mirror through which He may perceive His own perfection. This is why God loves humanity so deeply.

Related to these two explanations, *Sūrat Fuṣṣilat* (Qur'an 41:53) states, "We shall display Our signs upon the utmost horizons [of the universe] and within themselves until the Truth (*al-Ḥaqq*) becomes clear to them." Islamic scholars (*ulama*) identify two distinct categories of divine signs, namely *qawlīyah* and *kawnīyah*. The first category refers to messages from God recorded in scripture, while the second category refers to what is written in nature itself.

The first category (*qawlīyah*) describes how humans should live their lives. Religion provides moral and spiritual guidance, serving as an illuminated pathway through life, whose ultimate purpose is to help human beings return to God. The second category (*kawnīyah*) constitutes those aspects of the phenomenological world which, when they become the object of spiritual contemplation, may serve to open the eyes of the heart to experience God's presence. Clear manifestations of Divine perfection exist throughout the universe, which Muslims identify as "traces" of His Beautiful Names. For this reason all creatures are, in essence, as sacred as scripture itself. They contain and manifest both signs and traces of God. And because of these Divine traces, God loves His creatures.

In light of these considerations, how could God's scripture (His *qawlīyah* verses, or signs) command His servants to persecute or annihilate their fellow creatures? For the *kawnīyah* signs (*āyāt*), which God loves, are every bit as sacred as His *qawlīyah* verses (*āyāt*). In fact, the Arabic word for a verse from the Qur'an (*āyah*) literally means "a sign from God." When human beings interpret these two categories of signs in such a way as to negate either one or the other, something is clearly wrong. For example, whenever religious adherents weaponize scripture to legitimize tormenting their fellow creatures, their understanding and practice of religion is manifestly flawed. Only love, compassion, and a proper religious education can address this fundamental ignorance and neglect of religion's spiritual and ethical teachings. Conversely, the abandonment of religion altogether — along with the embrace of a purely mechanistic interpretation of the universe — tends to obscure God's *kawnīyah* signs. When such a worldview becomes widespread and assumes the form of militant secularism, it is likely to undermine the moral and spiritual foundations of a healthy society.

People of devout religiosity surely yearn for God's love and, as a result, feel spontaneously called to obey the voice of conscience. Paradise — or true happiness in this world and the next — cannot be obtained without God's love, compassion, mercy, and grace. In order to receive God's mercy and compassion, we must align our will with His and obey His command to love and protect others. This is the true meaning of *islām*.

PART III

10

Theology Matters: The Case of Jihadi Islam

Rüdiger Lohlker

SUMMARY

Islamist movements such as al-Qaeda, ISIS, and Boko Haram share a common ideology, which constitutes a very real threat to international peace and security. In 2014, senior Nahdlatul Ulama theologians joined world-class scholars from the University of Vienna's *Institut für Orientalistik*, to create the Vienna Observatory for Applied Research on Terrorism and Extremism (VORTEX). Dr. Rüdiger Lohlker, a Professor of Islamic Studies at the University of Vienna and respected Counter-terrorism Advisor to the European Union, headed VORTEX, supported by research fellows Dr. Nico Prucha and Dr. Ali Fisher. Their work with VORTEX convinced Nahdlatul Ulama leaders that it is essential to address "obsolete and problematic tenets of Islamic orthodoxy" that readily lend themselves to political weaponization.

The following essay originally appeared in the July–September issue of *Strategic Review: the Indonesian Journal of Leadership, Policy and World Affairs*. In this essay, Dr. Lohlker refutes the widely held and frequently asserted view that Western governments, scholars, and media outlets should neither critically examine, nor address the religious dimensions of Islamist terrorism. Dr. Lohlker writes that, "[W]ithout deconstructing the theology of violence inherent in jihadi communications and practice, these religious ideas will continue to inspire others to act, long after any given organized force, such as the Islamic State, may be destroyed on the ground."

This conceptual discussion is not an exercise in academic nit-picking. Rather, it implies that without deconstructing the theology of violence inherent in jihadi communications and practice, these religious ideas will continue to inspire others to act, long after any given organized force, such as the Islamic State, may be destroyed on the ground. This is not to deny the need for well-funded social work, interventions within families and institutions (such as schools and prisons), or even effective police action.

Flatly denying the importance of religion causes many in the West to overlook a crucial element of jihadi thought and action. This is particularly evident with regard to the mantra so often repeated in the wake of each new terrorist attack, viz.: "Islam is the religion of peace." The claim that religion motivates only positive behavior among human beings, and the implicit denial that religion may ever legitimize negative behavior, cannot withstand intellectual scrutiny. History provides countless examples of both positive and negative behavior legitimized by religion. Even if we abhor jihadis' use of Islamic religious concepts, we cannot deny the fact that they are trying to cut out, and render dominant, their own version of Islam as a religion of violence.

The only way to deconstruct this violent form of religion is to develop alternative forms of religion capable of resisting the theology of violence, which is characterized by apologetics that simultaneously demand and legitimize authoritarianism, socio-cultural and religious homogeneity, and the strict demarcation of boundaries, etc. (see below). This jihadi religion of violence is currently being disseminated throughout much of the world through a complex set of mechanisms, whose widely diverse forms and content are mutually reinforcing. The elements of this complex online and offline dissemination structure include more or less elaborate theological tracts; smaller booklets; condensed texts (such as four- to six-page leaflets); public speeches, events and propaganda meetings in mosques (*da'wa*); videos; posters in public spaces; the issuance of forms and declarations that individuals who have been accepted by a jihadi group are not unbelievers (*kufar*); and, of course, face-to-face communication itself. All these acts of communication convey one message in an extremely coherent manner: there is an Islamic entity, which is the organized form of *true* Islam.

It is understandable that many Muslims react by declaring that IS-Islam is "*un*-Islamic" and alien to their religion. However, since IS and other jihadi propaganda does not target persons who are firmly anchored in an alternate understanding of their faith, and *does* actually tap into significant elements of Islamic heritage, the aforementioned "denial response" may be viewed as that of believers who do not recognize — or do not *wish* to

10

Theology Matters: The Case of Jihadi Islam

Rüdiger Lohlker

Summary

Islamist movements such as al-Qaeda, ISIS, and Boko Haram share a common ideology, which constitutes a very real threat to international peace and security. In 2014, senior Nahdlatul Ulama theologians joined world-class scholars from the University of Vienna's *Institut für Orientalistik*, to create the Vienna Observatory for Applied Research on Terrorism and Extremism (VORTEX). Dr. Rüdiger Lohlker, a Professor of Islamic Studies at the University of Vienna and respected Counter-terrorism Advisor to the European Union, headed VORTEX, supported by research fellows Dr. Nico Prucha and Dr. Ali Fisher. Their work with VORTEX convinced Nahdlatul Ulama leaders that it is essential to address "obsolete and problematic tenets of Islamic orthodoxy" that readily lend themselves to political weaponization.

The following essay originally appeared in the July–September issue of *Strategic Review: the Indonesian Journal of Leadership, Policy and World Affairs*. In this essay, Dr. Lohlker refutes the widely held and frequently asserted view that Western governments, scholars, and media outlets should neither critically examine, nor address the religious dimensions of Islamist terrorism. Dr. Lohlker writes that, "[W]ithout deconstructing the theology of violence inherent in jihadi communications and practice, these religious ideas will continue to inspire others to act, long after any given organized force, such as the Islamic State, may be destroyed on the ground."

An intense debate has raged for many years in Europe and North America, as to whether the ideational products of jihadi groups are to be understood as religious or merely ideological. The dominant narrative among Western governments, policy experts and the mainstream media has been that al-Qaeda and other jihadi groups embrace a violent "ideology," rather than specific religious doctrines that pervade and drive their agenda.

The fact that jihadis have produced a significant volume of textual and audio/visual resources that directly address religious issues — most strikingly, beneath the umbrella of al-Qaeda (Lohlker 2009) and IS (Lohlker 2016a) — may justify our questioning this common assumption. Thousands of pages of text and countless gigabytes of audio/visual material have been devoted to the discussion of religious matters and the construction of a jihadi-type religion, which may be described as a "jihadi Islam." Indeed, it is crystal clear — to virtually anyone who the linguistic capacity to grasp and the opportunity to witness what jihadists are actually saying, writing and doing, both online and offline — that religion matters.

Since this not the place for a lengthy discussion about religion in general — as tempting as that may be for a scholar of religion — we will restrict ourselves to a more pragmatic distinction, and approach this issue from the perspective of jihadi communications. Specifically, we shall focus upon the establishment of a religious-ethical community of jihadis by means of communication. In doing so, let us bear in mind that terrorism itself may be regarded as a form of communication (Waldmann 2005, 13). We will talk about religion, so long as

> one pole of the communication has... [a] *non*-human, *non*-empirical, *transcendent*, or *'supernatural'* character, the communication may count as religious. It is the negative definition... that gives religion in modern global society its fluidity and ambiguity, allowing the construction of cultural entities as religion if only they can be convincingly established as such (Beyer 2001, 144).

Turning to IS, we may reliably state that it devotes significant resources to the production of explicitly religious material, including books that teach Islamic creed (*'aqīda*), Qur'anic exegesis (*tafsīr*), and Hadith (traditions ascribed to the Prophet Muhammad), to cite but a few examples. This is done intentionally — not in order to camouflage the "real" interests of IS (e.g., the acquisition of power, wealth or anything else), but because religion matters to IS and its followers, and constitutes the "real thing" for them.

If we understand ideology not merely as a set of ideas — be they political, economic, philosophical, or religious — we may discern a clear distinction between ideology and theology/religion.

10. Theology Matters: The Case of Jihadi Islam

Consulting standard texts on ideology, we may encounter — e.g., in Terry Eagleton's *Ideology: An Introduction* — a list of 16 types of ideology (Eagleton 1991, 1–2). Some are general and others particular; yet all refer to the ideas and behavior of social groups. Marxists, for example, describe religious belief as "false" and "inverted" consciousness (Rehmann 2013, 5). Other scholars tend to categorize and differentiate between three types of ideology: a) those characterized by certain errors caused by epistemological shortcomings, b) a system of ideas and values, and c) a social and political program (Tepe 2012, 1–2).

These ways of conceptualizing ideology all betray a reluctance to acknowledge that religion may still be "alive" in the post-modern era, and may even be part of the realms of evil — at least to some extent. Failure to recognize the importance of religion to others' motivation and behavior reflects a Western prejudice that emerged in the 1960s, for it conflicts with the the paradigm of "the inevitable decline of religion." Denial of the centrality of religion to jihadis' motivation and behavior may also constitute an attempt to absolve religion (and in particular, Islam) from the commission of violence, even if said violence is committed by persons acting from within an explicitly religious frame of reference. *Jihadists do not subscribe to this paradigm.* One reason for this may be glimpsed from Eagleton's remark, below, concerning ideology:

> The study of ideology is among other things an inquiry into the ways in which people may come to invest in their own unhappiness. It is because being oppressed sometimes brings with it some slim bonuses that we are occasionally prepared to put up with it. The most efficient oppressor is the one who persuades his underlings to love, desire and identify with his power; and any practice of political emancipation thus involves that most difficult of all forms of liberation: freeing ourselves from ourselves. The other side of the story, however, is equally important. For if such dominion fails to yield its victims sufficient gratification over an extended period of time, then it is certain that they will finally revolt against it. (Eagleton 1991, xiii–xiv)

Since the history of religion is full of cases of cognitive dissonance — which resulted in reinforcement of the same behavior that led to the experience of dissonance in the first place — we may assume that "the transcendent realm" (see above) helps to sustain belief, even if gratification does not appear in this world. A paradigmatic case is the repeatedly observed phenomenon, in which members of a religious community continue to believe in the wisdom and power of their leader, even after his or her prediction of the imminent end of the world has failed to materialize.

This conceptual discussion is not an exercise in academic nit-picking. Rather, it implies that without deconstructing the theology of violence inherent in jihadi communications and practice, these religious ideas will continue to inspire others to act, long after any given organized force, such as the Islamic State, may be destroyed on the ground. This is not to deny the need for well-funded social work, interventions within families and institutions (such as schools and prisons), or even effective police action.

Flatly denying the importance of religion causes many in the West to overlook a crucial element of jihadi thought and action. This is particularly evident with regard to the mantra so often repeated in the wake of each new terrorist attack, viz.: "Islam is the religion of peace." The claim that religion motivates only positive behavior among human beings, and the implicit denial that religion may ever legitimize negative behavior, cannot withstand intellectual scrutiny. History provides countless examples of both positive and negative behavior legitimized by religion. Even if we abhor jihadis' use of Islamic religious concepts, we cannot deny the fact that they are trying to cut out, and render dominant, their own version of Islam as a religion of violence.

The only way to deconstruct this violent form of religion is to develop alternative forms of religion capable of resisting the theology of violence, which is characterized by apologetics that simultaneously demand and legitimize authoritarianism, socio-cultural and religious homogeneity, and the strict demarcation of boundaries, etc. (see below). This jihadi religion of violence is currently being disseminated throughout much of the world through a complex set of mechanisms, whose widely diverse forms and content are mutually reinforcing. The elements of this complex online and offline dissemination structure include more or less elaborate theological tracts; smaller booklets; condensed texts (such as four- to six-page leaflets); public speeches, events and propaganda meetings in mosques (*da'wa*); videos; posters in public spaces; the issuance of forms and declarations that individuals who have been accepted by a jihadi group are not unbelievers (*kufar*); and, of course, face-to-face communication itself. All these acts of communication convey one message in an extremely coherent manner: there is an Islamic entity, which is the organized form of *true* Islam.

It is understandable that many Muslims react by declaring that IS-Islam is "*un*-Islamic" and alien to their religion. However, since IS and other jihadi propaganda does not target persons who are firmly anchored in an alternate understanding of their faith, and *does* actually tap into significant elements of Islamic heritage, the aforementioned "denial response" may be viewed as that of believers who do not recognize — or do not *wish* to recognize — the religion they profess when confronted with the brutal crimes committed by terrorists in the name of Islam, and thus refuse to acknowledge the terrorists' thoughts and actions as religiously-based.

Whatever motivates this reaction on the part of mainstream Muslims — and their counterparts in the West — this denial response will not solve the problem we face, nor destroy the religious appeal of jihadi Islam. Turning again to Eagleton, the critique of ideology he describes may also be relevant to the theology of violence — indicating that we must acknowledge and address, rather than ignore, the religious elements thereof:

> [O]nly those interventions will work which make sense to the mystified subject itself.... "Critique" is that form of discourse which seeks to inhabit the experience of the subject from inside, in order to elicit those "valid" features of that experience which point beyond the subject's present condition. (Eagleton 1991, xiv)

But now we must turn to theology and religion, leaving ideology aside.

RELIGION

In this section, we will turn away from discussing whether "ideology" is an accurate term to describe the phenomenon in question, and instead focus upon religion as a concept that may be useful to understand what is frequently and somewhat awkwardly described as "religiously motivated terrorism," in order to avoid eliciting a negative response from believers. As history clearly proves: violence is a contingent possibility in religion(s). Acknowledging this fact, and possibility, does not constitute an insult to — nor "defamation of" — religion. Rather, it is a necessary step if we are to understand, identify, marginalize and ultimately defeat those who advocate violence. By acknowledging the contingency of a violent turn, the possibility of religious adherents embracing non-violence is acknowledged as well.

Religion only exists through believers "doing," or practicing, religion. Alternative, non-violent ways of practicing religion are what is needed — and not merely for Islam.

Excluding religion from the picture — especially in the case of jihadi Islam — is an attempt to reproduce the constellation of politics and religion in European modernity on a theoretical level, and apply this to the Muslim world. Such an attempt fails to take into account that the configuration of politics and religion may differ in other regions of the world outside Western Europe. It also fails to take into account that what may be true at the level of governmental affairs in Europe, and to some extent within the framework of European theoretical/academic discussion, may not hold true at the grassroots level of Western societies themselves. Hence, the surprising "revival" of religion since the 1970s has occurred more in the realm of academic discussion than objective reality, as millions of people stubbornly refused to conform to the "decline of religion" paradigm.

Researchers in the field of new Islamic movements talk about the emergence of religious subcultures as the foundation of a lifestyle motivated by a certain religious ethos (Riesebrodt 2004, 27). Following James W. Jones we might say that the mingling of religion and politics in religiously motivated terrorism (and not only in jihadism) is one of the foremost challenges of the 21st century. The divine master plan claimed by these subcultures and movements gives them the mandate to act against societies at large (Lohlker 2012, 130).

As Jones expresses it, "the issues of national liberation, resisting domination, and economic justice are often intertwined with and sacralized by religious and spiritual motivations that cannot be ignored if contemporary terrorism is to be understood" (Jones 2008, 28).

In other words: switching from religious language advocating violence to violent action depends on recoding conflicts in a religious language enabling the believers to perceive themselves as threatened by satanic forces, by apocalyptic powers, by Babylon, etc., and thus legitimizing violent resistance and changing the way these conflicts will go on. It depends on specific situations, but religious language and symbolism advocating violence is necessary for the process of recoding (Kippenberg 2010; cf. Lohlker 2012, 131).

Coding or recoding conflicts in terms of religion leads to the practical logic (Bourdieu) of the actors thinking and acting in religious terms — even if this may occur in the most superficial forms thereof. To claim that the true cause or motivation for their actions is political, economic, psychological, criminal, etc., privileges academic-theoretical epistemology while ignoring the practical logic of religious actors themselves. To the extent that governments and civil society wish to intervene in the process of "violent radicalization" and thereby prevent acts of terror, it is necessary to assess the share and form (i.e., role) of religion in each individual case, in order to determine the most effective means of intervention. This requires careful analysis of, and response to, religious elements, as is obvious from the Arabic text embedded within the following IS propaganda image:

10. Theology Matters: The Case of Jihadi Islam 125

We will create supporters within your homes.
We will turn your sons into mujahidin.
We will raise them according to the Sunna of the Prophet Muhammad,
the trustworthy.
We will revive in their hearts
honour, moral elevation, pride.

Telegram (accessed January 29, 2016)

This illustration is a hybrid using a visual language that is easy to understand: the threat to parents; the reference to military jihad (in the context of IS, the most important religious duty); the reference to the Sunna (example) of the Prophet, which serves as the religious foundation of IS; and the psychological element of reclaiming honour and moral superiority vis-à-vis one's enemies, and thus overcoming feelings of inferiority (Lohlker 2016c). Eliminating religious references from this illustration — or any analysis thereof, by ignoring their existence — would neuter its effectiveness for IS recruitment purposes, and render it impossible for Western analysts to grasp the profound emotional and psychological power of IS propaganda and, hence, the precise nature of its threat.

The text in the following illustration reads:

O, God! This religion is Your religion, and we are Your warriors. We fight in Your path. O God! Our victory depends upon Your grace, favour and kindness. Their polytheism will not defeat our monotheism. Our disobedience will not vanquish their unbelief. O, God! Forgive us our sins. We seek Your forgiveness and turn to You in repentance. We believe in You and trust in You. Do not blame us for what the shameless are making of us. Bless, O God, our Prophet Muhammad, his family and his companions. **Our final prayer is that all praise may be for God alone, Lord of all the worlds.**

Telegram (accessed December 2, 2015)

This text is deeply imbued with religious emotion and hostility towards everyone who is outside "the community of believers." The message conveyed by the text — whose concluding prayer is derived from al-Fatihah, the very first chapter of the Qur'an, known to all Muslims — is reinforced by visual elements: one fighter stands guard while another presumably reads the Qur'an, with the Islamic State flag dominating the landscape. Again, we see violence and religion closely interwoven, for the combination of 'warrior–Islamic scholar' has become an integral part of IS iconography, as may be seen from the following illustration as well:

10. Theology Matters: The Case of Jihadi Islam

Telegram (accessed November 29, 2015)

We may cite many examples in which conflict has been recoded in religious language and symbols (Kippenberg 2010), without saying which came first: religion or conflict. In the present case, we may assume that the practical logic of jihadi actors allows for just one code: religious violence.

This (re-)coding may be very simple:

> "You will not enjoy peace unless and until we ourselves truly live in peace, in the lands of Muslims."

Telegram (accessed November 14, 2015)

The above example shows a contextualization of the November 2015 terrorist attacks in Paris, with bombings conducted by French airplanes in Syria appearing in the bottom-left corner. The text and images are intended to evoke antagonism between Muslims and non-Muslims, employing religion as a "code" to interpret what IS perceives and depicts as a conflict between two states.

One simple fact needs to be emphasized, at this point, in order to avoid a misconception that often results from the innate human tendency to think in terms of antitheses. Acknowledging and even stressing the importance of religion to contemporary jihadism does not imply that religion is the *sole* reason for the existence of jihadism, or any other form of religiously-motivated terrorism. Jihadism is, in fact, a multi-determined, multi-factorial phenomenon. The misconception referenced above leads many otherwise rational people — including Western policy makers, analysts, scholars and journalists — to deny the importance of religion in contemporary jihadism.

CASE STUDIES OF MISCONCEPTIONS REGARDING JIHADI ISLAM

In a recent book entitled *Jihad and the Nihilism of the West* (Manemann 2016), we read that relating Islam to jihadism means to assume a causality between religion and violence and, especially, between Islam and violence (ibid., 20). Shortly thereafter, the author acknowledges that Islam does in fact contain a set of symbols and ideas that are at times employed to legitimize violent conflict (ibid., 21). The author then turns to his counter-argument, by referencing the undeniable fact that for some Europeans who have become jihadists, religion was not the central element in the process of their radicalization and inducement to commit violence. Specifically, Manemann is referring to several widely publicized cases which demonstrate that the jihadists in question may indeed have had only a superficial knowledge of Islam. This leads Manemann to erroneously conclude that (IS-) Islam cannot be the cause of these Europeans' radicalization.

This often-voiced opinion ignores the fact that certain parts of the Internet have been heavily impregnated by jihadi propaganda, which does not consist of detailed theoretical-theological discourse, but rather, assumes the form of a highly compact, religious symbol- and slogan-waving (IS-) Islam, which facilitates the verbal and visual articulation of diverse grievances, while mobilizing opposition to those perceived to be responsible. IS propaganda sharply condemns the double standards of "Western" politics; the persecution of Muslims; the history of conflict between Islam and the West, ranging from the Crusades and colonialism to present-day bombings in Iraq and Syria that result in civilian casualties; systematic discrimination against Muslims (defined as a group targeted for religious reasons); and the creation of an ideal state based on (IS-) Islam. This propaganda is embedded within a larger structure that intertwines with theological doctrine, religious motivations and individual, social and broader political feelings of malaise (Löwenthal 1990).

To claim that converts are acting in a manner that violates certain rules of Islam (e.g., ibid.: 26) — with Islam itself portrayed as a non-contradictory system of thought — implicitly argues that only a religiously "well-educated" and "sufficiently knowledgeable" believer may be legitimately regarded as a representative of his or her faith. Such lines of discourse also imply that a recent convert cannot be termed a "true" believer. Certainly we are exaggerating the arguments in question. Yet, this exaggeration may serve to highlight the absurdity of such modes of reasoning. Setting benchmarks for accepting or viewing any given individual as a religious believer — and expecting believers to act in accordance with one specific mode of normative behavior — would consequently exclude the majority of religious believers throughout history.

The basic assumption made by those who deny jihadists' religious motivation, or legitimacy, is that religion itself cannot be complex, ambiguous or contradictory, which is in fact a quite modern idea (cf. Bauer 2011, Ahmed 2016). The author does not state that Islam has no role in jihadism, but would prefer to argue against mono-causal explanations of radicalization (Manemann 2016, 28). The author, however, does not offer a solution regarding how to approach the (in)compatibility of his claims: "religion plays no role" and "religions play a role." We would expect him to answer the question, "Which role?"

This conceptual unease is born out of a demarcation vis-a-vis other intellectual positions regarding jihadi Islam, which are characterized by different types of misconception, although they do display awareness of the importance of religion to jihadism. The first misconception is displayed by authors such as Graeme Wood (2015), who vigorously asserts that the barbaric variety of Islam practiced by the Islamic State is "medieval." In fact, IS-Islam is a modern variety of religion, which emerges from and is an integral part of the dark side of modernity itself. And yet it is, in fact, a profoundly *religious* variety. To construct a distinction between an evil, brutal and thus inherently "medieval" religion — which, by definition, cannot be modern and enlightened — is to subscribe to the widespread normative misconception of modernity as a homogenous, and altogether positive, force. Yet the past two centuries bear witness to innumerable cruelties that were based upon, and the product of, modern rationality. Even the concept of enlightenment is much more problematic and difficult to understand than the — at best naïve — defenders of the term "enlightenment" may imagine. *The Dialectics of Enlightenment,* by Adorno and Horkheimer, seems to have been forgotten.

A second misconception (Wood 2015) is that IS represents an attempt to re-constitute the age and circumstances of the earliest Muslim community. Close scrutiny of the Arabic-language material produced by the Islamic State demonstrates that IS is consciously engaged in a kind of archeological excavation of the Islamic tradition, from which diverse religious artifacts it is constructing IS-Islam.

The one-sided arguments referenced above are rooted in a flawed approach to jihadism and IS. Their shortcomings are partially due to a heavy reliance upon the few IS materials available in English and other European languages. To date, Western knowledge of the bulk of jihadi discourse — more than 80% of which occurs in Arabic — remains rudimentary at best, with the source material itself largely inaccessible and unexplored.

READING THEIR LIPS

Turning to jihadi Arabic language resources we may find, for example, a blog entitled *A'iddū! (Prepare yourself!)*[1] This title refers to a Qur'anic imperative. The blog offers resources (primarily documents and videos) that enable jihadis to wage "the military jihad" at different levels. As such, it is predominantly a "jihadi military" blog.

A'iddū! (Prepare yourself!) contains many files that provide detailed information regarding explosives, small arms, anti-tank weapons and intelligence operations, but also files that contain advice regarding the spiritual preparation of warriors. One file that discusses military tactics and the training of leaders, also describes 'Alī ibn Abi Tālib, the son-in-law of the Prophet Muhammad, and Abū Dharr, a prominent companion of the Prophet, as role models for cautious behavior. Another file that discusses security issues provides illustrations from the biography of the Prophet. We can even access a special file on this blog that is focused primarily upon military lessons derived from the biography of the Prophet, whilst among other files we encounter the story of Abū Mahjan al-Thaqafī, another

---

[1] We do not provide any URLs for jihadi material. All the material discussed is archived and available.

10. Theology Matters: The Case of Jihadi Islam

companion of the Prophet, who is cited as a example for those who have committed great sins and feel they are consequently forbidden to wage military jihad — quite the contrary, for sure.

The selected texts and videos have been assembled from various sources, including older al-Qaeda files, Hamas, Free Syrian Army documents, translations of Sun Tzu into Arabic, and even a translation of Israeli texts: a highly pragmatic selection indeed. And yet all of these technical military resources are explicitly embedded within a specific religious tradition which jihadis clearly regard as their own. In other words, the creators of this jihadi military blog regard their efforts as the natural, contemporary outgrowth of Islamic history and tradition. When reciting the *basmala* ("In the name of God, the Most Merciful, the Most Graceful"), etc., the authors of these texts are not mindlessly employing a culturally determined phrase. Rather, they consciously subscribe to a religiously impregnated discursive formulation and a history of contemporary jihadism that dates back to the Afghan Arab volunteers.

IS-CALIPH

The core of IS identity consists of two elements: the caliphate and violence (Lohlker 2015 and 2016a). One of the prerequisites for proclaiming a caliphate is to have a leader who possesses the requisite qualifications to serve as caliph. Leaving aside other elements of the theory of proclaiming a caliphate, we see that IS argues for al-Baghdādī's legitimacy as caliph by stating that he has proved to be a successful fighter, and that he is also a religious scholar who has authored several books. He fulfills another requirement for becoming caliph, due to having the appropriate genealogy. The following illustration, published on an IS-affiliated channel on *telegram,* traces al-Baghdādī's genealogy to the Prophet Muhammad through his daughter Fātima:

Telegram (accessed February 13, 2016)

A recent video entitled *Night Arrows* (*sihām al-layl*) demonstrates how IS-Islam makes powerful references to religion — and appropriates the symbols and emotions associated with Muslim religiosity — in its propaganda material.

The video depicts a city at night and a minaret, which evokes the idea of the call to prayer. The setting of the video is thus contextualized: it takes place within a Muslim city, in which the mosque is the most important structure. The film cuts to a man slowly rising from his sleep, taking a candle, and then proceeding to perform his ritual ablutions with water from a clay jug. Afterwards, the man enters another room to pray. An audio file can be heard featuring the voice of Abu Musab al-Zarqāwī, the founding father of al-Tawhid wal Jihad, a precursor organization to IS. The audio file begins with a call for Muslims [i.e., adherents of jihadi Islam] to pray for those who fight on their behalf, in service to God and Islam.

Golden, sparkling light descends into the hands of the praying man — symbolizing the blessed character of al-Zarqāwī's speech, which calls upon Muslims to pray for jihadi fighters — and this golden light becomes an integral part of the prayer. The candlelight slowly fades away, to reveal a landscape with two birds flying at sunset. A voice in the background tells viewers that "the Sunna," the obligatory example of the Prophet, must be followed as "established by God for his creatures," and that this includes the struggle (jihad) against oppressors. Once again, what may at first glance appear to be a political statement is embedded within a profoundly moving religious context.

The following sequence also contains a political statement, displaying video clips of Obama, Putin and Hollande speaking. In the background, a voice talks about the necessity of retaliating against the West for its "war against Islam and Muslims." The narrator continues to explain that the crimes of these aggressors are evident, and include the destruction caused by the anti-IS coalition's bombing campaign. The next video sequence shows buildings in ruins, people trying to help severely injured victims (especially children) and an enraged elderly man calling upon the wrath of God.

The film cross-fades to images from the Paris November 2015 attacks while the narrator continues to speak about retaliation, before fading once again to a sequence that shows fighters training for urban warfare. The narrator calls upon "those who arise in sincere belief to fight unbelief in the world" to take revenge for the Russians' bombing — Putin's image is shown — of "Muslims' homes." Such fighters, the speaker continues, prepare themselves for battle by trusting fully in God — armed IS-fighters are shown parading in their vehicles — and their first and most vital weapon is "belief" (*īmān*). Viewers are told that these IS warriors are conscious of their previous sins, and have repented them.

The film proceeds to show Muslims at prayer, in order to emphasize once again that all aspects of life should be oriented towards God. Prayer (which is an integral expression of belief) is considered to be "the most important weapon." While showing an old man praying alone, followed by a boy and an old man praying together, a brief Qur'anic recitation concludes this segment of the video. A man appears and elaborates upon the virtue of prayer, and again we experience a cross-fade to a congregation of men praying. The narrator explains that these men are beseeching God to aid them against their enemies.

Another man appears speaking in Turkish. He calls upon Muslims, to whom he refers as "jihadis," "to help the religion of God at least by praying." The "help" requested translates to waging war against the enemies of God. The speaker is sitting in front of row after row of books written in Arabic. They appear to be religious literature, suggesting that the man is a knowledgeable scholar of Islam. Again, the congregation of praying men appears and a song may be heard describing "those who stand in unity," which refers to Muslims — i.e., those who affirm the unity of God.

Another speaker tells viewers that the sky belongs to God, as does the earth, the rivers and the sea. Enormous mountains appear, along with beautiful forests and a waterfall. The film cross-fades to warplanes and the speaker tells viewers that God will ultimately destroy the aggressors' high-tech weapons. This will be accomplished through the devotion of IS fighters, who are shown recovering the corpses of their comrades who have been slain in battle, suggesting that Islamic State warriors will fight to the death. IS fighters within a city cross-fade between images of an erupting volcano and a stream of lava. Footage displays natural catastrophes that have occurred in the U.S., and the speaker proclaims that God will punish America through earthquakes and other disasters.

The video constitutes a true amalgamation of religious symbolism and ideas, which are visually manifest in the form of prayer and the film's adept use of religious formulae. This allows for an identification of jihadis with Muslims in general; for the religious justification of a political agenda; and for persuading viewers that nature, and the Islamic State, are expressions of God's omnipotent power. If one were to ignore the central role of religious symbolism and doctrine in the film *Night Arrows* (*sihām al-layl*), it would be impossible to comprehend, or describe, the substance and emotional power of its message.

ANTI-SHIISM

Anti-Shiism is a paradigmatic element which illustrates the religious dimension of Sunni jihadism. Enmity against Shiites — who are often dehumanized and referred to as "filth" etc. (e.g., Lohlker 2016b) — is embedded within a centuries-old discourse of marginalization and persecution which, in modern times, has been reinvigorated and disseminated throughout the world, with massive financial, logistical and political support from Saudi Arabia.

It may be tempting to interpret this sectarianism as a mere ideological disguise, meant to conceal the geopolitical interests at work (Saudi Arabia vs. Iran, IS vs. Iran, etc.). However, we may better understand the nature of the current Sunni–Shi'ite divide if we reconceptualise it as a political conflict that has succeeded in amalgamating centuries-old religious traditions, and strengthened the bitter antagonism felt by both sides, by tapping into these religious lines of force.

Conclusion

In addition to the considerations already put forward in this article, as evidence of the religious foundation of jihadism, we may add other elements of IS thought and the IS theology of violence (Lohlker 2015, 2016a), such as: the religious imperative to establish a caliphate based on violence; the prevailing apocalyptic mood; a thoroughly constructed set of gender rules based upon religious texts; the anti-smoking campaign waged by IS, on religious grounds; the internal structure of IS, which mirrors institutions mentioned in the history of Muslim communities; police/market control (*hisba*); social welfare (*zakāt*); and the introduction of new currency called the gold dinar, similar to that used in the early days of Islam. All this provides ample evidence of the religious foundation of jihadism, and the manner in which jihadis envision their overall strategic aims. As Scott Atran has written:

> This is the purposeful plan of violence that Abu Bakr al-Baghdadi, the Islamic State's self-anointed Caliph, outlined in his call for 'volcanoes of jihad': to create a globe-spanning jihadi archipelago that will eventually unite to destroy the present world and create a new-old world of universal justice and peace under the Prophet's banner. A key tactic in this strategy is to inspire sympathisers abroad to violence: do what you can, with whatever you have, wherever you are, whenever possible…. While many in the West dismiss radical Islam as simply nihilistic, our work suggests something far more menacing: a profoundly alluring mission to change and save the world (Atran 2015).

That is why religion matters: it is the fuel that enables the jihadi machine of destruction to rumble forward. Cutting off the "supply of fuel" requires offering alternative conceptions of religion — and many other things. Religion matters, but it is not the sole solution to the threat posed by jihadism. Hard power may be required, but soft power (youth workers, teachers, community and family empowerment, etc.) is required, too. Political, social and economic conditions may provide the soil for the rise of jihadist entities, but religion — in fact, a specific construction of religion — is an integral part of the problem.

We need to help the people affected by this theology of violence, both victims and perpetrators. In order to help those attracted to jihadi Islam create another form of self-identity, we must remind ourselves of Eagleton's remark: "only those interventions will work which make sense to the mystified subject itself" (Eagleton 1991, xiv).

BIBLIOGRAPHY

Ahmed, Shahab, *What Is Islam: The Importance of Being Islamic*, Princeton/Oxford: Princeton University Press, 2016

Atran, Scott, "ISIS is a Revolution," 2015 (https://aeon.co/essays/why-isis-has-the-potential-to-be-a-world-altering-revolution)

Bauer, Thomas, Kultur der Ambiguität. Eine andere Geschichte des Islams, Berlin: Verlag der Weltreligionen, 2011

Beyer, Peter, "What Counts as Religion in Global Society? From Practice to Theory," in: ibid. (ed.), *Religion im Prozeß der Globalisierung*, Würzburg: Ergon, 2001, pp. 125–150

Eagleton, Terry, *Ideology: An Introduction*, London/New York: Verso, 1991

Jones, James W., *Blood That Cries Out from the Earth: The Psychology of Religious Terrorism*, Oxford: Oxford University Press, 2008

Kippenberg, Hans G., "Religiöse Gewaltsprachen – religiöse Gewalthandlungen: Versuch einer Klärung ihres Verhältnisses," in Gabriel, Karl et al. (eds.), *Religion – Gewalt – Terrorismus. Religionssoziologische und ethische Analysen*, Paderborn: Ferdinand Schöningh, 2010, pp. 15–45

Lohlker, Rüdiger, "Theologie der Gewalt: Das Beispiel IS," Wien: facultas/wuv, 2016a

Lohlker, Rüdiger, "Roadmap to Terror in Saudi-Arabia," 2016b (https://islamicstudiespapers.files.wordpress.com/2016/02/astop-8.pdf)

Lohlker, Rüdiger, "Dschihadistischer Terror als Kompensation von Inferioritätsgefühlen?," 2016c

Lohlker, Rüdiger, "Die Gewalttheologie des IS: Gewalt, Kalifat und Tod," in Tück, Jan-Heiner (ed.), *Sterben für Gott – Töten für Gott?*, Freiburg i. Br.: Herder 2015, pp. 70–98

Lohlker, Rüdiger, "The Forgotten Swamp Revisited," in id. (ed.), *New Approaches to the Analysis of Jihadism: Online and Offline*, Göttingen: Vienna University Press 2012, pp. 125–139

Lohlker, Rüdiger, "Eine 'Bibliothek des Dschihad': Minbar at-tauhīd wa'l-gihād", in Pink, Johanna/Mathias Brückner, Mathias (eds.), *Von Chatforen bis Cyberjihad. Muslimische Internetnutzung in lokaler und globaler Perspektive*, Würzburg: Ergon, 2009, pp. 155–167

Löwenthal, Leo, *Falsche Propheten. Studien zum Autoritarismus. Schriften 3*, Frankfurt a. M.: Suhrkamp 1993

Manemann, Jürgen, "Der Dschihad und der Nihilismus des Westens. Warum ziehen junge Europäer in den Krieg?" Bielefeld: transcript, 2015

Mannheim, Karl, *Ideology and Utopia*, London: Routledge, 1936

Qabalan, Marwan, "The Armed Syrian Opposition: Common Aim but No Vision" (http://orientxxi.info/IMG/pdf/armed_20syrian_20opposition_20_5bakh_20final_5d.pdf)

Rehmann, Jan, *Theories of Ideology: The Powers of Alienation and Subjection*, Leden/Boston: Brill, 2013

Riesebrodt, Martin, "Was ist religiöser Fundamentalismus?," in Six, Clemens et al., *Religiöser Fundamentalismus: Vom Kolonialismus zur Globalisierung*, Innsbruck et al.: Studienverlag, 2004, pp.13-32

Tepe, Peter, *Ideologie*, Berlin/Boston: De Gruyter, 2012

Waldmann, Peter, *Terrorismus – Provokation der Macht*, Hamburg: Murmann, 2005

Wood, Graeme, "What ISIS Really Wants," *The Atlantic*, March 2015 (http://www.theatlantic.com/magazine/archive/2015/03/what-isis-really-wants/384980/)

11

Responding to a Fundamental Crisis Within Islam Itself

KH. Yahya Cholil Staquf

SUMMARY

In July of 2020, the General Secretary of Indonesia's 90-million-strong Nahdlatul Ulama called upon Muslims to lead by example and end the widespread, systematic, and ongoing persecution of religious minorities across the Islamic world. "Systemic prejudice and discrimination towards others, and the weaponization of 'tribal' identity — whether for self-preservation or self-aggrandizement — have been characteristic of nearly all societies throughout history," said Nahdlatul Ulama General Secretary Kyai Haji Yahya Cholil Staquf, in response to recent upheavals in the United States and Western Europe triggered by the death of George Floyd at the hands of a U.S. policeman.

Mr. Staquf issued his remarks in conjunction with the publication of his article, "Responding to a Fundamental Crisis Within Islam Itself," in *Public Discourse*, which is the online journal of the Witherspoon Institute, a non-profit research center located in Princeton, New Jersey. In this essay, Mr. Staquf discusses Stephen Rasche's book, *The Disappearing People*, "which paints a disturbingly vivid picture of the tragedy he witnessed in Iraq" and "[t]he calamitous fate of Iraq's Christians."

If we are to abolish the primordial cycle of hatred, tyranny, and violence that plagues humanity, and avert civilizational disaster, people of all faiths must work together to prevent the political weaponization of fundamentalist Islam. We should learn from the unique heritage of Muslims on the Indonesian island of Java, who

defeated Muslim extremists in the sixteenth century and restored freedom of religion for all citizens, two centuries before the Virginia Statute of Religious Freedom and the Bill of Rights led to the separation of state and religion in the United States.

When U.S. attorney Stephen Rasche left his practice and moved to northern Iraq to assist its long-suffering Christians, he confronted a grotesque reality that most Westerners have the luxury of ignoring. In *The Disappearing People*, Rasche paints a disturbingly vivid picture of the tragedy he witnessed in Iraq.

Rasche does not shy away from identifying the fundamental cause of Christianity's disappearance from its historic birthplace in the Middle East. The calamitous fate of Iraq's Christians — so diligently and movingly documented by Rasche's irrefutable first-hand testimony — is simply the latest chapter in a long and tragic history of religious persecution in the Muslim world. From sub-Saharan Africa to South and Southeast Asia, religious minorities often experience severe discrimination and violence inflicted by those who embrace a supremacist, ultraconservative interpretation of Islam that has been widely propagated in recent decades by Middle East states, including long-time US allies Saudi Arabia and Qatar.

This stark reality confronts each of us with a profound moral choice: shall we remain silent and ignore the suffering of others, so long as it does not directly affect us? Or shall we pursue the truth and obey the dictates of conscience, whatever the consequences may be?

The horrendous violence that has engulfed so much of the Islamic world threatens not only those who dwell in Nigeria, Sudan, Egypt, Lebanon, Syria, Iraq, Yemen, or Pakistan, but also those of us who live in seemingly tranquil societies far away. If we wish to end this primordial cycle of hatred, tyranny, and violence — which also periodically erupts, to tragic effect, on the streets of Jakarta, Mumbai, London, Paris, and New York — we must ask a number of questions that require difficult and honest answers.

Perhaps the most burning of these questions is "Why?" Why did the killers of the Islamic State in Iraq and Syria (ISIS), who stormed across the Nineveh plains in 2014, display such remarkable savagery towards Yazidis and Christians? Any informed and intellectually honest inquiry into this question will produce an unambiguous and profoundly disturbing answer: the doctrine, goals, and strategy of these extremists can be readily traced to specific tenets of orthodox, authoritative Islam and its historic practice, including those portions of *fiqh* (classical Islamic law, also known as *shari'ah*) that enjoin Islamic supremacy, encourage enmity towards non-Muslims and require the establishment of a universal Islamic state, or caliphate.

To prevent the further spread of violent Islamist extremism, Muslims and non-Muslims must work together, drawing on the peaceful aspects of Islamic teaching to encourage respect for religious pluralism and the fundamental dignity of every human being, regardless of creed.

THE ENDURING LEGACY OF THE OTTOMAN CALIPHATE

ISIS's quest to establish an Islamic state, and the inevitable consequences of this for anyone deemed to be "non-Muslim," is not a historical aberration in the Middle East. Rather, it is the historical norm. Throughout Islamic history, until the collapse of the Ottoman empire and the formal abolition of the Caliphate in 1924, the Middle East has been dominated by caliphs and/or those who ruled in their name, and governed according to the provisions of classical Islamic law.

There is nothing especially novel about ISIS, other than its eruption in the twenty-first century and its use of modern communications technology. Prior to the American and French Revolutions, and particularly the First World War, the political map of the world consisted primarily of competing empires, kingdoms and tribal confederations. Virtually all developed states embraced an official religion, whose orthodox tenets were shaped and/or enforced by the ruler and officials of the administrative state.

Within the Islamic world, the Ottoman Caliphate (1362 – 1924 CE) asserted its claim to embody the orthodox ideal of a unified Muslim community, led by a pious Muslim ruler who adhered to the basic tenets of Islamic (Sunni) orthodoxy. Similarly, the Safavid dynasty and its successors, in Iran, based their claim to political power on fundamental tenets of Islamic (Shi'ite) orthodoxy.

The full enjoyment of legal privileges by the subjects of these empires was predicated upon their religious identity conforming to that of the empire. For example, the Ottoman Caliphate systematically discriminated against non-Muslims by enforcing a wide range of orthodox Islamic tenets that govern the treatment of conquered non-Muslims, or *dhimmīyūn,* as did other Sunni and Shi'ite rulers throughout the Islamic world, with the exception of *Nusantara* (the Malay Archipelago) and of Java in particular.

Whilst the Ottoman Caliphate collapsed nearly a century ago, its operational assumptions and the classical corpus of Islamic jurisprudence, or *fiqh,* through which it was governed have remained deeply embedded within Muslim societies. As a result, obsolete and problematic elements of *fiqh* are still taught by most orthodox Sunni and Shi'ite institutions worldwide as authoritative and correct. These teachings, even when not enshrined in statutory law, nonetheless retain considerable religious authority and social legitimacy among Muslims, forming part of what Indonesia's Nahdlatul Ulama — the world's largest Islamic organization — has termed the "prevailing Muslim mindset."

A Threat to All Humanity

The fundamentalist/supremacist view of Islam that these obsolete and problematic tenets of Islamic orthodoxy endorse may be readily harnessed to serve the interests of those with a political agenda. This is evident from history and the savage conflicts now roiling much of the Islamic world. In 2017, the young adults movement of Nahdlatul Ulama published an 8,000-word analysis of the manner in which state and non-state actors have systematically "weaponized" orthodox Islamic teachings. The *Gerakan Pemuda Ansor Declaration on Humanitarian Islam* — which also provides a detailed road map for recontextualizing (i.e., reforming) these obsolete tenets — explicitly states:

> The Islamic world is in the midst of a rapidly metastasizing crisis, with no apparent sign of remission. Among the most obvious manifestations of this crisis are the brutal conflicts now raging across a huge swath of territory inhabited by Muslims, from Africa and the Middle East to the borders of India; rampant social turbulence throughout the Islamic world; the unchecked spread of religious extremism and terror; and a rising tide of Islamophobia among non-Muslim populations, in direct response to these developments.
>
> Most of the political and military actors engaged in these conflicts pursue their competing agendas without regard to the cost in human lives and misery. This has led to an immense humanitarian crisis, while heightening the appeal and dramatically accelerating the spread of a de facto Islamist revolutionary movement that threatens the stability and security of the entire world, by summoning Muslims to join a global insurrection against the current world order.
>
> In other words, the crisis that engulfs the Islamic world is not limited to armed conflicts raging in various and sundry regions. Due to the transcendent value ascribed to religious belief by the vast majority of Muslims, the competition for power in the Islamic world necessarily includes a major sectarian/ideological (i.e., religious) component.
>
> Various actors — including but not limited to Iran, Saudi Arabia, ISIS, al-Qaeda, Hezbollah, Qatar, the Muslim Brotherhood, the Taliban and Pakistan — cynically manipulate religious sentiment in their struggle to maintain or acquire political, economic and military power, and to destroy their

enemies. They do so by drawing upon key elements of classical Islamic law (*fiqh*), to which they ascribe divine authority, in order to mobilize support for their worldly goals.

ISIS is no exception to this rule. Its claim to notoriety lies in the fact that, for a time, it successfully filled the power vacuum left in Sunni Arab areas of Mesopotamia in the wake of the withdrawal of American troops from Iraq and the Arab Spring. This enabled ISIS to implement a program for government that, prior to its emergence, had been a mere aspiration for modern Islamist extremists, derived from *fiqh* manuals written by medieval Muslim jurists.

THE STATUS OF RELIGIOUS MINORITIES

The consequences of these *fiqh* teachings for religious minorities in the Middle East are clear, for the conduct of ISIS towards these minorities is consistent with historical patterns and a fundamentalist reading of Islamic orthodoxy. This orthodoxy posits the existence of a supreme leader of the Muslim community (*Imām*), in whom is vested absolute political authority, and upon whom the rights of non-Muslims depend.

According to the dictates of this legal system, non-Muslims have no rights independent of those granted to them by the Imam, who is responsible for preserving order. In the absence of an Imam, "infidels" are in danger of losing their protected status. Throughout Islamic history, political chaos has often been accompanied by the murder, robbery, rape, and/or enslavement of non-Muslims. This feature of Islamic orthodoxy explains, in part, the recurrent cycles of persecution, expulsion, and/or violence to which non-Muslim populations have been subjected in Iraq and throughout the Middle East.

After the fall of Mosul to ISIS in 2014, for example, leaders of the city's Christian community were summoned to a council to "negotiate" a new *dhimmī* (literally "protection") contract, by which their rights and status would ostensibly be guaranteed by Abu Bakr al-Baghdadi, Imam of the newly proclaimed ISIS Caliphate. Naturally fearing for their safety, and rejecting the punitive conditions that would likely be imposed upon them by ISIS as part of this *dhimmī* contract, Mosul's Christians refused to attend the council. Lacking protection from the Imam, the status of Christians in and around Mosul reverted, in the view of ISIS, to that of unprotected infidels who may be killed or enslaved on sight. ISIS's subsequent treatment of Christians was in accordance with this designation and in line with a fundamentalist reading of Islamic law.

A Crisis in the Middle East

It is precisely this lack of rights for non-Muslims within classical *fiqh* — apart from those granted at the sufferance of a Muslim autocrat — to which the Chaldean Catholic Archbishop Bashar Warda of Erbil referred in a heartfelt speech titled, "The Future of Religious Pluralism in Iraq," delivered at Georgetown University under the auspices of the Religious Freedom Project (the precursor organization of the Religious Freedom Institute) on February 15, 2018:

> We Christians, a people who have endured persecution in patience and faith for 1,400 years, now confront an existential struggle. It is possibly the last struggle we will confront in Iraq. The most immediate cause is the ISIS attacks that led to the displacement of more than 125,000 Christians from our historical homelands and rendered us, in a single night, without shelter and refuge, without work or properties, without churches and monasteries, without the ability to participate in any of the things which give one a life of dignity: family visits, celebration of weddings and births, the sharing of sorrows. Our tormentors confiscated our present while also seeking to wipe out our history and destroy our future.
>
> And yet we are still there. Scourged, battered, and wounded. Yet still there. And having survived thus far, to this point of near finality, we have been granted a position of clarity and courage that we have perhaps lacked, or avoided, up until this day. We can no longer ignore the fundamental cause of what has been a relentless persecution of our people for nearly a millennium and a half. Having faced for 1400 years a slow-motion genocide that began long before the ongoing ISIS genocide today, the time for excusing this inhuman behavior and its causes is long since past.
>
> When a people have nothing left to lose, in some sense it is very liberating, and from this position of clarity and new-found courage, I must speak to you honestly on behalf of my people and speak to you the truth.
>
> The truth is that there is a fundamental crisis within Islam itself and if this crisis is not acknowledged, addressed, and fixed then there can be no future for Christians or any other form of religious plurality in the Middle East. Indeed, there is little reason to see a future for anyone in the Middle East, including within the Muslim world itself, other than in the context of continued violence, revenge, and hatred. And as we have seen too many times, this violence seeks to overtake us all, and destroy vulnerable innocent lives wherever it can find them...
>
> Prior to the ISIS horror of 2014, we Iraqi Christians had historically endeavored to maintain a dialogue of life with Muslims. In this dialogue we refrained from speaking honestly and truthfully to our oppressors in order to simply survive and live quietly. We would not openly face the long history

of violence and murder inflicted upon us. We did not push back against the constantly recurring periods of extremism that inflicted such pain and violence against the innocents, both Muslim and Christian alike. But following the horror of ISIS there is nothing left for us now but to speak plainly and unreservedly: there is a crisis of violence in Islam and for the sake of humanity, including the followers of Islam themselves, it must be addressed openly and honestly.

At the root of all of this we must be straightforward about the reality of the teachings of Jihad, which are the justification for all these acts of violence. Apologists for the history of the last 1,400 years of oppression against Christians will point to the various periods of Muslim tolerance regarding Christians, as the possible and desired alternative to the other periods of violence and persecution. One cannot deny that such periods of relative tolerance have existed. And yet all such periods of tolerance have been a one-way experience, in which the Islamic rulers decide, according to their own judgment, whether the Christians and other non-Muslims are to be tolerated in their beliefs or not. It is never, and has never, ever, been a question of equality. Fundamentally, in the eyes of Islam, we Christians and all other non-Muslims are not equal, and are not to be treated as equal, only to be tolerated or not, depending upon the intensity of the spirit of Jihad that prevails at the time.

Such is the cycle of history that has recurred in the Middle East over the past 1,400 years, and with each successive cycle the number of Christians and other non-Muslims has decreased until we have reached the point which exists in Iraq today — the point of extinction. Argue as you will, but this coming extinction will likely soon be fact, and what then will anyone be able to say? That we were made extinct by natural disaster, or gentle migration? That the ISIS attacks were unprecedented? Or in our disappearance will the truth emerge: that we were persistently and steadily eliminated over the course of 1,400 years by a belief system which allowed for regular and recurring cycles of violence against us...

The math of this equation is not complicated. One group is taught that they are superior and legally entitled to treat others as inferior human beings on the sole basis of their faith and religious practices. This teaching inevitably leads to violence against any "inferiors" who refuse to change their faith. And there you have it — the history of Christians and religious minorities in the Middle East for the last 1,400 years.

ISLAM IN ANOTHER CONTEXT

Far from the Islamic "heartland" of the Arab, Turkish, and Persian Middle East, Indonesia has never been a part of any of that region's historic caliphates. This separation has enabled the *Nusantara* ("East Indies") civilization to develop a spiritual view of Islam that tends to view *shari'ah* as a set of universal principals that all religions recognize and acknowledge, rather than an inflexible set of rules developed by classical Muslim jurists for running a pre-modern state. This unique civilizational heritage enabled Muslims on the island of Java — which constitutes the geographic, political and economic center of Indonesia — to defeat Muslim extremists in the sixteenth century, and restore freedom of religion for all Javanese two centuries before the Virginia Statute of Religious Freedom and the Bill of Rights led to the separation of state and religion in the United States.

It was this "civilizational wisdom" that inspired the creation of Indonesia as a multi-religious and pluralistic nation state in 1945. It also enabled Indonesia's first democratically elected president, H.E. KH. Abdurrahman Wahid — backed by Indonesia's Nahdlatul Ulama — to transform it into the world's third largest democracy following the overthrow of President Suharto's authoritarian regime in 1998. In spite of these enormous advantages, however, Indonesia has continued to grapple with the tension that exists between Islamic orthodoxy and the ideals of equality of citizenship and equality before the law, which form the bedrock of both its political settlement and the modern nation state.

Obsolete and problematic tenets of Islamic orthodoxy do in fact exist. These enjoin religious enmity, supremacy, and violence, fuelling Islamist extremism among Muslim communities throughout the world, including Indonesia.

So long as obsolete, medieval tenets within Islamic orthodoxy remain the dominant source of religious authority throughout the Muslim world, Indonesian Islamists will continue to draw power and sustenance from developments in the world at large. This is especially true so long as key state actors — including Iran, Turkey, Saudi Arabia, Qatar and Pakistan — continue to weaponize problematic tenets of Islamic orthodoxy in pursuit of their respective geopolitical agendas.

These considerations have led key figures within the NU — including Abdurrahman Wahid in the months and years prior to his death, and former NU Chairman Kyai Haji A. Mustofa Bisri — to conclude that it would be impossible to permanently resolve the tension that is inherent between Islamic orthodoxy and NKRI/UUD-45 (the Indonesian nation state and its constitution), so long as we confine our efforts to the domestic, or purely Indonesian, context of the perennial Islamist threat.

Preserving Indonesia's unique civilizational heritage — which gave birth to NKRI as a multi religious and pluralistic nation state — requires the successful implementation of a global strategy to develop a new

Islamic orthodoxy that reflects the actual circumstances of the modern world in which Muslims must live and practice their faith.

This global effort, already launched by key elements of the Nahdlatul Ulama — including its five-million-strong young adults organization, Gerakan Pemuda Ansor — is not just an inevitable corollary of efforts to defeat Islamist subversion of Indonesia. It is vital to the well-being and preservation of virtually every other nation in the world, whose laws are derived from modern political processes and whose people and governments do not wish to be subsumed in a universal Islamic caliphate or exhausted by the struggle to prevent its establishment.

The recontextualization and reform of Islamic orthodoxy is thus crucial to the welfare of Muslims and non-Muslims alike, for it constitutes the one indispensable prerequisite of any rational and humane solution to the multi-dimensional crisis that has plagued the Muslim world for over a century and not only shows no sign of abating — despite an ever-growing toll of human lives and misery — but, rather, increasingly threatens to spill over and engulf humanity as a whole.

A Chain Reaction of Violence

ISIS's genocidal campaign in Iraq and the Levant has set off a chain reaction of violence and retaliation with profound global implications. Across a vast arc of territory stretching from the Western Sahel to the Southern Philippines, Islamist groups inspired by ISIS's "success" are pursuing their own campaigns of mass killing, displacement, and terror that threaten to break the already badly frayed bonds of trust that make a shared communal life between Muslims and non-Muslims possible.

Jihadis' highly symbolic acts of desecration and astute use of propaganda have associated Islam with terrorism in the minds of many non-Muslims, strengthened politically opportunistic elements worldwide, and fuelled an intensifying cycle of retaliatory violence that threatens all of our futures. Whether it be a white supremacist slaughtering Muslims at prayer at a mosque in Christchurch, New Zealand; the wholesale and systematic campaign of ethnic cleansing perpetrated against Rohingya Muslims by the government of Myanmar; the hi-tech, totalitarian repression of millions of Uyghur Muslims in Xinjiang; or the weaponization of Islam for political gain in the West, innocent Muslims are suffering the consequences of this global reawakening of "tribal" identities.

The cycle of retaliatory bloodshed we are witnessing is deeply rooted in history, including ancient animosities embedded within the collective memory of entire ethnic and religious groups. It is precisely these hatreds that extremists seek to awaken through heinous and shocking acts of terror. If we are to avert disaster and stem this primordial cycle of hatred, tyranny, and violence it is imperative for people of goodwill of every faith and nation to join in building a global consensus to prevent the political weaponization of Islam, whether by Muslims or non-Muslims, and to curtail the spread of communal hatred by fostering the emergence of a truly just and harmonious world order, founded upon respect for the equal rights and dignity of every human being.

Dismantling the Theology that Underlies Islamist Violence

The spiritual leadership of Nahdlatul Ulama is working to ensure that the world's largest Muslim organization plays its part in this tremendous undertaking, by dismantling and replacing the theology that underlies and animates Islamist violence. In 2019, the NU Central Board published *fiqh* rulings based upon a gathering of nearly 20,000 Muslim religious scholars from across Indonesia's vast archipelago ("2019 Munas") that endorsed the concept of a nation-state rather than caliphate; recognized all citizens, irrespective of their ethnicity or religion, as having equal rights and obligations; decreed that Muslims must obey the laws of any modern nation-state in which they dwell; and affirmed that Muslims have a religious obligation to foster peace rather than automatically wage war on behalf of their co-religionists, whenever conflict erupts between Muslim and non-Muslim populations anywhere in the world.

A central feature of these 2019 Munas rulings is the abolition of the legal category of infidel (*kāfir*) within Islamic law (*fiqh*), so that non-Muslims may enjoy full equality as fellow citizens in their own right, rather than rely on protection at the sufferance of a Muslim ruler.

And so, we return to the story with which we started: *The Disappearing People*. Stephen Rasche has provided a vivid account of an entire religious community's near-extinction in the very place of its birth, the ancient Middle East. By implication, Stephen has also described an existential threat that confronts all of us, Muslim and non-Muslim alike. It simply remains to be seen whether we will heed his warning and act in time to prevent similar disasters from befalling those of us who dwell in blessed lands, seemingly distant from the horrifying chaos that engulfs so much of the Islamic world.

12

Gerakan Pemuda Ansor Declaration on Humanitarian Islam

SUMMARY

On May 21 and 22, 2017, over 300 Indonesian religious scholars gathered with colleagues from South Asia, the Middle East, Europe, and North America to address "obsolete tenets of classical Islamic law, which are premised upon perpetual conflict with those who do not embrace or submit to Islam." The event was held at Pondok Pesantren (*Madrasah*) Bahrul 'Ulum in Jombang, East Java — birthplace of the Nahdlatul Ulama and its five-million-strong young adults movement, Gerakan Pemuda Ansor.

Kyai Haji A. Mustofa Bisri — former Chairman of the Nahdlatul Ulama Supreme Council and co-founder of the Humanitarian Islam movement — opened the event with a prayer that the assembled scholars' deliberations would constitute "a humble act of religious piety and a blessing for all humanity... [as well as] the starting point of a movement that may bring the rays of enlightenment to a desperate world." The two-day international gathering of *ulama* concluded with the adoption of the *Gerakan Pemuda Ansor Declaration on Humanitarian Islam*, an 8,000-word analysis of the manner in which state and non-state actors have "weaponized" orthodox Islamic teachings, and detailed road map that calls for "a serious, long-term socio-cultural, political, religious and educational campaign to transform Muslims' understanding of their religious obligations, and the very nature of Islamic orthodoxy."

What follows are excerpts from the *Gerakan Pemuda Ansor Declaration on Humanitarian Islam*.

بِسْمِ اللهِ الرَّحْمٰنِ الرَّحِيْمِ

In the Name of God, the Most Beneficent, the Most Compassionate

Gerakan Pemuda Ansor (GP Ansor) and Bayt ar-Rahmah li ad-Da'wa al-Islamiyah Rahmatan li al-'Alamin hosted an international gathering of *ulama* (Islamic scholars) on 21 and 22 May 2017 at Pondok Pesantren Bahrul 'Ulum in Tambak Beras, Jombang, East Java — birthplace of the Nahdlatul Ulama and its young adults movement, GP Ansor.

After extensive discussion and consultation with experts in a variety of related fields who participated in this gathering of *ulama*, GP Ansor has resolved to adopt the **"Gerakan Pemuda Ansor Declaration on Humanitarian Islam,"** as follows:

PART I: THE CONTEXT

1. In the theory of classical Islamic law (*usul fiqh*), religious norms (*ahkam*; singular, *hukm*) constitute a response to reality. The purpose of religious norms (*maqasid al-shari'ah*) is to ensure the spiritual and material well-being of humanity.
2. The authoritative Sunni jurists, Imam al-Ghazali and Imam al-Shatibi, identified five primary components of *maqasid al-shari'ah*, viz., the preservation of faith, life, progeny, reason and property.
3. Religious norms may be universal and unchanging — e.g., the imperative that one strive to attain moral and spiritual perfection — or they may be "contingent," if they address a specific issue that arises within the ever-changing circumstances of time and place.
4. As reality changes, contingent — as opposed to universal — religious norms should also change to reflect the constantly shifting circumstances of life on earth. This was in fact the case during the early centuries of Islam, as various schools of Islamic law (*madzhab*) emerged and evolved. For the past five centuries, however, the practice of *ijtihad* (independent legal reasoning, employed to create new religious norms) has generally lapsed throughout the Sunni Muslim world.
5. When contemporary Muslims seek religious guidance, the most widely-accepted and authoritative reference source — indeed, the standard of Islamic orthodoxy — is the corpus of classical Islamic thought (*turats*) — and especially *fiqh* (jurisprudence) — that

reached its peak of development in the Middle Ages and was then frozen in place, largely unchanged to the present day.
6. A wide discrepancy now exists between the structure of Islamic orthodoxy and the context of Muslims' actual (lived) reality, due to immense changes that have occurred since the teachings of orthodox Islam grew ossified towards the end of the medieval era.
7. This disjunct between key tenets of Islamic orthodoxy and the reality of contemporary civilization can, and often does, lead Muslims into physical, moral and spiritual danger, if they insist upon observing certain elements of *fiqh*, regardless of their present context. Among the complex issues that lie at the heart of this discrepancy are:
    - Normative practices governing relations between Muslims and non-Muslims, including the rights, responsibilities and role of non-Muslims who live in Muslim-majority societies, and vice versa;
    - Relations between the Muslim and non-Muslim world, including the proper aims and conduct of warfare;
    - The existence of modern nation states and their validity — or lack thereof — as political systems that govern the lives of Muslims; and
    - State constitutions and statutory laws/legal systems that emerged from modern political processes, and their relationship to *shari'ah*.
8. Social and political instability, civil war and terrorism all arise from the attempt, by ultraconservative Muslims, to implement certain elements of *fiqh* within a context that is no longer compatible with said classical norms.
9. Any attempt to establish a universal Islamic state — *al-imamah al-udzma* (the Great Imamate), also known as *al-khilafah* (the Caliphate) — will only lead to disaster for Muslims, as one aspirant battles with another for dominion of the entire Islamic world.
10. The history of Islam following the death of the Prophet's (saw.) son-in-law, Sayyidina Ali, demonstrates that any attempt to acquire and consolidate political/military power in the form of a Caliphate will inevitably be accompanied by the slaughter of one's opponents, and tragedy for the Muslim community as a whole, particularly at the outset of a new dynasty.
11. When this effort is fused with the orthodox injunction to engage in offensive war against non-Muslims — until they convert or submit to Islamic rule, so that the entire world may be united beneath the

banner of Islam — this constitutes a summons to perpetual conflict, whose ever-widening appeal to Muslims is rooted in the very history and teachings of Islam itself.

12. Indeed, authoritative elements of *fiqh* describe such conflict as a religious obligation — which, at times, is incumbent upon the Muslim community in general, and others, upon every Muslim adult male, depending on the circumstances involved — for these religious norms emerged at a time when conflict between Islam and non-Muslim neighboring states was nearly universal.

13. If Muslims do not address the key tenets of Islamic orthodoxy that authorize and explicitly enjoin such violence, anyone — at any time — may harness the orthodox teachings of Islam to defy what they claim to be the illegitimate laws and authority of an infidel state and butcher their fellow citizens, regardless of whether they live in the Islamic world or the West. This is the bloody thread that links so many current events, from Egypt, Syria and Yemen to the streets of Mumbai, Jakarta, Berlin, Nice, Stockholm and Westminster.

14. Civil discord, acts of terrorism, rebellion and outright warfare — all pursued in the name of Islam — will continue to plague Muslims, and threaten humanity at large, until these issues are openly acknowledged and resolved.

15. Clearly, the world is in need of an alternative Islamic orthodoxy, which the vast majority of Muslims will embrace and follow.

16. The question that confronts humanity — Muslims and non-Muslims alike — is: how can we encourage, and ultimately ensure, that such an alternative not only arises, but becomes the dominant orthodoxy?

THE HISTORY OF EFFORTS TO RECONTEXTUALIZE ISLAMIC TEACHINGS WITHIN THE MALAY ARCHIPELAGO

17. In contrast to the disjunct between key tenets of Islamic orthodoxy and the actual reality that exists in much of the Muslim world, Indonesia has been blessed by the historic example of those, known as the *Wali Songo* (or "Nine Saints"), who proselytized *Islam Nusantara* ("East Indies Islam"). These Nine Saints and their followers stressed the need to contextualize Islamic teachings and adapt these to the ever-changing realities of space and time, while pre-

senting Islam not as a supremacist ideology or vehicle for conquest, but rather, as one of many paths through which humans may attain spiritual perfection.
18. In line with their teachings, Islam gradually took root throughout much of the East Indies Archipelago, contributing to the depth and beauty of preexisting Nusantara civilization while preserving, rather than disrupting, social harmony.
19. The Nahdlatul Ulama (NU) and its young adults movement, GP Ansor, stand heir to this noble tradition. For nearly a century, NU theologians have developed an extensive body of religious discourse that not only secures the legitimacy of Indonesia as a multi-religious and pluralistic nation state, but may also serve as a "pilot project" that demonstrates the feasibility of cooperation between *ulama* and statesmen to develop theologically-legitimate modern socio-political systems that promote the welfare of Muslims and non-Muslims alike.
20. During its 27th national congress held in Situbondo, East Java in 1984, the elected chairman of the NU Supreme Council, Kyai Haji Achmad Shiddiq, established a theological framework for the concept of brotherhood that was not limited to Muslims (*ukhuwwah islamiyah*), but also encompassed all the citizens of a nation (*ukhuwwah wathaniyah*) and, indeed, the brotherhood of all humanity (*ukhuwwah basyariyah*).
21. In 1992 — at a National Gathering of Religious Scholars held in Lampung, under the leadership of H.E. Kyai Haji Abdurrahman Wahid — the NU explicitly acknowledged that the changing context of reality *necessitates* the creation of new interpretations of Islamic law and orthodox Islamic teaching.
22. At this same Congress, the NU issued a formal decree stating that if the Muslim community cannot find individuals who meet the exacting criteria of a *mujtahid* (one qualified to exercise independent reasoning to create Islamic law), then *ulama* must assume the burden of responsibility and perform collective *ijtihad* (the use of independent reasoning to formulate Islamic law), which is called "*al-istinbath al-jama'iy*."
23. *Ulama* have endowed the Indonesian nation state (NKRI) with profound theological legitimacy, by advancing a number of strong religious arguments in its favor. The theological rationale that Indonesian *ulama* employed to legitimize NKRI were the product of new *ijtihad*, which cannot be found within the authoritative texts of *fiqh* from the canon of classical Islamic thought.

24. Moreover, this new *ijtihad* succeeded at securing the support of an overwhelming majority of Indonesian Muslims, while simultaneously helping to shape their religious views and mentality.

A Threat to All Humanity

25. The Islamic world is in the midst of a rapidly metastasizing crisis, with no apparent sign of remission. Among the most obvious manifestations of this crisis are the brutal conflicts now raging across a huge swath of territory inhabited by Muslims, from Africa and the Middle East to the borders of India; rampant social turbulence throughout the Islamic world; the unchecked spread of religious extremism and terror; and a rising tide of Islamophobia among non-Muslim populations, in direct response to these developments.
26. Most of the political and military actors engaged in these conflicts pursue their competing agendas without regard to the cost in human lives and misery. This has led to an immense humanitarian crisis, while heightening the appeal and dramatically accelerating the spread of a de facto Islamist revolutionary movement that threatens the stability and security of the entire world, by summoning Muslims to join a global insurrection against the current world order.
27. In other words, the crisis that engulfs the Islamic world is not limited to armed conflicts raging in various and sundry regions. Due to the transcendent value ascribed to religious belief by the vast majority of Muslims, the competition for power in the Islamic world necessarily includes a major sectarian/ideological (i.e., religious) component.
28. Various actors — including but not limited to Iran, Saudi Arabia, ISIS, al-Qaeda, Hezbollah, Qatar, the Muslim Brotherhood, the Taliban and Pakistan — cynically manipulate religious sentiment in their struggle to maintain or acquire political, economic and military power, and to destroy their enemies. They do so by drawing upon key elements of classical Islamic law (*fiqh*), to which they ascribe divine authority, in order to mobilize support for their worldly goals.
29. Mirroring this phenomenon, Western populists, Hindu nationalists and Buddhist monks in Sri Lanka and Myanmar often cite the identical elements of Islamic orthodoxy, and the behavior of

Muslims, to justify their perception of Islam as a subversive political ideology, rather than as a religion deserving of constitutional protections and respect.

THE 2016 ISOMIL NAHDLATUL ULAMA DECLARATION IDENTIFIED THE PRIMARY CAUSE OF THIS RAPIDLY ESCALATING CRISIS

30. As the International Summit of Moderate Islamic Leaders (ISOMIL) Nahdlatul Ulama Declaration, promulgated in May of 2016, explicitly states:
    8. The Nahdlatul Ulama regards specific modes of interpreting Islam (*tafsir*) as the most significant factor causing the spread of religious extremism among Muslims.
    9. For many decades past, various governments in the Middle East have exploited religious differences, and a history of enmity between sects, without regard to the consequences thereof for humanity at large. By "weaponizing" sectarian differences, these governments have sought to exercise both soft and hard power, and exported their conflict to the entire world. These sectarian propaganda campaigns have deliberately nurtured religious extremism, and stimulated the spread of terrorism throughout the world.
    10. This spread of religious extremism, and terrorism, is directly contributing to the rise of Islamophobia throughout the non-Muslim world.
    11. Certain governments in the Middle East derive their political legitimacy from precisely those problematic interpretations of Islam that underlie and animate religious extremism and terror. These governments need to develop an alternate source of political legitimacy if the world is to overcome the threat of religious extremism and terror.
    12. The Nahdlatul Ulama is prepared to help in this effort.
    15. The Nahdlatul Ulama calls upon people of goodwill of every faith and nation to join in building a global consensus not to politicize Islam, and to marginalize those who would exploit Islam in such a way as to harm others.
    16. The Nahdlatul Ulama will strive to consolidate the global *ahlusunnah wal jamaah* (Sunni Muslim) community, in order to bring about a world in which Islam, and Muslims, are truly beneficent and contribute to the well-being of all humanity.

A Critical Juncture

31. Whether conscious or not, willing or not, Muslims face a choice between starkly different visions of the future. Will they strive to recreate the long-lost ideal of religious, political and territorial unity beneath the banner of a Caliphate — and thus seek to restore Islamic supremacy — as reflected in their communal memory and still firmly entrenched within the prevailing corpus, and worldview, of orthodox, authoritative Islam? Or will they strive to develop a new religious sensibility that reflects the actual circumstances of our modern civilization, and contributes to the emergence of a truly just and harmonious world order, founded upon respect for the equal dignity and rights of every human being?
32. The first choice obviously leads in the direction of cataclysmic — or, to use the language of Sunni and Shiite extremists, *apocalyptic* — global conflict. To imagine the devastation that would ensue, one need not contemplate the likelihood of Muslims prevailing in an existential struggle with the non-Muslim world, whose military powers include the United States, Russia and China.
33. Any effort to consolidate political and military leadership of the entire Muslim world would, in and of itself, unleash havoc on an immense scale. Nuclear proliferation, mass urbanization, the fragile, interconnected nature of the world economy and the geographic dispersal of Muslims guarantee that any such attempt would threaten the very pillars of civilization itself.
34. The second choice — to develop a new religious sensibility that reflects the actual circumstances of our contemporary world — demands an altogether different type of courage, as well as a vast depth of wisdom and knowledge of the world we inhabit. For it requires Muslims to reevaluate a number of obsolete concepts that remain firmly entrenched within Islamic orthodoxy; develop new religious teachings suitable to the modern era; and mobilize the political support necessary to establish an alternative religious authority that is capable of propagating and defending these new teachings as they gradually come to be accepted and observed in practice by the Muslim community as a whole, and eventually constitute a *new* authoritative orthodoxy.

13

The Battle for the Soul of Islam

James M. Dorsey

SUMMARY

In October of 2020, a leading U.S. think tank published an in-depth analysis of "The Battle for the Soul of Islam," reporting that Indonesia's Nahdlatul Ulama has emerged as a formidable contender in the Islamic world's competition for religious soft power and leadership — capable of operating on the same level as states such as Saudi Arabia, the United Arab Emirates, Turkey, and Iran.

The article by Dr. James M. Dorsey — a Middle East expert who is a senior fellow at prominent universities in Singapore, Germany, and Israel — appeared in the journal *Current Trends in Islamist Ideology*, which is published by Hudson Institute's Center on Islam, Democracy, and the Future of the Muslim World. Soon after its publication, the article was nominated for the prestigious European Press Prize, amidst the intense debate that followed the beheading of a French school teacher and other Islamist attacks committed in Nice, Vienna, and Dresden.

Jordanian ruler Abdullah I bin Al-Hussein gloated in 1924 when Mustafa Kemal Ataturk, the visionary who carved modern Turkey out of the ruins of the Ottoman empire, abolished the Caliphate.

"The Turks have committed suicide. They had in the Caliphate one of the greatest political forces, and have thrown it away... I feel like sending a telegram thanking Mustapha Kemal. The Caliphate is an Arab institution. The Prophet was an Arab, the Koran is in Arabic, the Holy Places are in Arabia and the Khalif should be an Arab of the tribe of Khoreish,"

Abdullah told *The Manchester Guardian* at the time, referring to the tribe of the Prophet Mohammed.[1] "Now the Khaliphate has come back to Arabia," he added.

It did not. Arab leaders showed no interest in the return of the Caliphate even if many Muslim intellectuals and clerics across the Middle East and the Muslim World criticized Ataturk's abolition of it. Early Islamist political movements, for their part, largely declared the revival of caliphate as an aspiration rather than an immediate goal. A century later it is not the caliphate that the world's Muslim powerhouses are fighting about. Instead, they are engaged in a deepening religious soft power struggle for geopolitical influence and dominance.

This battle for the soul of Islam pits rival Middle Eastern and Asian powers against one another: Turkey, seat of the Islamic world's last true caliphate; Saudi Arabia, home to the faith's holy cities; the United Arab Emirates, propagator of a militantly statist interpretation of Islam; Qatar with its less strict version of Wahhabism and penchant for political Islam; Indonesia, promoting a humanitarian, pluralistic notion of Islam that reaches out to other faiths as well as non-Muslim centre-right forces across the globe; Morocco which uses religion as a way to position itself as the face of moderate Islam; and Shia Iran with its derailed revolution.

In the ultimate analysis, no clear winner may emerge. Yet, the course of the battle could determine the degree to which Islam will be defined by either one or more competing stripes of ultra-conservativism — statist forms of the faith that preach absolute obedience to political rulers and/or reduce religious establishments to pawns of the state. Implicit in the rivalry is a broader debate across the Muslim World that goes to the heart of the relationship between the state and religion. That debate centers on what role the state, if at all, should play in the enforcement of religious morals and the place of religion in education, judicial systems and politics. As the battle for religious soft power between rival states has intensified, the lines dividing the state and religion have become ever more blurred, particularly in more autocratic countries. This struggle has and will affect the prospects for the emergence of a truly more tolerant and pluralistic interpretation of one of the three Abrahamic religions.

---

[1] *The Manchester Guardian*, "Hussein The New Khalif: Special Interview In His CAMP in TrandJordania. Arab Claims to Moslem Leadership. Dangers to Hedjaz From Arabia: Reproach For the Allies. Emir Abdullah Confident," 13 March 1924, ProQuest Historical Newspapers: The Guardian and The Observer.

AN EVER MORE COMPETITIVE STRUGGLE

A survey of the modern history of the quest for Muslim religious soft power reveals an ever more competitive struggle with the staggered entry of multiple new players. Initially, in the 1960s, the Saudis, with Pakistani and a degree of West African input, had the playing field more or less to themselves as they created the building blocks of what would emerge as the world's most focused, state-run and well-funded Islamic public diplomacy campaign. At the time, Western powers saw the Saudi effort in fostering conservative Islam as part of the global effort to contain communism. Ultimately, it far exceeded anything that the Soviets or the Americans undertook.

The Saudi endeavor, in contrast to the United States that could rely on its private sector and cultural attributes, was by necessity a top-down and largely government-financed initiative that overtime garnered widespread public support. The bulk of Saudi money went to non-violent, ultra-conservative religious, cultural and media institutions in countries stretching from China across Eurasia and Africa into the Americas. Some recipients of Saudi largesse were political, others were not. More often than not, funding was provided and donations were made with the tacit approval and full knowledge of governments, if not their active cooperation.

Following the 1979 Iranian revolution, the kingdom's religious outreach no longer focused on containing communism alone, and Saudi practice increasingly mirrored Iran's coupling of religious soft power with hard power through the selective use of proxies in various Middle Eastern countries. Rarely publicly available receipts of donations by Saudis to violence-prone groups and interviews with past bagmen suggest that the kingdom directly funded violent militants in select countries in response to specific circumstances. This included Afghanistan during the anti-Soviet jihad in the 1980s, Pakistan to support anti-Shiite and anti-Iranian militants, Bosnia Herzegovina in aid of foreign fighters confronting Serbia in the 1990s, Palestine, Syria where Islamists were fighting the regime of Bashar al-Assad, Iraq wracked by an anti-Shiite insurgency and Iran in a bid to fuel ethnic unrest.

Money was often hand carried to recipients or channelled through businessmen, money exchangers and chosen banks. Receipts of donations to Sipah-e-Sahaba, a banned virulently anti-Shia group that attacked Shias in Pakistan, and its successors and offshoots, bear the names of a Saudi donor who is hard to trace. They suggest that the dividing lines between private and officially-sanctioned funding are blurred.

To be sure, the level of Saudi funding and the thrust of the kingdom's religious soft power diplomacy has changed with the rise of Crown Prince Mohammed bin Salman. The drive today is to project the kingdom and its Islam as tolerant, forward-looking, and outward- rather than inward-looking. Saudi religious outreach also aims to open doors for the kingdom through demonstrative acts like the visit to the Nazi concentration camp Auschwitz in Poland by a delegation of 25 prominent Muslim clergymen led by Mohammed al-Issa, the head of the Muslim World League. The League, which was once a prime vehicle for the kingdom's global promotion of religious ultra-conservatism, has also been forging closer ties with Jewish and Christian evangelist communities.

Indeed, Prince Mohammed has turned the League into a propagator of his vaguely defined notion of a moderate Islam. Meantime, Saudi Arabia's retreat from religiously packaged foreign funding[2] has created opportunity for the kingdom's competitors.

Facts on the ground in the kingdom and beyond, nonetheless, tell at times a different story. Schoolbooks are being cleansed of supremacist and racist references in a slow and grinding process initiated after the 9/11 Al-Qaeda attacks in New York and Washington.

The United States Commission on International Religious Freedom said in its 2020 report that "despite progress in recent years, Saudi textbooks have seen some backsliding regarding language inciting hatred and violence toward non-Muslims. While the 2019 – 2020 textbooks showed marginal improvements in the discussion of Christians, textbooks still teach that Christians and Jews 'are the enemy of Islam and its people,' and that members of the LGBTQI community will 'be struck [killed] in the same manner as those in Sodom.'"[3]

Prince Mohammed's nominal embrace of religious tolerance and interfaith dialogue has produced far more public interactions with Jewish and Christian leaders but not led to a lifting on the ban on public non-Muslim worship and the building of non-Muslim houses of worship in the kingdom itself. Access to holy sites like Mecca and Medina remains banned for non-Muslims, as it has been for most of Islam's history, and often entry into mosques is also barred.

---

[2] Jonathan Benthall, "The Rise and Decline of Saudi Overseas Humanitarian Charities," Georgetown University Qatar, 2018, https://repository.library.georgetown.edu/bitstream/handle/10822/1051628/CIRSOccasionalPaper20JonathanBenthall2018.pdf?sequence=1&isAllowed=y

[3] United States Commission on International Religious Freedom, *Annual Report 2020*, 28 April 2020, https://www.uscirf.gov/sites/default/files/Saudi%20Arabia.pdf

While Saudi Arabia has implemented strict regulations on donations for charitable purposes abroad, the source and the channelling of funding to militants that serve the kingdom's geopolitical purpose remains unclear at best. Militant Pakistani bagmen described in interviews in 2017 and 2018 the flow of large amounts of money to ultra-conservative madrassas that dot Pakistan's borders with Iran and Afghanistan. They said the monies were channelled through Saudi nationals of Baloch origin and often arrived in suitcases in an operation that they believed had tacit Saudi government approval. The monies, according to bagmen interviewed by this writer, were being transferred at a time when U.S. policymakers like former national security adviser John Bolton were proposing to destabilize the Iranian regime by supporting ethnic insurgencies.[4] Saudi Arabia was also publicly hinting that it may adopt a similar strategy.[5]

No Longer in a Class of Its Own

The 1979 Islamic Revolution in Iran marked the moment when Saudi religious soft power was no longer in a class of its own. It also launched a new phase in Saudi-Iranian rivalry that progressively has engulfed the Middle East and North Africa and beyond. Competition for religious soft power and influence is a fixture of the rivalry. So is the marked difference in Saudi and Iranian concepts of religious soft power.

Although both had sectarian traits, Saudi Arabia's primary focus was religious and theological while revolutionary Iran's was explicitly political and paramilitary in nature and geared toward acquiring hard power. Iranian outreach in various Arab countries focused on cultivating Shiite militias, not on greater religious piety.

The Iran-Iraq War in the 1980s in which Sunni Gulf states funded Iraqi leader Saddam Hussein's war machine shifted Iran's focus from export of its revolution to a greater emphasis on Iranian nationalism. Iran also moved to nurturing Shiite militias that would constitute the country's first line of defense.

---

[4] John R. Bolton, "How to Get Out of the Iran Nuclear Deal," *The National Interest*, 28 August 2017, https://www.nationalreview.com/2017/08/iran-nuclear-deal-exit-strategy-john-bolton-memo-trump/

[5] James M. Dorsey, "Pakistan caught in the middle as China's OBOR becomes Saudi-Iranian-Indian battleground," *The Turbulent World of Middle East Soccer*, 5 May 2017, https://mideastsoccer.blogspot.com/2017/05/pakistan-caught-in-middle-as-chinas.html

Gone were the days of Tehran's emphasis on groups like the Islamic Front for the Liberation of Bahrain that gathered regularly in a large sitting room in the home of Ayatollah Hussein-Ali Montazeri, a one-time designated successor of revolutionary leader Ayatollah Ruhollah Khomeini, and the exploits of his son, Mohammed Montazeri, who was nicknamed Ayatollah Ringo and founded an armed group in Lebanon and Syria that aimed to liberate Muslim lands.

The watershed shift has shaped Iran and its religious strategy, including its support for and recruitment of Shiite and other groups and communities in the Middle East, Pakistan, and Afghanistan. It constituted Iran's soft and hard power response to the Saudi effort to infuse Muslim communities worldwide with an ultra-conservative, anti-Shiite, anti-Iranian interpretation of the faith. Elsewhere, like in Southeast Asia and West Africa, the thrust of Iranian religious diplomacy was, like much of the Saudi effort, focused primarily on religious and social issues.

The shift was evident early on in emotive debates in Iran's parliament in 1980 about the utility of the occupation of the U.S. embassy in Tehran at a time that Iran was at war with Iraq. Men like Hojatoleslam Hashemi Rafsanjani, the speaker of the parliament who later became President, Ayatollah Mohammed Beheshti, the number two in the Iranian political hierarchy at the time, and chief jurist Ayatollah Sadegh Khalqali, who was known as the hanging judge for his penchant for the death penalty, argued unsuccessfully in favour of a quick resolution of the embassy crisis so that Iran could focus on the defense of its territory and revolution.

The debates signalled a shift from what was initially an ideological rivalry to a geopolitical fight that continues to this day and that is driven by the perception in Tehran that the United States and the Gulf states are seeking to topple the Islamic regime.

An Ever More Complex Battle

If the first phase of the battle for the soul of Islam was defined by the largely uncontested Saudi religious soft power campaign, and the second phase began with the emergence of revolutionary Iran, the third and most recent phase is the most complex one, not only because of the arrival on the scene of new players but also because it entails rivalries within rivalries.

The new players are first and foremost the United Arab Emirates, Turkey, Qatar, and Indonesia. Their entry into the fray has further blurred the dividing lines between purely religious and cultural soft power, nationalism, and the struggle within Muslim societies over values, including various freedoms, rights, and preferred political systems.

The third phase is complicated by the fact that all of the players with the exception of Indonesia have embraced Iran's model of coupling religious soft power with hard power and the use of proxies to advance their respective agendas. This is apparent in the Saudi-UAE-led war to counter Iran in Yemen; Emirati, Egyptian and Turkish support for opposing sides in Libya's civil war; and Turkish and Gulf state involvement in Syria.

The intensifying violence lays bare the opportunism adopted by most players. Saudi Arabia, for example, has been willing to forge or maintain alliances with groups aligned with the Muslim Brotherhood even though it has designated the organization as a terrorist entity,[6] while the UAE, which claims the mantle of moderation but still supports the forces of Libyan rebel leader Khalifa Haftar whose ranks include a significant number of Salafist fighters.[7]

The resurgence of political Islam as a result of the 2011 popular Arab revolts that toppled leaders in Egypt, Tunisia, Libya, and Yemen, fuelled the worst fears of men like Saudi Crown Prince Mohammed, Egyptian General-turned President Abdel Fattah al-Sisi and UAE Crown Prince Mohammed bin Zayed.

The upheaval also created an opportunity for the UAE, a country that prides itself on being a cutting-edge, cosmopolitan home to people from some 190 countries. It launched a multi-faceted effort to project itself as an open and tolerant society that is at the forefront of Islamic moderation and tolerance, and to respect religious diversity and inter-faith dialogue.

Bin Zayed's acquiescence of the Salafis, who have sought to impose strict Islamic law on Haftar's eastern Libyan stronghold of Benghazi, is based on their association with an ultra-conservative strand of the faith that preaches absolute obedience to the earthly ruler in power. That acquiescence contradicts Bin Zayed's otherwise dim view of ultra-conservative interpretations of Islam like Wahhabism.

Speaking in 2005 to then U.S. ambassador James Jeffrey, Bin Zayed compared Saudi Arabia's religious leaders to "somebody like the one we are chasing in the mountains," a reference to Osama bin Laden who at the time

---

[6] James M. Dorsey, "Indonesia: A major prize in the battle for the soul of Islam," *The Turbulent World of Middle East Soccer*, 30 July 2020, https://mideastsoccer.blogspot.com/2020/07/indonesia-major-prize-in-battle-for.html

[7] David Kirkpatrick, "A Police State With an Islamist Twist: Inside Hifter's Libya," *The New York Times*, 20 February 2020, https://www.nytimes.com/2020/02/20/world/middleeast/libya-hifter-benghazi.html

was believed to be hiding in a mountainous region of Afghanistan.⁸ In an email to *New York Times* columnist Thomas Friedman twelve years later, Yusuf al-Otaiba, a confidante of Bin Zayed and the UAE's ambassador in Washington, asserted that "Abu Dhabi fought 200 years of wars with Saudi over Wahhabism."⁹

Al Otaiba's comment came a year after the UAE, in a bid to undermine Saudi religious diplomacy, sponsored a gathering of prominent Sunni Muslim leaders in the Chechen capital of Grozny that effectively excommunicated Wahhabism.¹⁰ Western officials refrained from publicly commenting, but they privately commended Emirati efforts to confront a worldview that they feared provided a breeding ground for social tensions and extremism.¹¹

Bin Zayed has played a key role in shaping Bin Salman's policies to shave off Wahhabism's rougher edges and to bring the UAE's and Saudi Arabia's religious soft power endeavors closer together. This alignment has resulted in what author Shadi Hamid calls non-political politicized Islam, or a "third trend in political Islam."¹² That trend, in the words of scholar Gregory Gause, "is tightly tied to state authority and subservient to it."¹³

Bin Zayed's efforts have paid off. Despite ruling at home with an iron fist, Bin Zayed has been able to promote a state-controlled Islam that styles itself as tolerant and apolitical and preaches obedience to established rulers without addressing outdated or intolerant concepts embedded in the faith such as the notion of kafirs or infidels, slavery, and Muslim supremacy that remain reference points even if large numbers of Muslims do not heed them in their daily life.

His success, backed by armies of paid Western lobbyists, is evidenced by the fact that the UAE is widely perceived as a religiously tolerant,

---

8   United States Embassy in the United Arab Emirates, "MBZ Meeting with Senior Advisor on Iraq Jeffrey," Wikileaks, 15 October 2005, https://wikileaks.org/plusd/cables/05ABUDHABI4308_a.html
9   Leaked emails of Yusuf al Otaibah shared in 2017 with this author by GlobalLeaks.
10 James M. Dorsey, "Fighting for the Soul of Islam: A Battle of the Paymasters," *RSIS Commentary No. 241*, 20 September 2016, https://www.rsis.edu.sg/wp-content/uploads/2016/09/CO16241.pdf
11 Interviews with the author in September and October 2016.
12 Shadi Hamid, "The false promise of 'pro-American' autocrats," *Brookings*, 19 March 2020, https://www.brookings.edu/blog/order-from-chaos/2020/03/19/the-false-promise-of-pro-american-autocrats/
13 F. Gregory Gause III, "What the Qatar crisis shows about the Middle East," *The Washington Post*, 28 June 2017, https://www.washingtonpost.com/news/monkey-cage/wp/2017/06/27/what-the-qatar-crisis-shows-about-the-middle-east/

pluralistic, and enlightened society. This is in stark contrast to Bin Salman and Saudi Arabia's reputational problems as a result of the 2018 killing in Istanbul of journalist Jamal Khashoggi and the arrests and alleged torture of dissidents and others deemed a potential threat.

The UAE has also successfully projected itself as a secular state despite the fact that its constitution requires legislation to be compatible with Islamic law. In doing so, Emirati leaders walk a fine line. Islamic scholars with close ties to the UAE felt a need to rush to defend Al Otaiba, the UAE ambassador,[14] against accusations of blasphemy for telling Charlie Rose in a television interview that "what we would like to see is more secular, stable, prosperous, empowered, strong government."[15]

To avert criticism, the UAE government rolled out Mauritanian philosopher Adballah Seyid Ould Abah who insisted that it was "obvious that (Al Otaiba) did not mean secularism according to the concept of 'laïcite' or according to the social context of the term. Saudi Arabia, the UAE and other countries in the region are keen on sponsoring a religion, maintaining its role in the public field, and protecting it from ideological exploitation which is a hidden manifestation of secularization."[16]

The UAE scored one of its most significant successes with the first ever papal visit to the Emirates by Pope Francis during which he signed a Document on Human Fraternity with Al Azhar's Grand Imam, Ahmad El-Tayeb. The pope acknowledged the UAE's growing influence, when in a public address he thanked Egyptian judge and his late advisor Mohamed Abdel Salam, who was close to both the Emiratis and Egypt's Al-Sisi, for drafting the declaration. Abdel Salam ensured that the UAE and the Egyptian president rather than Al Azhar put their stamp on the document.

CREATING THE UAE'S RELIGIOUS ECOSYSTEM

To bolster the Emirati version of "counter-revolutionary" Islam and counter influential Qatari-backed groups associated with the Muslim Brother-

---

[14] Adballah Seyid Ould Abah, "What does the UAE envoy to Washington mean by 'secularism?'" *Al Arabiya*, 12 August 2017, https://english.alarabiya.net/en/views/news/middle-east/2017/08/12/What-does-the-UAE-envoy-to-Washington-mean-by-secularism-.html

[15] Charlie Rose, "Qatar and the Middle East," 26 July 2017, https://charlierose.com/videos/30799

[16] Adballah Seyid Ould Abah, "What does the UAE envoy to Washington mean by 'secularism?'" *Al Arabiya*, 12 August 2017, https://english.alarabiya.net/en/views/news/middle-east/2017/08/12/What-does-the-UAE-envoy-to-Washington-mean-by-secularism-.html

hood and other strands of political Islam, Bin Zayed launched a multi-pronged offensive involving geopolitical as well as religious building blocks.

Bin Zayed drew a line in the sand when in 2013 he helped orchestrate a military coup that toppled Mohammed Morsi, a Muslim Brother who won Egypt's first and only free and fair election.[17] His engineering of the 2017 debilitating UAE-Saudi-Bahraini-Egyptian diplomatic and economic boycott of Qatar, which is accused of being a pillar of political Islam, further strengthened Bin Zayed's drawing of the religious soft power battle lines.

The battles that have ensued between the UAE and Qatar have been as much in the realm of ideology and ideas as they have been in war theatres like Libya, where the UAE has funded and armed Libyans fighting the elected, internationally recognized Islamist Government of National Accord based in Tripoli.

Bin Zayed signaled his ideational intentions with the creation of religious organizations of his own, the launch of Emirati-run training programs for non-UAE imams, and a visit a year after the 2013 coup in Egypt to Al Azhar's sprawling 1000-year-old mosque and university complex in Cairo. The visit was designed to underline the Emirati ruler's determination to steer Al Azhar's adoption of moderate language and counter extremism and fanaticism.[18]

Meantime, the new Emirati imam-training programs put the UAE in direct competition with Saudi Arabia, Turkey, and Morocco, major purveyors of Muslim clerical training. The UAE scored initial successes with the training of thousands of Afghan clerics[19] and an offer to provide similar services to Indian imams.[20]

The UAE's growing world influence was evident in those who participated in the 2016 Grozny conference that effectively excommunicated Wahhabism. Participants included the imam of the Al-Azhar Grand Mosque, Ahmed El- Tayeb, Egyptian Grand Mufti Shawki Allam, former

---

[17] David D. Kirkpatrick, "Recordings Suggest Emirates and Egyptian Military Pushed Ousting of Morsi," *The New York Times*, 1 March 2015, https://www.nytimes.com/2015/03/02/world/middleeast/recordings-suggest-emirates-and-egyptian-military-pushed-ousting-of-morsi.html

[18] WAM, "Mohamed bin Zayed visits Al Azhar, meets Grand Imam – UPDATE," 18 September 2014, http://wam.ae/en/details/1395269811015

[19] Haneen Dajani, "Afghan imams learn from UAE counterparts," *The National*, 16 April 2015, https://www.thenational.ae/uae/afghan-imams-learn-from-uae-counterparts-1.70308

[20] Charu Sudan Kasturi, "UAE keen on Indian imams," *The Telegraph*, 11 February 2016, https://www.telegraphindia.com/india/uae-keen-on-indian-imams/cid/1487085

Egyptian Grand Mufti and Sufi authority Ali Gomaa, a strident supporter of Egyptian President Abdel Fattah Al-Sisi, Al Sisi's religious affairs advisor, Usama al-Azhari, the mufti of Damascus Abdul Fattah al-Bizm, a close confidante of Syrian President Bashar al-Assad, influential Yemeni cleric Habib Ali Jifri, head of the Abu Dhabi-based Islamic Tabah Foundation who has close ties to Bin Zayed, Indian grand mufti Sheikh Abubakr Ahmad, and his Jordanian counterpart, Sheikh Abdul Karim Khasawneh.

The participation of El-Tayeb, a political appointee and salaried Egyptian government official, and other Egyptian religious luminaries who had supported Al-Sisi's military coup, said much about the UAE's inroads into Al Azhar, an institution that was for decades a preserve of Saudi ultra-conservatives. El-Tayeb signaled the shift when in 2013 he accepted the Sheikh Zayed Book Award for Cultural Personality of the Year in recognition of his "leadership in moderation and tolerance."

El-Tayeb was lauded "for encouraging a culture of tolerance, dialogue and protection of civil society" at a moment that Morsi, the embattled Egyptian president, was fighting for his political life, and Bin Zayed was cracking down on Emirati Muslim Brothers.[21]

The Grozny conference was co-organized by the Tabah Foundation, the sponsor of the Council of Elders, a UAE-based group founded in 2014 that aims to dominate Islamic discourse that many non-Salafis assert has been hijacked by Saudi largesse. The Council, like the Forum for Promoting Peace in Muslim Societies, another UAE-funded organization, was created to counter the Doha-based International Union of Muslim Scholars (IUMS) headed by Yusuf Qaradawi, one of the world's most prominent and controversial Muslim theologians who is widely viewed as a spiritual leader of the Muslim Brotherhood.

The Tabah Foundation is headed by Saudi-based Mauritanian politician and Islamic scholar Abdullah Bin Bayyah as well as El-Tayeb. Before he established the Emirati-supported group, Bin Bayyah was vice president of Qaradawi's European Council for Fatwa and Research, created to provide guidance to European Muslims through the dissemination of religious opinions. He also heads the Emirates Fatwa Council that oversees the issuing of religious opinions and trains and licenses clerics.

Bin Bayyah as well as other prominent traditionalists with past ties to the Brotherhood and/or political Islam, including Hamza Yusuf, an American convert to Islam, and Aref Ali Nayed, a former Libyan ambassador to

---

[21] Mohammed Eissa, "Azhar Grand Imam el-Tayyeb Wins Cultural Personality Award," *Ahram Online*, 30 April 2013, http://english.ahram.org.eg/NewsContent/18/0/70444/Books/Azhar-Grand-Imam-ElTayyeb-wins-Cultural-Personalit.aspx

the UAE, found common ideological ground in the assertion that the Brotherhood and jihadist ideology are offshoots of ultra-conservative strands of Islam. They saw the UAE's position as rooted in decades of animosity between Al Azhar and the Brotherhood that Egyptian presidents Gamal Abdel Nasser, Anwar Sadat and Hosni Mubarak exploited to counter the Brothers and Wahhabism.

Born Mark Hanson, Yusuf, a disciple of Bin Bayyah, is widely viewed as one of the most influential and charismatic Western Islamic preachers.

Nayed, an Islamic scholar, entrepreneur, and onetime supporter of the 2011 popular "Arab Spring" revolts, moved Kalam Research & Media, a Muslim think tank that he founded in 2009, to Dubai and aligned it with the UAE's strategy.

"I believe that the entire region is undergoing an identity crisis in reality. Who are we? And what is the Islam we accept as our religion?... It is an existential question and there is a major struggle. I believe that there is fascism in the region as a whole that dresses up as Islam, and it has no relation to true Islam... Let me be explicit: there are countries that support the Muslim Brothers, and there are countries that are waging war against the Muslim Brothers... This is a regional war — we do not deny it," Nayed told BBC Arabic.[22]

Embracing Machiavelli's notion of religion as a powerful tool in the hands of a prince, members of the Abu Dhabi ruling family, including Bin Zayed and his foreign minister, Abdullah bin Zayed Al Nahyan, began courting Bin Bayyah in early 2013. They invited the cleric to the Emirates the same month that Morsi was toppled.[23]

In a letter three months later to Qaradawi's IUMS that bitterly opposed the overthrow of Morsi and condemned the Egyptian military government's subsequent brutal repression of the Brotherhood, Bin Bayyah wrote that he was resigning from the group because, "the humble role I am attempting to undertake towards reform and reconciliation [among Muslims] requires a discourse that does not sit well with my position at the International Union of Muslim Scholars."[24]

Bin Bayyah published the letter to demonstrate to Emirati leaders that he had ended his association with Qatari-supported Islamist groups. He has

---

[22] BBC News, "Without Restrictions (بلا قيود)," YouTube, 23 September 2015, https://www.youtube.com/watch?v=Yx9WRaYvOfw

[23] BinBayyah.net, Net, 2013, http://binbayyah.net/arabic/archives/category/news/page/15

[24] Usaama al-Azami, "Abdullāh bin Bayyah and the Arab Revolutions: Counter-revolutionary Neo-traditionalism's Ideological Struggle against Islamism," *The Muslim World Today*, Vol. 101:4, pp. 427–440.

since acknowledged that he speaks on behalf of the UAE government.[25] The courting of Bin Bayyah emanated from Bin Zayed's realization that he needed religious soft power to justify the UAE's wielding of hard power in countries like Yemen and Libya. The timing of Bin Zayed's positioning of Bin Bayyah as what Usaama Al-Azami, an Islamic scholar,[26] dubs "counter-revolutionary Islam's most important scholar," was hardly coincidental. It coincided with the gradual withdrawal from public life of the far more prolific and media savvy Qaradawi, who had become a nonagenarian.

Al-Azami argues that the UAE's financial and political clout rather than intellectual argument will decide to what degree the Emirates succeed in their religious soft power campaign.

"The counter-revolutionary Islamic political thought that is being developed and promoted by Bin Bayyah and the UAE suffers from certain fundamental structural problems that means its very existence is precariously predicated on the persistence of autocratic patronage. Its lack of independence means that it is not the organic product of a relatively unencumbered engagement with political modernity that might be possible in freer societies than counter-revolutionary Gulf autocracies," Al-Azami wrote.[27]

Yahya Birt, a British Muslim scholar of UAE-supported clerics, argues that their need to project their sponsors at times is at odds with reality on the ground. "The extracted price of government patronage is high for ulema in the Middle East. Generally speaking, they have to openly support or maintain silence about autocracy at home, while speaking of democracy, pluralism, and minority rights to Western audiences," Birt said.

"What does this mean for the soft power dimension of the UAE with projects such as the Forum for Promoting Peace? On the face of it the Forum seems benign enough: promoting ideas of peace, minority rights and citizenship in the Arab and Muslim world, but at what price? Any criticism of the UAE's human rights violations... seems impossible," Birt went on to say.[28]

LONGING FOR PAST IMPERIAL GLORY

Slick public relations packaging is what gives the UAE an edge in its rivalry with both Saudi Wahhabism as well as with Qatar and Turkey. Saudi Arabia

---

[25] The UAE Council for Fatwa, 4 February 2019, http://binbayyah.net/english/wp-content/uploads/2019/02/Popes-Visit-to-Abu-Dhabi-English.pdf
[26] Ibid. Al-Azami.
[27] Ibid. Al-Azami.
[28] Ibid. Birt.

is hobbled by the image of an austere, ultra-conservative and secretive kingdom that it is trying to shed and a badly tarnished human rights record magnified by hubris and a perceived sense of entitlement. For its part, Turkey's religious soft power drive has a raw nationalist edge to it that raises the spectre of a longing for past imperial glory.

Inaugurated in 2019, Istanbul's Camlica Mosque, Turkey's largest with its six minarets, symbolizes President Recep Tayyip Erdogan's ambitions. So does the controversial return a year later of the Hagia Sophia, the 1,500-year-old-church-turned-mosque-turned museum, to the status of a Muslim house of worship. In contrast to Mustafa Kemal Ataturk, the general who turned Hagia Sophia into a museum to emphasize the alignment with the West of the state he had carved out of the ruins of the Ottoman empire, Erdogan embarked on a campaign of support for mosques and Muslim communities in former imperial holdings and beyond.

In doing so, Erdogan was following in the footsteps of Ottoman sultans who sought legacy in grandiose mosque construction. He was signaling his intention to restore Turkish glory by positioning his country as the leader of the Islamic world, willing and able to defend Muslims across the globe. His was a worldview outlined by Ahmet Davutoglu, Erdogan's onetime prime and foreign minister, who argued that Turkey's geography, history, and religious and cultural agency empowered it to be a regional hegemon.[29]

Erdogan underlined the importance of religious soft power in his geopolitical strategy by granting his Religious Affairs Department or Diyanet a key role in foreign and aid policy. Established by Ataturk in 1924 to propagate a statist, moderate form of Islam that endorsed secularism, Erdogan infused the directorate with his version of political Islam.

Erdogan harnessed the Diyanet to legitimize his military escapades in Syria, Libya, and Iraq[30] in much the same way that Iran and now the UAE blends hard power with religious soft power. Diyanet regularly instructs imams at home and abroad to recite a Quranic verse, Sura Al-Fath or the Verse of the Conquest, to legitimize the Turkish president's adventures. The sura conveys a message of victory and conquest as well as the favor God conferred upon the Prophet Mohammed and his followers. It promises

---

[29] Ahmet Davutoglu, "The Clash of Interests: An Explanation of the World (Dis)Order," *Perceptions Journal of International Affairs*, Vol. 2:4, December 1997–February 1998), p.1.

[30] *Hurriyet Daily News*, "'Conquest' prayers performed across Turkey's mosques for Afrin operation," 21 June 2018, https://www.hurriyetdailynews.com/conquest-prayers-performed-across-turkeys-mosques-for-afrin-operation-126072

increased numbers of faithful as well as forgiveness of worldly mistakes by those who do jihad on the path of God.

The construction of mosques and the dispatch of Diyanet personnel who serve as imams, religious counselors, and political commissars have been an important component of a multi-pronged Turkish strategy to build influence. The strategy also included development and humanitarian aid, the funding and building of infrastructure, private sector investment, and the opening of universities.

The meshing of religious soft power and aid has served Turkey well. Perhaps nowhere more so than in Somalia where US$1 billion in aid channelled through Diyanet and other NGOs funded the building of the Recep Tayyip Erdogan Hospital in the capital Mogadishu[31] and the establishment of Turkey's foremost foreign military base.[32] Somalia is at the eastern end of a major Turkish diplomatic, economic and cultural push across the African continent that is part of policy designed to position Turkey as a major Middle Eastern, Eurasian and African player.

The price tag attached to Turkish largesse often was that beneficiaries handed over schools operated by the exiled preacher Fethullah Gulen, a onetime Erdogan ally who Turkish officials accuse of building a state within a state and engineering the 2016 failed military attempt to unseat Erdogan with the backing of the UAE. Beneficiaries were often required to extradite suspected Gulen followers and look the other way when Turkish intelligence agents kidnapped alleged followers of the preacher and return them to Turkey.[33]

Turkey's quest for religious soft power kicked into high gear in the wake of the failed 2016 coup with Erdogan repeatedly defining Turkish identity as essentially Ottoman. It is an identity that obliged Turkey in Erdogan's view to come to the defense of Muslims around the world, starting with the 45 modern-day states that once were Ottoman territory. Erdogan, for instance, embraces Palestinian nationalist aspirations as well as Hamas, the Islamist group that controls the Gaza Strip, and the struggle for

---

[31] Pınar Akpınar, *From Benign Donor to Self-Assured Security Provider: Turkey's Policy in Somalia*, Istanbul Policy Center, IPC Policy Brief, 3 December 2017, https://www.researchgate.net/publication/323219525_From_Benign_Donor_to_Self-Assured_Security_Provider_Turkey's_Policy_in_Somalia

[32] Ash Rossiter and Brendon J. Cannon, "Re-Examining the 'Base': The Political and Security Dimensions of Turkey's Military Presence in Somalia," *Insight Turkey* 21:1, Winter 2019.

[33] Die Morina, "Kosovo Minister and Spy Chief Sacked Over Turkish Arrests," *Politico*, 30 March 2018, https://balkaninsight.com/2018/03/30/kosovo-intelligence-director-and-internal-minister-dismissed-over-turkish-arrested-men-03-30-2018/

independence of Kosovo because they are Muslim. Erdogan is not the first Turkish leader to root Turkey's Islamic identity in its Ottoman past.

So did Turgut Ozal, who in the 1980s and early 1990s put Turkey on the path towards an export-driven free market economy. Ozal, as president, also pioneered the opening to post-Soviet Central Asia and encouraged Turkish investment in the Middle East and North Africa. But he shied away from de-emphasizing Turkey's ties to the West. Erdogan's contribution has been that by breaking with Turkey's Kemalist past, he was able to put Islam as a religion and a foundational civilization at the core of changing Turkish educational and social life and positioning the country on the international stage.

If Ozal, a former World Banker, was the more cosmopolitan expression of Turkish Islamism, Erdogan veered towards its more exclusivist, anti-Western bent. Ozal embraced Westernization as empowering Turkey. Erdogan rejected it because it deprived the state of its religious legitimacy, ruptured historic continuity, and produced a shallow identity. It is a strategy that has paid dividends. Erdogan emerged as the most trusted regional leader in a 2017 poll that surveyed public opinion in 12 Middle Eastern countries. Forty percent of the respondents also recognized Erdogan as a religious authority even though he is not an Islamic scholar.[34]

The irony of Erdogan's fallout with Gulen as well as the souring of Turkish-Saudi relations, initially as a result of Turkish suspicions of Gulf support for the failed coup and the 2018 killing in Istanbul of Khashoggi, is that both the Turkish preacher and the Saudi journalist were nurtured in Saudi-backed organizations associated with the Muslim Brotherhood.

Gulen played a key role in the 1960s in the founding of the Erzurum branch of the Associations for the Struggle against Communism, an Islamist-leaning Cold War Turkish group that had ties to Saudi Arabia.[35] Erdogan, former Turkish president Abdullah Gul and former parliament speaker Ibrahim Karatas, among many others, were formed in nationalist and Islamic politics as members of the Turkish National Students Union, which represented the Muslim World League in Turkey.[36]

Turkey has a leg up on its competitors in the Balkans, Central Asia, and Europe. Centuries of Ottoman rule as well as voluntary and forced migration have spawned close ethnic and family ties. Millions of Turks pride

---

[34] Yusuf Sarfati, "Religious Authority in Turkey: Hegemony and Resistance," Baker Institute for Public Policy, Rice University, March 2019, https://www.bakerinstitute.org/media/files/files/c873dd82/cme-pub-luce-sarfati-031119.pdf

[35] Ertuğrul Meşe, *Komünizmle Mücadele Dernekleri* (İstanbul: İletişim, 2016), p. 134–135.

[36] Uğur Mumcu, *Rabıta* (Ankara: UMAG, 2014), p. 199.

themselves on their Balkan roots. The names of Istanbul neighbourhoods, parks and forests reflect the Balkans' Ottoman history. Central Asians identify themselves as Turkic, speak Turkic languages and share cultural attributes with Turks.

In Europe, Turkish operatives often enjoy the goodwill of large well-integrated Diaspora communities even if the fault lines run deep between Turks and Kurds opposed to the Turkish government's repression of Kurdish political aspirations.

Turkey's Achilles Heel may be that the Ottoman-style Islam it projects is a misreading of the empire's history. In another twist of irony, Erdogan embraced a Kemalist vision of the Ottomans as a religiously driven empire rather than one that perceived itself as both Muslim and European and that was pragmatic and not averse to aspects of secularism. It is that misreading that in the words of Turkey scholar Soner Cagaptay has produced "an ahistorical, political Islam-oriented, and often patronising foreign policy concoction" and has informed Turkey's soft power strategy.[37]

Turkey has sought to bolster its bid for religious soft power by positioning itself alongside Malaysia as the champion of the rights of embattled Muslim communities like Myanmar's Rohingya. Turkey's claim to be the defender of the Muslim underdog is however called into question by its refusal, with few caveats, to criticize the brutal crackdown on Turkic Muslims in China's northwestern "autonomous region" of Xinjiang.

Turkey's perfect opportunity to project itself arose with Gulf acquiescence to the U.S.'s official recognition of Israeli annexation of East Jerusalem and the Golan Heights, as well the launch of a peace plan that buried hopes for a two-state solution of the Israeli-Palestinian conflict. To the chagrin of the UAE and Saudi Arabia, Turkey convened a summit in Istanbul of the Riyadh-based, Saudi-dominated Organization of Islamic Cooperation that groups 54 Muslim countries to denounce the U.S.'s recognition of Jerusalem as Israel's capital. Erdogan vowed two years later to prevent Israel from annexing parts of the West Bank and declared that Jerusalem was "a red line for all Muslims in the world."[38] Erdogan has also condemned

---

[37] Soner Cagaptay, *Erdogan's Empire* (London: I. B. Tauris, 2020), p. 54.
[38] *Haaretz*, "Erdogan Vows to Defend Palestinians Against Israel's 'Annexation Project' in Holiday Message to U.S. Muslims," 26 May 2020, https://www.haaretz.com/israel-news/.premium-erdogan-warns-against-israel-s-annexation-project-in-message-to-u-s-muslims-1.8872356?utm_source=smartfocus&utm_medium=email&utm_campaign=daily-brief&utm_content=https://www.haaretz.com/israel-news/.premium-erdogan-warns-against-israel-s-annexation-project-in-message-to-u-s-muslims-1.8872356

the UAE and Bahrain's recent diplomatic recognition of Israel even though he has never reversed Turkey's own ties with the Jewish state.

The New Kid on the Block

Indonesia, the new kid on the block in the competition for Muslim religious soft power and leadership, has proven to be a different kettle of fish. Nahdlatul Ulama, the world's largest Muslim movement, rather than the government of President Joko Widodo, has emerged as a formidable contender, one that is capable of operating on the same level as the states with which it competes.

As a result, the Indonesian state takes a back seat in the global competition among Muslims. It benefits from its close ties to Nahdlatul Ulama as well as the movement's ability to gain access to the corridors of power in world capitals, including Washington, London, Berlin, Budapest, the Vatican, and Delhi. Nahdlatul Ulama was instrumental in organizing a visit to Indonesia in 2020 by Pope Francis that had to be postponed because of the coronavirus pandemic.[39]

The movement also forged close working ties to Muslim grassroots communities in various parts of the world as well as prominent Jewish and Christian groups. Nahdlatul Ulama's growing international influence and access was enabled by its embrace in 2015 of a concept of "Nusantara (archipelago) Islam" or "humanitarian Islam" that recognized the United Nations Declaration of Human Rights.[40] The movement has also gone beyond paying lip service to notions of tolerance and pluralism with the issuance of fatwas intended to re-contextualize the faith by eliminating categories like infidels.[41]

Nahdlatul Ulama's evolution towards a process of re-contextualization of Islam dates back to a 1992 gathering of religious scholars chaired by Abdurrahman Wahid, the group's leader at the time and later president of Indonesia. The gathering noted that "the changing context of reality necessitates the creation of new interpretations of Islamic law and orthodox Islamic teaching."[42]

---

[39] Multiple interviews with Nahdlatul Ulama officials.
[40] Bayt ar-Rahmah, *The Nusantara Manifesto*, 25 October 2018, https://www.baytarrahmah.org/media/2018/Nusantara-Manifesto.pdf
[41] Bayt ar-Rahmah, "Political Communique 2018_10_25 Nusantara Manifesto," 25 October 2018, https://baytarrahmah.org/2018_10_25_nusantara-manifesto/
[42] Bayt ar-Rahmah, *Joint Resolution and Decree*, 25 October 2018, https://www.baytarrahmah.org/media/2018/Ansor_BaR_Joint-Resolution-and-Decree_2018.pdf

Speaking to a German newspaper 25 years later, Nahdlatul Ulama General Secretary Yahya Cholil Staquf laid out the fundamental dividing line between his group's notion of a moderate Islam and that of Indonesia's rivals without identifying them by name. Asked what Islamic concepts were problematic, Staquf said: "The relationship between Muslims and non-Muslims, the relationship of Muslims with the state, and Muslims' relationship to the prevailing legal system wherever they live ... Within the classical tradition, the relationship between Muslims and non-Muslims is assumed to be one of segregation and enmity... In today's world such a doctrine is unreasonable. To the extent that Muslims adhere to this view of Islam, it renders them incapable of living harmoniously and peacefully within the multi-cultural, multi-religious societies of the 21st century."[43]

Widodo initially hoped that Nahdlatul Ulama's manifesto on humanitarian Islam would empower his government to position Indonesia as the beacon of a moderate interpretation of the faith. Speaking at the laying of the ground stone of the International Islamic University (UIII) in West Java, Widodo laid down a gauntlet for his competitors in the Middle East by declaring that it was "natural and fitting that Indonesia should become the (authoritative) reference for the progress of Islamic civilization."[44]

Widodo saw the university as providing an alternative to the Islamic University of Medina, that has played a key role in Saudi Arabia's religious soft power campaign, and the centuries-old Al Azhar in Cairo, that is influenced by financially-backed Saudi scholars and scholarship as well as Emirati funding. The university is "a promising step to introduce Indonesia as the global epicenter for 'moderate' Islam'," said Islamic philosophy scholar Amin Abdullah.[45]

Saudi and Emirati concerns that Indonesia could emerge as a serious religious soft power competitor were initially assuaged when Widodo's aspirations were thwarted by critics within his administration. A six-page proposal to enhance Indonesian religious soft power globally put forward in 2016 by Nahdlatul Ulama at the request of Pratikno, Widodo's minister

---

[43] Marco Stahlhut, "Terrorismus und Islam hängen zusammen," *Frankfurter Algemeine Zeitung*, 18 August 2017, https://www.reddit.com/r/de/comments/6uorfx/faz_islam_und_terrorismus_h%C3%A4ngen_zusammen_volltext/

[44] Fabian Januarius Kuwado, "Harapan Jokowi pada Universitas Islam Internasional Indonesia," *Kompas*, 5 June 2018, https://nasional.kompas.com/read/2018/06/05/12232491/harapan-jokowi-pada-universitas-islam-internasional-indonesia

[45] Luthfi T. Dzulfikar, "How Indonesia's new international Islamic university will host global research for 'moderate Islam,'" *The Conversation*, 16 December 2019, https://theconversation.com/how-indonesias-new-international-islamic-university-will-host-global-research-for-moderate-islam-128785

responsible for providing administrative support for his initiatives, was buried after the foreign ministry warned that its adoption would damage relations with the Gulf states.[46]

That could have been the end of the story. But neither Saudi Arabia nor the UAE anticipated Nahdlatul Ulama's determination to push its concept of humanitarian Islam globally, including at the highest levels of government in western capitals as well as in countries like India. Nor did they anticipate Mr. Widodo's willingness to play both ends against the middle by supporting Nahdlatul Ulama's campaign while engaging on religious issues with both the Saudis and the Emiratis.

The degree to which Nahdlatul Ulama is perceived as a threat by the UAE and Saudi Arabia is evident in battles in high level inter-faith meetings convened by the Vatican, U.S. Ambassador at Large for International Religious Freedom Sam Brownback, and others over principles like endorsement of the UN human rights declaration.

Nahdlatul Ulama's rise to prominence was also what persuaded Muhammad bin Abdul Karim Al-Issa, the head of the Muslim World League, to visit the Indonesian group's headquarters in Jakarta in early 2020.[47] It was the first visit to one of the world's foremost Islamic organizations in the League's almost 60-year history. The visit allowed him to portray himself as in dialogue with Nahdlatul Ulama in his inter-faith contacts as well as in conversation with Western officials and other influential interlocutors.

Al-Issa had turned down an opportunity to meet two years earlier when a leading Nahdlatul Ulama cleric and he were both in Mecca at the same time. He told a Western interlocutor who was attempting to arrange a meeting that he had "never heard" of the Indonesian scholar and could not make time "due to an extremely previous busy schedule of meetings with international Islamic personalities" that included "moderate influential figures from Palestine, Iraq, Tunisia, Russia and Kazakhstan."[48]

Saudi Arabia was forced several months later in the run-up to the 2019 Indonesian presidential election to replace its ambassador in Jakarta, Osama bin Mohammed Abdullah Al Shuaib. The ambassador had denounced in a tweet — that has since been deleted — Ansor, the Nahdlatul

---

[46] Interview with the author of the paper, 13 July 2020
[47] *Antaranews*, "World Muslim League supports NU's harmonization mission," 28 February 2020, https://en.antaranews.com/news/142430/world-muslim-league-supports-nus-harmonization-mission
[48] James M. Dorsey, "Indonesia: A major prize in the battle for the soul of Islam," The Turbulent World of Middle East Soccer, 30 July 2020, https://mideastsoccer.blogspot.com/2020/07/indonesia-major-prize-in-battle-for.html

13. The Battle for the Soul of Islam 177

Ulama young adults organization, as heretical and he had supported an anti-government demonstration.[49]

Nahdlatul Ulama's ability to compete is further evidenced by its increasingly influential role in Centrist Democrat International or CDI, the world's largest alliance of political parties, that grew out of European and Latin American Christian Democratic movements. Membership in CDI of the National Awakening or PKB, the political party of Nahdlatul Ulama, arguably gives it a leg up in the soft power competition with the UAE and Saudi Arabia, which both ban political parties. Meantime, the PKB is far more pluralistic than Turkey's ruling Justice and Development Party (AKP), which has shown increasingly authoritarian tendencies.

CDI's executive committee met in the Javan city of Yogyakarta in January 2020. Participants included prominent Latin American leaders and former heads of state, Hungarian Prime Minister Victor Orban, Slovenian Prime Minister Janez Jansa and Elmar Brock, a close associate of German Chancellor Angela Merkel.

Nahdlatul Ulama's sway was apparent in CDI's adoption of a resolution that called for adherence to universal ethics and humanitarian values based on Western humanism, Christian democracy, and Humanitarian Islam. The resolution urged resistance to "the emergence of authoritarian, civilizationalist states that do not accept the rules-based post-WWII order, whether in terms of human rights, rule of law, democracy or respect for international borders and the sovereignty of other nations."[50]

Nahdlatul Ulama benefits from what journalist Muhammad Abu Fadil described as rejection of an "Arab face of Islam" that in his words was "hopelessly contorted by extremism" in Western perceptions. Abu Fadil suggested that "certain elements in the West have become interested in 'Asian Islam,' which appears to be more moderate than Arab Islam; less inclined to export radical ideology; less dominated by extremist interpretations of religion; and possessed of a genuine and sincere tendency to act with tolerance."[51]

---

[49] Bayt ar-Rahmah, "NU and netizens demand Saudi ambassador to Indonesia leave the country over pro-212 tweet," 4 December 2018, https://www.baytarrahmah.org/media/2018/coconuts-jakarta_nu-netizens-demand-saudi-ambassador-indonesia-leave-country-pro-212-tweet_12-04-18.pdf

[50] IDC-CDI, *Draft resolution on promoting a rules-based international order founded upon universal ethics and humanitarian values*, 23 January 2020, https://www.idc-cdi.com/wp-content/uploads/2020/04/Resolution-on-promoting-a-rules-based-international-order-founded-uponuniversal-ethics-and-humanitarian-values.pdf

[51] Muhammad Abu Fadil, "Political Horizons for Indonesian Islam," 15 June 2015, *Al Arab*, https://alarab.co.uk/آفاق-سياسية-أمام-الإسلام-الإندونيسي

Conclusion

A major battle for Muslim religious soft power that pits Saudi Arabia, Iran, the United Arab Emirates, Qatar, Turkey, and Indonesia against one another is largely about enhancing countries' global and regional influence. This battle has little to do with implementing notions of a moderate Islam in theory or practice despite claims by the various rivals, most of which are authoritarian states with little regard for human and minority rights or fundamental freedoms.

Muslim-majority Indonesia, the world's third largest democracy, is the odd-man out. A traditionalist and in many ways conservative organization, Nahdlatul Ulama, the world's largest Muslim movement, has garnered international respect and recognition with its embrace of a Humanitarian Islam that recognizes the United Nations Universal Declaration of Human Rights and the principles enshrined in it and has taken tangible steps to address Islamic concepts that it considers outdated. In doing so, Nahdlatul Ulama has emerged as a formidable challenger to powerful state actors in the battle for the soul of Islam. But it still faces the challenge of overcoming the Arab view, expressed by Abdullah I of Jordan after the end of caliphate, that Muslim leadership must somehow return to the Arabs.

14

Humanitarian Islam: Fostering Shared Civilizational Values to Revitalize a Rules-Based International Order

Timothy S. Shah and Thomas G. Dinham

Summary

In this essay, originally published in July 2020 in *Strategic Review,* Indonesia's top foreign affairs journal, Timothy Shah and Thomas Dinham describe how the world's largest Muslim organization, Nahdlatul Ulama (NU), is spearheading a mass, grassroots, multi-faith campaign to revitalize the post-World War II rules-based international order and forge a positive role for Islam upon the world stage.

The post-World War II rules-based international order is under severe stress, challenged by the emergence of "authoritarian, civilizationist states that do not accept [this] order, whether in terms of human rights, rule of law, democracy or respect for international borders and the sovereignty of other nations."[1] What also distinguishes "civilizationist" states —

---

[1] Cf. *Resolution on promoting a rules-based international order founded upon universal ethics and humanitarian values*, which was submitted by Indonesia's National Awakening Party (PKB) and unanimously adopted by Centrist Democrat International (CDI) in Yogyakarta, Indonesia, on January 23, 2020. Previously known as Christian

including Communist China and Putin's Russia — is the weaponization of ethnic, religious and/or cultural identities, including their history and symbols, in order to consolidate and wield power vis-à-vis both internal and external enemies.

"Civilizationism" is part of a global resurgence of identity-based, supremacist politics unfolding in tandem with profound shifts in economic and geopolitical power in the 21st century. Simultaneously, socio-cultural and political developments in recent decades have precipitated a crisis of confidence in Europe and North America regarding the traditional values and legitimacy of Western civilization. These developments have profoundly undermined the philosophical, spiritual, and moral foundation upon which the post-war international order was built.

Many of the most powerful and respected institutions in the West — which reflect the views of dominant cultural, intellectual, political and economic elites — have embraced a new, constantly-evolving "orthodoxy" that seeks to compel the universal adoption of a hypertrophied human rights agenda that differs dramatically from that which accompanied the birth of the post-war international order. Ironically, these elites are themselves heirs to the Christian "civilizing mission" of 19th-century European imperialists, and to a centuries-old system of Western hegemony. This de facto neo-colonial project — in effect, a contemporary manifestation of Western civilizationism — is deeply offensive to a majority of the world's population and is thus accelerating the breakdown of a rules-based international order, whose key principles were widely ratified in the 20th century, but only superficially implemented by most nations.

In recent decades, Western human rights discourse has increasingly deviated from the clear, concise and rigorously defined principles articulated in the thirty articles of the *Universal Declaration of Human Rights* (UDHR), which were adopted by the United Nations General Assembly on December 10, 1948, as a concrete means to promote "universal respect for, and observance of, human rights and fundamental freedoms for all without distinction as to race, sex, language, or religion" (*United Nations Charter*, Article 55). Having emerged in the aftermath of WWII and all its horrors, UDHR embodied the values of mid-20th-century Western humanism and Christian democracy. Although these values "may be regarded as universal, and have found expression in other religious traditions,"[2] the human

---

Democrat International, CDI and its European affiliate, the European People's Party (EPP), is the world's largest network of political parties.

[2] Cf. *Resolution on the consolidation of a global consensus regarding key ethics and values that should guide the exercise of power so that the geopolitical landscape of the 21st century*

14. Humanitarian Islam: Fostering Shared Civilizational Values

rights framework established by UDHR has never been fully embraced by the world's other great civilizations and religious faiths.

Humanity thus stands at a crossroads. On the one hand, cumulative and rapidly accelerating scientific, technological, and economic progress have created an historically unparalleled opportunity for the collective flourishing of humanity, particularly when accompanied by a rules-based international order that safeguards national sovereignty and policies founded upon respect for the equal rights and dignity of every human being. On the other hand, civilizationist leaders — who instrumentalize and mobilize tribal identity, political and economic power, and technology to tyrannize others — pose an immense threat to the future of humanity.

Recognizing and responding to this threat, Gerakan Pemuda Ansor — the 5-million-member young adults movement of the world's largest Muslim organization, Indonesia's Nahdlatul Ulama (NU) — assembled a coalition of international religious and political figures at the Second Global Unity Forum held in Yogyakarta, Indonesia, in October of 2018 and promulgated the *Nusantara Manifesto*. This 40-page *Manifesto* is part of a systematic and institutional campaign by NU spiritual leaders who seek to address "obsolete and problematic (i.e., historically contingent, or *mutaghayyirāt*) elements within Islamic orthodoxy that lend themselves to tyranny, while positioning these efforts within a much broader initiative to reject any and all forms of tyranny, and foster the emergence of a global civilization endowed with nobility of character."[3] The *Manifesto* states:

> The *Gerakan Pemuda Ansor Declaration on Humanitarian Islam*[4] discussed, at length, the threat to modern civilization posed by "obsolete tenets of classical Islamic law, which are premised upon perpetual conflict with those who do not embrace or submit to Islam" (point 42). Yet these problematic tenets of Islamic orthodoxy do not constitute the sole — and perhaps not even the

---

may be characterized by a truly just and harmonious world order, which was submitted by Indonesia's National Awakening Party (PKB) and unanimously adopted by Centrist Democrat International (CDI) in Rome, Italy, on October 11, 2019.

[3] Gerakan Pemuda Ansor and Bayt ar-Rahmah, *The Nusantara Manifesto*, adopted through a *Joint Resolution and Decree* signed by both organizations on October 25, 2018 in Yogyakarta, Indonesia. Published in *Hasil-Hasil Musyawarah Nasional 'Alim Ulama Nahdlatul Ulama 2019* (*Findings of the 2019 National Conference of Nahdlatul Ulama Religious Scholars*), Jakarta: Nahdlatul Ulama Central Board.

[4] Gerakan Pemuda Ansor and Bayt ar-Rahmah, *Gerakan Pemuda Ansor Declaration on Humanitarian Islam*, promulgated on May 22, 2017 in Jombang, Indonesia. Published in *Hasil-Hasil Musyawarah Nasional 'Alim Ulama Nahdlatul Ulama 2019* (*Findings of the 2019 National Conference of Nahdlatul Ulama Religious Scholars*), Jakarta: Nahdlatul Ulama Central Board.

primary — threat to the future of humanity. For dogmatism, which naturally lends itself to tyranny, may readily manifest under various ideological guises, both religious and secular.

Nevertheless, the ease with which Islamists have been able to exploit problematic elements of Islamic orthodoxy to clothe their political agenda in religious authenticity has had the far-reaching and catastrophic result of strengthening dogmatic forces worldwide. The full ramifications of this process are still unfolding and threaten to produce an enduring radicalization of politics on a global level. This is a particularly alarming development, as it comes at a time when the diverse peoples, cultures and civilizations of the world are increasingly interconnected, interdependent and interfused.

In the Islamic world and those regions with localized Muslim majorities, Islamist groups have used the clarion call of establishing an Islamic state to launch civil wars, insurgencies and campaigns of terrorism that have left cities in ruin, countless dead and millions displaced over a vast arc of territory stretching from the Western Sahel to the southern Philippines. Many of these conflicts have lasted for decades and, in spite of their terrible toll, show no sign of abating in the decades to come.

The widespread perception of Muslims and Islam as a threat to non-Muslim societies is a direct and intentional result of Islamist groups' actions, and their astute use of propaganda, which transmits powerfully symbolic images of the dystopian reality they seek to create. Horrors of the past such as slavery, crucifixion and the public execution of alleged homosexuals, adulterers, infidels, apostates and magicians are resurrected, re-instituted as valid components of an Islamic social order and broadcast to a disgusted global audience.

Islamist terrorism has strengthened politically opportunistic elements in non-Muslim societies, as those seeking to maintain or acquire power exploit such violence to buttress their own political agendas.

The Communist Party of China's determination to build a hi-tech totalitarian surveillance state threatens not only the inhabitants of China, but potentially all who dwell within its sphere of influence, as the native populations of Tibet and Xinjiang can testify. Indeed, the CPC has exploited global concern about Islamist terrorism to shield this project from international criticism, and millions of Uyghur Muslims in Xinjiang have seen their homeland converted into a testing ground for radically new methods of totalitarian oppression, which could be exported worldwide. (See Ansor Decree Number 04/KONBES-XXI/IV/2017, *Gerakan Pemuda Ansor's View Regarding the Republic of Indonesia's Strategic Interests and National Security Agenda within the Cauldron of Current Geopolitical Dynamics*.)

In South and South-East Asia, the perceived threat of Islam has been exploited to confer legitimacy on local brands of exclusivist and authoritarian religious and political ideologies. Buddhist supremacism threatens Muslim minorities in Myanmar and Sri Lanka, while [supremacist ideologies and movements] aim to subordinate Muslims, Christians and others in South Asia.

In the Western world, Islamist terrorism — and, in the case of Europe, the influx of refugees and migrants from the broader Middle East and Africa — have significantly contributed to a profound polarization that threatens the integrity of those societies' democratic systems. On both the political left and right, attitudes towards Islam have become a proxy battleground in a wider struggle for power that politicizes Islam and renders Muslims highly vulnerable to any breakdown in political order.

Efforts by corporations, ideological movements and governments in the West to harness technology, including artificial intelligence, to manipulate public opinion and restrict freedom of expression pose a different but no less alarming threat of tyranny, particularly when wedded to social-cultural, economic, legislative and administrative efforts to accomplish the same agenda.

Although superficially distinct, these threats share a number of traits in common. Each is inextricably linked to the innate human tendency to dominate, or seek to dominate, others. And each illustrates the danger posed by welding dogma — whether secular or religious — to a political agenda backed by powerful economic interests and the use of technology to impose conformity (in effect, a "tribal identity") upon others, and crush the spirit of anyone who opposes this agenda.[5]

Alarmed by the threat that a resurgent Islamist current poses to the unity of Indonesia and its people — and to the future of humanity as a whole — the spiritual leadership of NU has launched a long-term, systematic, and institutional campaign to reform what they describe as "obsolete and problematic tenets of Islamic orthodoxy" that lend themselves to political weaponization and enjoin religious hatred, supremacy, and violence.[6] This global "Humanitarian Islam" movement grew out of the 2014 *Islam Nusantara* campaign, which was the brainchild of NU spiritual leaders Kyai Haji A. Mustofa Bisri — then Chairman of the Nahdlatul Ulama Supreme Council — and his nephew, NU General Secretary Kyai Haji Yahya Cholil Staquf. This wildly successful drive popularized the term *"Islam Nusantara,"* deployed it as a powerful cultural motif for re-enlivening Indonesians' appreciation of their distinct civilizational heritage, and rallied Muslims across Indonesia's vast archipelago against Islamist extremism at a time when the Islamic State, or ISIS, was wreaking havoc across the Middle East.[7]

---

[5] Gerakan Pemuda Ansor and Bayt ar-Rahmah, *The Nusantara Manifesto*, points 77–86.

[6] Cf. Gerakan Pemuda Ansor and Bayt ar-Rahmah, *Gerakan Pemuda Ansor Declaration on Humanitarian Islam and The Nusantara Manifesto.*

[7] Bayt ar-Rahmah, "Bayt ar-Rahmah," https://baytarrahmah.org/2014_12_09_bayt-ar-rahmah/

Building upon the *Islam Nusantara* campaign's success, Mustofa Bisri and Yahya Staquf founded *Bayt ar-Rahmah li ad-Da'wa al-Islamiyah Rahmatan li al-'Alamin* (Home of Divine Grace for Revealing and Nurturing Islam as a Blessing for All Creation) with American businessman and LibForAll/International Institute of Qur'anic Studies (IIQS) co-founder C. Holland Taylor, whose organization helped facilitate the *Islam Nusantara* campaign. *Bayt ar-Rahmah* serves as a hub for the worldwide expansion of NU operations and leads the global Humanitarian Islam movement, which seeks to restore *rahmah* (universal love and compassion) to its rightful place as the primary message of Islam, by addressing obsolete and problematic elements within Islamic orthodoxy that lend themselves to tyranny.

Drafted by Nahdlatul Ulama spiritual leaders who govern Bayt ar-Rahmah, the Humanitarian Islam movement's foundational texts were promulgated between 2016 and 2018 by Gerakan Pemuda Ansor, then formally adopted and expanded upon by Nahdlatul Ulama through a series of rulings issued at a mass gathering of nearly 20,000 Islamic scholars in February of 2019. In a book published by the NU Central Board, which contains the *Findings of the 2019 National Conference of Nahdlatul Ulama Religious Scholars*, NU theologians: (a) analyzed the manner in which state and nonstate actors around the world weaponize orthodox Islamic teachings; (b) outlined "a serious, long-term socio-cultural, political, religious and educational campaign to transform Muslims' understanding of their religious obligations, and the very nature of Islamic orthodoxy"; (c) formally endorsed the concept of a modern nation state rather than caliphate; (d) recognized all citizens, irrespective of their ethnicity or religion, as having equal rights and obligations within a modern nation state; (e) decreed that Muslims must obey the laws of any nation in which they dwell; (f) stated that Muslims have a religious obligation to foster peace rather than automatically wage war on behalf of their co-religionists, whenever conflict erupts between Muslim and non-Muslim populations anywhere in the world; and (g) abolished the legal category of infidel (*kāfir*) within Islamic law (*fiqh*), so that non-Muslims may enjoy full equality as fellow citizens in their own right, rather than rely on protection at the sufferance of a Muslim ruler.[8]

Addressing the Islamist threat to Indonesia, Mr. Staquf states:

---

[8] Bayt ar-Rahmah, "World First: Nahdlatul Ulama Abolishes the Legal Category of 'Infidel' within Islamic Law," October 16, 2019, https://baytarrahmah.org/2019_10_16_world-first-nahdlatul-ulama-abolishes-the-legal-category-of-infidel-within-islamic-law/

14. Humanitarian Islam: Fostering Shared Civilizational Values

There can be little doubt that the outcome of this struggle, within Indonesia, will be impacted by the forces of globalization, which bring people and ideas from the far corners of the earth into daily contact with Indonesian Muslims, for both good and ill. So long as obsolete, medieval tenets within Islamic orthodoxy remain the dominant source of religious authority throughout the Muslim world, Indonesian Islamists will continue to draw power and sustenance from developments in the world at large.[9]

Bayt ar-Rahmah and Gerakan Pemuda Ansor have also developed — and begun to operationalize — a global strategy to reconcile Islamic teachings with the reality of contemporary civilization, whose context and conditions differ significantly from those in which classical Islamic law emerged.

This strategy is built upon nine foundational documents: the *International Summit of Moderate Islamic Leaders (ISOMIL) Nahdlatul Ulama Declaration* (2016); the *First Global Unity Forum Declaration* (2016); the *Gerakan Pemuda Ansor Declaration on Humanitarian Islam* (2017); the *Nusantara Statement* and *Nusantara Manifesto* (2018); the *Findings of the 2019 National Conference of Nahdlatul Ulama Religious Scholars*; a *Resolution on acknowledging that universal human fraternity is essential to the emergence of a global civilization founded upon respect for the equal rights and dignity of every human being* (2019); a *Resolution on the consolidation of a global consensus regarding key ethics and values that should guide the exercise of power so that the geopolitical landscape of the 21st century may be characterized by a truly just and harmonious world order* (2019); and a *Resolution on promoting a rules-based international order founded upon universal ethics and humanitarian values* (2020), adopted by Centrist Democrat International.

As a result of these pioneering efforts, a large body of Sunni Muslim authorities are now engaged in a wide-ranging, concerted and explicit project of theological reform for the first time since the late Middle Ages.[10]

---

[9] Yahya Cholil Staquf, "Enduring threat, global ramifications," *Strategic Review: The Indonesian Journal of Leadership, Policy and World Affairs*, (July-September 2018): pp. 12–17.

[10] The Ottoman Reform Edict of 1856 (*Hatt-i Humayan*), adopted under pressure from Great Britain, France and the Austro-Hungarian Empire, proclaimed equality between Muslims and non-Muslims. For example, the *jizyah* tax was abolished and non-Muslims permitted to enter military service. However, widespread Muslim rejection of these attempted reforms helped trigger the Armenian genocides of the 1890s (which were instigated by Sultan Abdul Hamid II) and the First World War (orchestrated by a Young Turks administration), and also contributed to the ethnic cleansing of Anotolia during the 1920s. Ultimately, the effect of these reforms was the virtual elimination of non-Muslims within the territory that

These efforts have been extensively cited by sponsors of an international campaign to award the Nobel Peace Prize to Nahdlatul Ulama and Muhammadiyah. Bayt ar-Rahmah also has access to the world's largest political network — Centrist Democrat International/European People's Party (CDI/EPP) — via Indonesia's largest Islamic political party, the National Awakening Party, or PKB, which is rooted within the spiritual wing of Nahdlatul Ulama and was founded by NU leaders including President Abdurrahman Wahid and Kyai Haji A. Mustofa Bisri.

In fact, PKB's membership in Centrist Democrat International was the direct result of a senior CDI/EPP figure's participation in the 2018 Second Global Unity Forum, which gave birth to the *Nusantara Statement* and *Nusantara Manifesto*. PKB is systematically advancing the Humanitarian Islam agenda through its membership in CDI and its fraternal relationship with member parties worldwide. In January of 2020, CDI adopted a resolution submitted by PKB, which concludes:

The CDI states the following:

- *As the world's economic center of gravity shifts towards Eurasia — and geopolitical competition threatens to undermine peace and security throughout this vast landmass — widespread acknowledgment of, and adherence to, universal ethics and humanitarian values may help ensure that this transition can be navigated more peacefully;*
- *CDI and its member parties are in a unique position to facilitate this process, for they embrace a common set of humane and universal values, rooted in their respective religious and cultural traditions;*
- *These traditions — which include but are not limited to Western humanism, Christian democracy and Humanitarian Islam — may serve as the foundation for a 21st century alliance to promote a rules-based international order founded upon universal ethics and humanitarian values;*
- *Centrist Democrat International invites people of good will of every faith and nation, as well as political parties and governments worldwide, to join in this alliance to safeguard human dignity and foster the emergence of a truly just and harmonious world order, founded upon the equal rights and dignity of every human being.*

This resolution — unanimously adopted by the CDI Executive Committee at a meeting held on January 23, 2020 in Yogyakarta, Indonesia — established a concrete mechanism for cooperation between the Humanitarian

---

became the modern Turkish nation state. Cf. Peter Balakian, *The Burning Tigris: The Armenian Genocide and America's Response* (New York: HarperCollins, 2009).

Islam movement, CDI, and its member parties worldwide, including those that govern many European nations and EU institutions, such as Germany and the Presidency of the European Commission.

In order to strengthen the existing rules-based international order and facilitate its acceptance by Muslims worldwide, NU spiritual leaders have established a theological framework for the emergence of what they describe as "Islamic jurisprudence for a global civilization, whose constituent elements retain their distinctive characteristics" (*fiqh al-ḥaḍārah al-'ālamīyah al-mutaṣahirah*). These spiritual leaders seek to "address the need for social harmony at a global level and in each of the world's regions where Muslims actually live and work, through a process of recontextualizing and 'indigenizing' Islam, as historically occurred in *Nusantara* (the Malay Archipelago)."[11]

They are also working to consolidate South and Southeast Asia as an alternate pillar of support for a rules-based international order through a strategy called the "Ashoka Approach," which seeks to reawaken the ancient spiritual heritage of the Indianized cultural sphere ("Indosphere") to foster humility, compassion, and respect for the equal rights and dignity of every human being.

Roughly co-extensive with South and Southeast Asia, the Indosphere is a vast geographic and cultural zone stretching from Pakistan to Indonesia, which was formatively and permanently shaped by the great spiritual traditions — particularly Hinduism and Buddhism — that originated in the Indian subcontinent.

Throughout the Indosphere and the world at large, state and non-state actors are increasingly weaponizing ethnic, religious, and cultural identities to maintain or acquire political power. Their actions pose a significant threat to the post-World War II international order, which is built upon a philosophical and moral framework that regards every human being as "born free and equal in dignity and rights" (Preamble, *Universal Declaration of Human Rights*). This global authoritarian resurgence threatens to recreate in the 21st century the horrors of the past. For amidst an increasingly multi-polar world, Western power and Western culture alone are insufficient to sustain, much less strengthen and enhance, a rules-based international order dedicated to safeguarding national sovereignty and fundamental human rights.

In response to this crisis, leaders of the Humanitarian Islam movement have developed — and begun to implement — a strategy to foster,

---

[11]   Cf. Part XI of the *Nusantara Manifesto* (points 99–173) and especially Section 11.5 (points 157–173).

among regional actors, an awareness of their shared civilizational heritage and their common interest in shaping the future of humanity. This entails examining the nature of the historic engagement between Indian civilization and indigenous cultures throughout the region. It also requires building a de facto alliance among the peoples and nations of the Indosphere, enabling them to cope more effectively with a wide range of challenges to their sovereignty, and their respective cultures, in the 21st century.

To stimulate this awareness of the region's common interests, NU leaders are posing a simple question to key interlocutors from government and civil society institutions throughout the Indosphere: "Should we simply 'yield' and accept cultural, ideological, economic, and political domination of our individual nations by self-interested global actors, including China, Western nations, and the Gulf states? Or shall we stand together to voice our perspectives and defend our interests from a position of dignity, as independent cultures and nations acting upon the world stage?"

NU leaders are uniquely positioned to ask such questions, as the Nahdlatul Ulama's cultural heartland lies within the heavily populated island of Java, which constitutes the geographic, political and economic center of Indonesia, and boasts ancient ties to both Hindu-Buddhist and Islamic civilizations. A majority of Javanese Muslims continue to cherish their pre-Islamic heritage as an intrinsic part of their identity, giving rise to the uniquely pluralistic and tolerant expression of Islamic teachings known as *Islam Nusantara* (East Indies Islam). A distinguishing feature of *Islam Nusantara* is its tendency to prioritize religion's spiritual essence over its purely formal and dogmatic elements, which "readily lend themselves to weaponization and, in the wrong hands, foster conflict rather than social unity" (*Nusantara Manifesto*, point 88). *Islam Nusantara* remains a vibrant, powerful, and — as demonstrated in the 2014 and 2019 national elections — politically decisive force within Indonesia.

Bayt ar-Rahmah leaders — including NU General Secretary KH. Yahya Cholil Staquf and C. Holland Taylor, who serves as GP Ansor's Emissary to the UN, Americas and Europe — maintain that in order to engage in political, economic and civilizational dialogue on the basis of equality, the nations of the Indosphere must rediscover their shared civilizational legacy, whose cultural and spiritual heritage is equal to that of the Sinosphere, Europe, and the Middle East. By re-enlivening the region's own spiritually informed and benevolent narratives regarding the nature of religious and cultural identity — as enshrined in Ashoka's Major Rock Edicts and the teachings of *Islam Nusantara* — the Ashoka Approach[12] is intended to strengthen the Indosphere and enable it to resist both internal and external disruptive influences, including those originating from China, the Middle East, and elsewhere.

Building on their transformative work in support of religious pluralism in Indonesia and the global Humanitarian Islam movement, NU spiritual leaders are seeking to mobilize like-minded religious and political figures throughout South and Southeast Asia to foster a renewed appreciation for the spirituality and respect for pluralism that were once defining features of the Indianized cultural sphere, and forge concrete avenues of cooperation between profoundly spiritual and humanitarian expressions of Hinduism, Buddhism, and Islam. Their explicit goal is for South and Southeast Asia to re-emerge as a cohesive, vital, and proactive civilizational sphere, which functions as a powerful, independent pillar of support for a rules-based international order founded upon shared civilizational values.

Leaders of the Humanitarian Islam movement are acutely aware of the last time Indonesia played a prominent role upon the world stage: viz., when President Soekarno joined India's Jawaharlal Nehru, Egypt's Gamal Abdel Nasser and Yugoslavia's Josip Broz Tito in establishing the Non-Aligned Movement in the 1950s. However, the NU leaders' agenda is expressly spiritual, and seeks to unite all of humanity rather than simply steer a neutral course between the world's great powers. The global Humanitarian Islam movement represents one aspect of the transformational legacy of Indonesia's first democratically elected president and long-time NU Chairman H.E. Kyai Haji Abdurrahman Wahid (1940 – 2009). In fact, the Humanitarian Islam movement was directly inspired by President Wahid and its leadership consists of close friends and disciples of a man widely revered by Indonesian Catholics, Hindus and Buddhists, and regarded as a saint by many of the NU's 90 million followers.

This global movement to establish a rules-based international order founded upon shared civilizational values seeks to "abolish the primordial cycle of hatred, tyranny and violence that has plagued humanity since time immemorial";[13] derail the juggernaut of "tribal" politics, whether

---

[12] Cf. Timothy S. Shah and C. Holland Taylor, *The Ashoka Approach,* Magelang, Indonesia and Bangalore, India, 2020: Bayt ar-Rahmah and Religious Freedom Institute. Conceived and written in collaboration with Kyai Haji Yahya Cholil Staquf, General Secretary of the Nahdlatul Ulama Supreme Council and Bayt ar-Rahmah Director of Religious Affairs.

[13] Cf. *Resolution on the consolidation of a global consensus regarding key ethics and values that should guide the exercise of power so that the geopolitical landscape of the 21st century may be characterized by a truly just and harmonious world order,* presented by PKB to the Executive Committee of Centrist Democrat International. The *Resolution* was unanimously adopted by CDI on October 11, 2019 in Rome, Italy.

rooted in ethnic, religious or secular/ideological identities; shift the focal point of authority in the Islamic world from the Middle East to South and Southeast Asia, where a majority of the world's Muslims reside; and re-enliven the profound civilizational values of the Indosphere, in order to buttress the rules-based post-WWII international order as the world's geopolitical center of gravity shifts from the North Atlantic axis into the heart of Eurasia.

As Bernard Adenay Risakotta writes in *Living in a Sacred Cosmos: Indonesia and the Future of Islam* (New Haven: Yale Southeast Asia Studies, 2019):

> *The center of Islam in the world today is neither Saudi Arabia nor the Middle East. Rather, it is Indonesia. Indonesia is the most important country in the world about which most people know practically nothing. Just as the center of Christianity is no longer in Europe or North America, but has shifted to the Southern Hemisphere (Jenkins, 2012), so the center of Islamicate civilization has shifted from the Middle East to Asia.*

15

"Positive Deviance" Within the Indosphere & the Muslim World

Timothy Samuel Shah[1]

SUMMARY

In conjunction with the 75th anniversary of Indonesia's declaration of independence on August 17, 1945, the U.S.-based Religious Freedom Institute published a groundbreaking study titled *Indonesia Religious Freedom Landscape Report 2020*. The report's analytical framework is informed by the concept of "positive deviance," a term coined by development scholars in the 1960s to describe individuals or groups that outperform their peers even though they face similar problems and enjoy similar resources. The report concludes that Indonesia is a remarkable example of positive deviance in the area of religious freedom, both within the "Indosphere" and the Muslim world at large.

Roughly co-extensive with South and Southeast Asia, the Indosphere is a vast geographic and cultural zone stretching from Pakistan to Indonesia, which was formatively and permanently shaped by the great spiritual traditions — particularly Hinduism and Buddhism — that originated in the Indian subcontinent. Today, however, the region is increasingly beset by exclusionary religious nationalisms and other politically weaponized ethnic and religious identities. The fruit of an intensive three-year project led by Timothy Shah and Rebecca Shah and funded by the Templeton Religion Trust, the

---

[1] This chapter originally appeared as the concluding section of *Indonesia Religious Freedom Landscape Report 2020*, authored by Timothy S. Shah (Washington, D.C.: Religious Freedom Institute, 2020), available at https://static1.squarespace.com/static/57052f155559869b68a4f0e6/t/5f34524992021e34b58624ac/1597264467556/Indonesia+Landscape+Report+ONLINE.pdf

report describes how Nahdlatul Ulama spiritual leaders are working to preserve Indonesia's ancient traditions of religious pluralism and tolerance, and leverage these to project strategic influence worldwide. What follows is the concluding section of the 88-page *Indonesia Religious Freedom Landscape Report 2020*.

THE REGIONAL AND GLOBAL CONTEXT

From 2017 to 2020, the Religious Freedom Institute's South and Southeast Asia Action Team (SSEA-AT) analyzed the religious freedom landscape in eight of the most important countries in the region. The fruit of this multi-year collaborative analysis, which drew heavily on the expertise of SSEA-AT's senior fellows along with dozens of other experts, is a monograph-length study titled: *Surveying the Religious Freedom Landscape in South and Southeast Asia: Strengths, Weaknesses, Opportunities, and Threats Shaping the Present Condition and Future Direction of Religious Freedom in Pakistan, India, Nepal, Bangladesh, Sri Lanka, Burma, Malaysia, and Indonesia* (Washington, D.C.: Religious Freedom Institute, 2020).

The nations covered by this landscape report include the most populous and strategically significant countries of South and Southeast Asia, and approximately 86% of the region's population. These nations dominate the Indosphere — a vast geographic and cultural zone stretching from Pakistan to Indonesia. Moreover, the Indosphere constitutes the western half of the Indo-Pacific region and is thus a vital theater of competition between the world's current and emerging great powers.[2]

---

[2] The Indosphere, or the historically "Indianized" civilizational sphere, includes the eight nations covered in RFI SSE-AT's regional landscape report and several countries not covered in the report, including Thailand, Cambodia, Laos, Vietnam, and Singapore.

15. "Positive Deviance" Within the Indosphere & the Muslim World 193

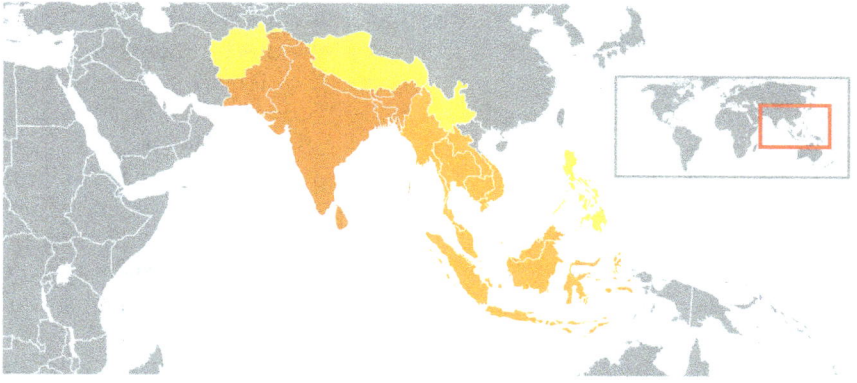

The historic Indianized cultural zone, or Indosphere
Dark orange: Indian subcontinent.
Light orange: the Indianized states of Southeast Asia.
Yellow: peripheral regions subject to considerable Indian influence.
(Indian cultural zone, Wikimedia, CC BY-SA 3.0)

RFI SSEA-AT's regional landscape analysis provides a detailed assessment of the current state and likely trajectory of religious freedom in each of the eight focus countries, evaluating numerous factors that influence the free exercise of religion, either positively or negatively. This includes not only "weaknesses" and "threats" but also "strengths" and "opportunities," as befits a standard "SWOT" analysis. Among the factors analyzed are: government laws, regulations and policies; theological frameworks and religious beliefs; levels of social tolerance among the general population; and relevant civil society groups. The report examines these factors within the context of each nation's unique history, culture, and politico-religious dynamics.

Although the landscape of each country is unique, many of these nations face similar challenges (e.g., ethnic and/or religious conflict), and certain geopolitical dynamics are impacting the entire region (e.g., China's influence operations, including the Belt and Road Initiative, and the spread of Islamist extremism). Therefore, RFI SSEA-AT's regional landscape analysis goes beyond a series of individual country-level assessments to identify the broad characteristics of the current state and trajectory of religious freedom in the region as a whole. The two-fold purpose of this regional analysis is to elucidate what trends and causes underlie these common features and to begin to plot a constructive path toward greater religious freedom for the whole region.

One relatively unusual feature of this landscape report is that it analyzes both positive and negative aspects of religious freedom conditions throughout the region, including "strengths," which are generally long-term, structural and deep-seated, as well as "opportunities" that may be leveraged therefrom. In contrast, virtually all available religious freedom reports focus exclusively on where and how religious freedom is weak rather than where and how it is strong, along with "naming and shaming" bad actors. However, we can fully understand the drivers and dynamics of religious freedom violations in a particular locale only if we carefully investigate why similar locales may have better religious freedom conditions.

Too often it is assumed that religious persecution in a particular locale will disappear if we could just eliminate certain negative dynamics or suppress a few bad actors. In many cases, however, religious persecution may be occurring in one locale not only because of the *presence of negative dynamics*. It may also be occurring because of the *absence of positive dynamics* that might be present elsewhere, and which could mitigate religious persecution more widely if only they were encouraged or activated. Yet, again, we seldom study cases of robust religious pluralism and religious freedom with the same systematic seriousness with which we study cases of religious persecution.

Despite the existence of major threats and challenges to religious freedom in Indonesia, it is nevertheless home to powerful actors that are systematically and institutionally maneuvering to strengthen the prospects for religious liberty in Indonesia, the Indosphere, and the world at large. Viewed from a regional or even global perspective, Indonesia thus embodies what scholars of child nutrition in the developing world — beginning in the 1960s and 1970s — came to describe as "positive deviance."

As the Positive Deviance Collaborative notes, "Positive Deviance is based on the observation that in every community there are certain individuals or groups whose uncommon behaviors and strategies enable them to find better solutions to problems than their peers, while having access to the same resources and facing similar or worse challenges."[3] Cases of "positive deviance" are pregnant with positive examples and lessons that

---

[3] The Positive Deviance Collaborative goes on to say, "The Positive Deviance approach is an asset-based, problem-solving, and community-driven approach that enables the community to discover these successful behaviors and strategies and develop a plan of action to promote their adoption by all concerned"; from the website of the Positive Deviance Collaborative: https://positivedeviance.org. The Fetzer Institute in Kalamazoo, Michigan has been an important supporter of the "positive deviance" approach.

we seldom scrutinize, analyze, or disseminate in a form that can be of practical benefit to the cause of promoting religious freedom.

THE MOST PROMISING INDIGENOUS ACTORS AND STRATEGIES WITHIN THE INDOSPHERE

RFI SSEA-AT's operational base within the region and its years of careful networking and engagement have enabled it to identify a number of promising local religious freedom actors and strategies. At the broadest level, these investigations have led SSEA-AT to conclude that Indonesia is the South and Southeast Asian country with the greatest "cultural and spiritual capital" conducive to religious freedom.[4] In fact, the Republic of Indonesia is built upon what Templeton Religion Trust and Dr. Christopher Seiple, founder and president *emeritus* of the Institute for Global Engagement, describe as the principles of "covenantal pluralism."[5] Indonesia's state ideology, *Pancasila*, represents a living and enduring manifestation of covenantal pluralism that is not only embedded within the Constitution of the largest Muslim-majority nation and democracy in the world, but also rooted in its centuries-old religious and civilizational traditions. Indeed, a strong case can be made that Indonesia provides the most striking example of "positive deviance" in an otherwise discouraging neighborhood.

Where all other countries among the eight that we have studied — Pakistan, India, Nepal, Bangladesh, Sri Lanka, Burma, and Malaysia — have become increasingly shaped and in many cases overrun by toxic religious nationalism and other supremacist ideologies (such as Islamism) in the last 10-20 years, Indonesia has not only preserved but successfully doubled down on its culturally and constitutionally grounded traditions of religious freedom and pluralism. Despite many severe challenges, the truth is that Indonesia celebrated its 75th anniversary of independence from Dutch colonial rule — on August 17, 2020 — with a degree of commitment to religious freedom that is undeniable and impressive.

---

[4] A. Mustafa Bisri and C. Holland Taylor, "Indonesia's 'Big Idea': Resolving the Bitter Global Debate on Islam," *Strategic Review: The Indonesian Journal of Leadership, Policy and World Affairs,* July-September 2012; available at https://www.libforall.org/lfa/media/2012/Strategic-Review_Indonesia-s_Big_Idea_Jul-Sep-12.pdf

[5] Cf. the 22nd Annual Templeton Lecture on Religion & World Affairs, delivered by Dr. Christopher Seiple on October 30, 2018; available at https://www.fpri.org/article/2018/11/the-call-of-covenantal-pluralism-defeating-religious-nationalism-with-faithful-patriotism/

Moreover, this robust and deep-seated commitment to religious pluralism is not held merely by a few Westernized elites or isolated pockets of Indonesian society. Rather, it is actively embraced by a wide range of powerful forces, which include a majority of its political, military and business leaders, with the nation's current president, Joko Widodo, among them; the country's mainstream national, cultural, and religious traditions, embodied in the five pillars, or *Pancasila,* of the Indonesian Constitution; and powerful, broad-based religious and civil society organizations such as the Muhammadiyah and the 90-million-member Nahdlatul Ulama. The NU in particular is increasingly committed not only to defending but also to expanding the strength and scope of religious freedom in Indonesia and throughout the world.

Significantly, Indonesia is the only Muslim-majority country in the modern world that has witnessed *a dramatic increase in the size and influence of its Christian population* since it became an independent nation-state. This is in sharp and dramatic contrast to the near collapse of Christian minority populations in most of the Muslim-majority countries of the Middle East, North Africa, and even South Asia, Pakistan foremost among them.[6] RFI SSEA-AT Senior Fellow Robert Hefner underscored this point in his analysis of Indonesia for the book SSEA-AT Director Timothy Shah edited with Daniel Philpott, supported by the Templeton Religion Trust, entitled, *Under Caesar's Sword: How Christians Respond to Persecution* (Cambridge University Press, 2018).

The Under Caesar's Sword (UCS) Project, a joint effort between the University of Notre Dame, the Religious Freedom Project at Georgetown, and the Religious Freedom Institute, has been roughly coterminous and closely conjoined with the RFI's TRT-funded work on South and Southeast Asia, and has significantly informed SSEA-AT's findings and proposals for further work in the region. Above all, the UCS Project highlighted that one of the most effective responses by Christian minorities to persecution world-wide is bridge-building with powerful pro-pluralism actors in the relevant majority community.[7] In particular, as Robert Hefner empha-

---

[6] The dramatic decline that Pakistan's religious minorities — including its Christian community — have experienced in their security, freedom, and numbers since independence in 1947 has been powerfully documented and explained by RFI SSEA-AT senior fellow Farahnaz Ispahani in her monograph, *Purifying the Land of the Pure: A History of Pakistan's Religious Minorities* (Oxford and New York: Oxford University Press, 2017).

[7] This finding is relevant not only to Christian minorities living under threat, but also to Western governments and NGOs seeking to mitigate and prevent religious persecution and foster religious freedom around the world. In fact, *In Response to*

sizes in his treatment of Indonesia, Christians and members of the Muslim majority community have built strong bridges of cooperation — over many decades — to create and sustain a basic cultural and political framework of religious pluralism and religious freedom. Despite significant and ongoing challenges since 1945, the result is that Indonesia's Christian minority has experienced a remarkable degree of freedom and security. According to Hefner:

> Although Christians comprise just less than 10 percent of the population, their national influence is proportionally far greater. Christians are well represented in the ranks of the middle class and university graduates; own several of the country's largest and most respected media conglomerates; figure prominently in the ranks of artists, public intellectuals, and celebrities; and occupy mid-level or senior leadership positions in most of the country's non-Muslim political parties. No less tellingly, at the time of Indonesia's declaration of independence in August 1945, Christians comprised less than 3 percent of the country's population but were well represented in the ministerial cabinets that served during Indonesia's vibrant parliamentary era (1950-7). The single most striking index of the community's relative social health, however, is that in the seven decades since Indonesian independence Christians have seen their percentage share of the national population triple in size.[8]

As one Christian leader active in Indonesian politics over the course of more than fifty years, Marsillam Simanjuntak, told Hefner in the early 2000s, "In my entire social life, I have never felt that my primary experience here in Indonesia is that of being a minority. I have always felt like an Indonesian citizen, an equal citizen."[9]

Persecution, the report summarizing the findings of the Under Caesar's Sword Project, specifically calls on governments and multilateral institutions to "[d]etermine if there are locally available social and ethical resources that can enhance local initiatives and also make international human rights norms more culturally relevant and thus effective — for instance, building bridges in Indonesia to the many Muslims who adhere to its tradition of plurality and multi-confessional citizenship" ("Recommendations for Action: External Governments and Multilateral Institutions," in Daniel Philpott, *In Response to Persecution,* Under Caesar's Sword Project, 2017, p. 51).

[8] Robert W. Hefner, "Christians and Multireligious Citizenship in Muslim Indonesia," in Daniel Philpott and Timothy Shah, eds., *Under Caesar's Sword: How Christians Respond to Persecution* (Cambridge and New York: Cambridge University Press, 2018), p. 359.

[9] Hefner, "Christians and Multireligious Citizenship," p. 389.

It is often said that religious minorities are like the proverbial canary in the coal mine — an early and sensitive indicator of the quality of the religious freedom atmosphere in a given society. "The most certain test by which we judge whether a country is really free," wrote Lord Acton, "is the amount of security enjoyed by minorities." Indonesia is far from perfect. During its transition from authoritarian rule to democracy, Christians living on several islands in eastern Indonesia were engulfed in a violent conflict with Muslim neighbors that claimed approximately 10,000 lives and rendered over 500,000 people homeless.[10] Groups considered heretical from the standpoint of mainstream Islamic orthodoxy, such as the Ahmadiyya, are still subject to periodic abuse. Government regulations complicate and sometimes impede the construction of churches in various parts of Indonesia. Overall, however, Indonesia stands out for maintaining a distinctive socio-cultural and religious ecology vis-à-vis its minority communities, based upon the principle of *bhinneka tunggal ika*, or unity amid diversity.

Indonesia's pluralistic social ecology is especially striking when one considers the increasingly pervasive rhetorical and physical assaults targeting religious minorities in nearly every major country in South and Southeast Asia, often with the complicity or even overt support of the highest government officials. In sharp contrast to what has unquestionably become a more toxic atmosphere for religious minorities in Pakistan, India, Sri Lanka, Bangladesh and Burma, where levels of toxicity continue to rise, the atmosphere in Indonesia remains relatively clear and healthy, enabling Christians and most other religious minorities not only to survive but to flourish.

Though many factors are at work, one crucial reason that Indonesia is a relative bright spot within the religious freedom landscape of South and Southeast Asia and the Muslim world is a single civil society organization: the Nahdlatul Ulama. Now the largest mass Islamic organization in the world, the NU was founded nearly a century ago, in 1926, almost simultaneously with the Muslim Brotherhood, founded in 1925 in Egypt. However, while the Muslim Brotherhood and its numerous ideological offspring — such as Hizb ut-Tahrir, Hamas, al-Qaeda and ISIS — have consistently pursued militant, integralist, and anti-pluralist agendas, with fateful consequences for Egypt and the world, the NU has become an increasingly robust and creative defender and advocate of a distinctively Indonesian vision of religious pluralism and tolerance. This vision

---

[10] Cf. Kyai Haji Abdurrahman Wahid and C. Holland Taylor, "In Indonesia, Songs against Terrorism," *Washington Post*, October 7, 2005.

15. "Positive Deviance" Within the Indosphere & the Muslim World

is rooted in the country's own unique religious tradition — that of *Islam Nusantara* (East Indies Islam).

With some 90 million followers, the NU is without parallel within the Indosphere and the Muslim world. Nahdlatul Ulama illustrates the power and significance of the proposition that underlies the RFI's Freedom of Religious Institutions in Society (FORIS) Project: the more religious institutions are free from arbitrary state interference and repression, the more they are free to innovate, to develop according to their own spiritual logic, and ultimately to serve society. Ever since its founding, the NU has been independent, self-organizing and free of government control. It has participated in every major phase of Indonesia's modern history and consistently determined outcomes, including the establishment of Indonesia as a multi-religious and pluralistic (*Pancasila*) nation-state; the defeat of Dutch colonialism (1945 – 1949); defeat of a communist rebellion in 1948; the defeat of Islamist insurgencies, including Darul Islam (1949 – 1962) and the CIA-backed PRRI-Permesta rebellion (1958 – 1961); the tragedy that followed in the wake of an abortive Communist uprising in 1965, which led to the mass slaughter of suspected Communists (in which many NU leaders and members participated); and Indonesia's successful transition to democracy in the late '90s. Nahdlatul Ulama's institutional independence and deeply rooted theological commitment to serving the common good — as opposed to a narrow political program — have enabled it to develop and mature into a remarkably powerful and effective organization in defending Indonesia's traditions of religious pluralism and tolerance.

The NU's youth wing, Gerakan Pemuda Ansor, is the world's largest Muslim young adults movement. All five million of its members also belong to *Barisan Ansor Serbaguna Nahdlatul Ulama*, or Banser — an active militia force. GP Ansor constitutes the front line and primary kinetic element within Nahdlatul Ulama and the primary vehicle for the grassroots mobilization of NU followers. GP Ansor's principal mission includes the defense of NKRI (the Indonesian nation state); the 1945 Constitution, which established Indonesia as a multi-religious and pluralistic nation; *Pancasila*; *Bhinneka Tunggal Ika* ("Oneness Amid Diversity"); and the profoundly spiritual — i.e., *humanitarian* — values of Sunni Islam, which flourished in harmony with pre-existing East Indies civilization and cultures to produce *Islam Nusantara*.

The heart of NU's strategy — articulated in a number of documents drafted by its spiritual leaders over a period of nearly a century[11] — is to

---

[11] For example, see Kyai Haji Abdurrahman Wahid, ed., *Ilusi Negara Islam (The Illusion of an Islamic State)* Jakarta, Indonesia: LibForAll Foundation, Wahid Institute and

restore *rahmah* (universal love and compassion) to its rightful place as the primary message of Islam, in order to eliminate the widespread practice of using religion to incite hatred and violence towards others. To quote Christopher Seiple, the NU seeks to mobilize "the best of faith" to defeat "the worst of religion."[12] As a central component of this strategy, NU spiritual leaders are developing "an Islamic jurisprudence for a global civilization, whose constituent elements retain their distinctive characteristics (*fiqh al-ḥaḍārah al-'ālamīyah al-mutaṣahirah*)." As stated in the *Nusantara Manifesto*, these NU leaders — most notably, Bayt ar-Rahmah co-founders Kyai Haji A. Mustofa Bisri and KH. Yahya Cholil Staquf — seek to "address the need for social harmony at a global level and in each of the world's regions where Muslims actually live and work, through a process of recontextualizing and 'indigenizing' Islam, as historically occurred in *Nusantara* (the Malay Archipelago)."

In a region where much wrong is being perpetrated by many governments and non-state actors, Indonesia is doing something right. Now is a good time for the rest of us to take note and learn all that we can from Indonesia's remarkable and multi-faceted example of "positive deviance."

Maarif Institute, 2009/2011) and Kyai Haji Yahya Cholil Staquf, et al, *Hasil-Hasil Musyawarah Nasional Alim Ulama Nahdlatul Ulama 2019* (*Findings of the 2019 National Conference of Nahdlatul Ulama Religious Scholars*), Jakarta: Nahdlatul Ulama Central Board, 2019.

[12] Christopher Seiple, "Can the best of faith defeat the worst of religion?" *World Economic Forum*, September 13, 2013, https://www.weforum.org/agenda/2013/09/can-the-best-of-faith-defeat-the-worst-of-religion/

16

The Universal Values of Indonesian Islamic Civilization

KH. A. Mustofa Bisri

SUMMARY

In this essay — originally published in the January–March 2017 issue of *Strategic Review* — Nahdlatul Ulama spiritual leader and co-founder of the global Humanitarian Islam movement, Kyai Haji A. Mustofa Bisri, analyzes the threat to international peace and security posed by a de-facto Islamist insurrection against the current rules-based international order. He contrasts the supremacist, politicized understanding of religion that underlies and animates this global insurrection with the spiritual, pluralistic, and tolerant Islam that developed in the Malay Archipelago — *"Islam Nusantara."*

According to the author, the universal values that lie at the heart of *Islam Nusantara* — also known as Humanitarian Islam — are capable of discrediting and ultimately defeating Islamist radicalism. In this article, KH. A. Mustofa Bisri outlines a detailed, systematic, and institutional strategy for accomplishing this objective and invites people of goodwill of every faith and nation to join a global movement to defeat religious extremism and "restore the majesty of Islamic teachings as a source of universal love and compassion (*rahmatan lil 'alamin*)."

Let us begin by regarding the roots of global extremism and Islamophobia. Centuries of conflict have left deep scars upon the collective psyche of Muslims and non-Muslims alike, in many parts of the world. The spread of Islamist extremism and terror in recent decades has revived, and exacerbated, this ancient trauma. And although this long history of conflict is inextricably tied to military and political rivalries — rather than the substantive (i.e., spiritual) teachings of religion — the fact remains that Muslims and non-Muslims alike have been deeply enmeshed in nearly 14 centuries of armed conflict.

This, in turn, has led to a biased perception, characterized by widespread stereotyping, unfounded generalizations and prejudice, among Muslims regarding non-Muslims and vice versa. As a result, conflicts that have nothing to do with the substantive teachings of religion are often attributed to religion itself.

The spread of a shallow understanding of Islam renders this situation critical, as highly vocal elements within the Muslim population at large (i.e., extremist groups) justify their harsh and often savage behavior by claiming to act in accord with God's commands, although they are grievously mistaken.

According to the Sunni view of Islam, every aspect and expression of religion should be imbued with *rahmah* (love and compassion) and foster the perfection of human nature, as expressed through sublime moral character (*akhlaqul karima*). This may be achieved — in fact, may only be achieved — if one's understanding and practice of the exoteric norms of religion such as ritual prayer, fasting and so forth are augmented by a full grasp of its inner, spiritual dimension.

When Muslim extremists act in ways that contradict the substantive teachings of religion, while loudly claiming to represent the true teachings of Islam, it is only natural that many non-Muslims will take these extremists at their word and develop (or, in light of history, "rediscover") an aversion toward Islam itself.

Certain steps are essential to address the complex and deep-rooted problems of Islamist extremism and Islamophobia:

- Recognize that efforts to defeat religious extremism are inseparable from, and integral to, efforts to create a just and peaceful world order.
- Marginalize and discredit Islamist ideology, which arises from a superficial understanding of religion and simultaneously seeks to render Muslims' understanding of Islam more shallow. This shall be done by disseminating the teachings of *ulama* (religious scholars) who grasp the profound essence of religion and its fundamental message of *rahmah* (universal love and compassion) in other words, *ahlus sunnah wal jama'ah ulama* (traditional/spiritual Sunni religious scholars).

- Consolidate and mobilize spiritual *ahlus sunnah wal jama'ah ulama* throughout the world to guide Muslims to an understanding of Islam that is deeply imbued with universal love and compassion, so that this view becomes a powerful societal consensus among Muslims worldwide and a force for good in the world.
- Establish close cooperation between moderate Muslim groups and non-Muslims who hold an objective view of the issues at stake, to stem a rising tide of Islamist extremism and a corollary backlash against Muslims living in the West.

ISLAM NUSANTARA (INDONESIAN ISLAM)
AS A "CAPITAL ASSET"

For more than six centuries, Islam Nusantara has been carefully nurtured by extensive networks of Sunni *ulama*, who combined spiritual wisdom with detailed knowledge of Islamic law and extensive engagement with the daily lives of local inhabitants in their respective environments. As a result, the Muslim populations that emerged in the East Indies archipelago traditionally maintained a close relationship with Sunni *ulama* and their lives generally reflected the compassion-centered teachings of Islam.

As a civilization, Nusantara (the East Indies Archipelago) embraced and came to represent what experts have termed "the smiling face of Islam" — conspicuous for its tolerance and emphasis on social harmony. This occurred because Sunni *ulama* provided religious guidance that emphasized a contextual and profoundly spiritual view of religion, while prioritizing coexistence with others who worship differently and unity of the nation as a whole.

Indeed, Indonesia's Nahdlatul Ulama, the world's largest Islamic organization, played a vital role in securing independence and establishing the Unified State of the Republic of Indonesia upon the harmonious foundation of *Pancasila* (i.e., as a multireligious rather than purely "Islamic" state), the Basic Constitution of 1945 and the national motto *"Bhinneka Tunggal Ika"* (Unity in Diversity). These founding principles of the Indonesian nation-state reflect the Sunni Muslim view of Islam, whose core message is *rahmah* and whose sole purpose is to serve as an unconditional blessing for all creation, by enabling human beings to rise to the state of *khalifatullah fil ardh* (God's vicegerent on earth, i.e., sainthood).

Nahdlatul Ulama (NU) was established in 1926 following the Wahhabi conquest of Mecca and Medina, to preserve and strengthen the solidarity of Sunni *ulama* networks throughout the Indonesian archipelago and support their traditional role of guiding the larger community of Muslims. Because of NU, "Islam Nusantara," which we may define as the localized expression of Islam as a source of universal love and compassion, through the development of noble character, has remained vibrant among the predominantly Muslim population of Indonesia. Islam Nusantara represents a form of "spiritual capital" that may contribute significantly to the cause of international peace and security.

Key elements of Islam Nusantara include:

- An epistemological community: a large group of *ulama* (religious scholars) engaged in the continuous development of Islam Nusantara as a system of profound values, practically applied in order to address actual problems as they emerge from time to time and age to age.
- An effective social leadership structure, with *ulama* in the foremost position.
- A mass following — more than 40 percent of Indonesia's population, according to exit polls from Indonesia's 2014 national elections — with a high degree of cohesiveness that gives rise to, and expresses, the values of Islam Nusantara in daily life.

THE INDONESIAN GOVERNMENT'S ROLE

In June 2015, nearly 40,000 Nahdlatul Ulama followers gathered at Masjid Istiqlal, Indonesia's national mosque, in Jakarta, to attend an *Istighosah* ceremony heralding the arrival of Ramadan, the Islamic fasting month. Titled "Nurturing Spiritual Traditions; Safeguarding National Unity," the ceremony was designed to launch a two-day national conference of NU religious scholars (*ulama*), who gathered to make final preparations for the quinquennial NU Congress to be held in Jombang, East Java, in early August of that year.

Indonesian President Joko Widodo delivered the keynote address at the ceremony, which was also attended by Said Aqil Siradj, chairman of the NU Executive Board; Lukman Hakim Saifuddin, a prominent NU theologian and Indonesian minister of religion; Nusron Wahid, chairman of Ansor, the NU's young adults organization; Ibu Sinta Nuriyah Wahid, the widow of former Indonesian president and NU chairman Abdurrahman Wahid; and Yahya Cholil Staquf, secretary for political and international affairs to the NU Supreme Council.

16. The Universal Values of Indonesian Islamic Civilization

"The NU has the primary responsibility for preserving and promoting Islam Nusantara," said Siradj during his introductory address. "Islam Nusantara was proselytized [by Muslim saints] who embraced local culture, strengthened and preserved local culture, respected local culture. They did not seek to destroy local culture [unlike Muslim extremists]," he later told BBC Indonesia in an interview.

In his keynote address, President Joko proclaimed: "I am profoundly concerned by the political upheavals and bloodshed in the Muslim Middle East. Syria and Iraq are being wrenched apart by devastating convulsions. Praise be to God, our Islam is Islam Nusantara. Islam that is gentle and polite. Islam that is civilized. That is Islam Nusantara — Islam full of tolerance." His remarks, reported by hundreds of media outlets, quickly went viral, garnering massive public attention via print, broadcast and Internet social media.

Additional media reports soon emerged, stating that Islam Nusantara is "being unofficially supported by the government" (*Tempo* magazine, July 9, 2015). During a state visit to Britain in April of 2016, President Joko addressed the British Parliament, where he affirmed Indonesia's commitment to become a nation that upholds the values of universal humanity, pluralism and tolerance, and expressed pride in the fact that Islam in Indonesia has played a vital role in consolidating democracy, promoting moderation and opposing religious extremism and terror.

President Joko emphasized the role of soft power, including religious and cultural approaches, to counter Islamist extremism, and voiced his belief that Indonesia is destined to become a blessing (*rahmah*) for the entire world, by promoting peace and cooperation among civilizations.

THE ROLE OF NAHDLATUL ULAMA

Regardless of what policy the Indonesian government adopts, and what measures it may pursue in regard to the international crisis facing Islam, Nahdlatul Ulama is moving to address this crisis and will continue to do so by nurturing and widely propagating the values of Sunni Islam. For example, Nahdlatul Ulama is taking concrete steps to consolidate Sunni *ulama* throughout the world and to establish collaborative relationships with like-minded individuals, organizations and governments worldwide.

In Afghanistan, after a long and extremely difficult process, the NU succeeded in facilitating the establishment of a diverse, multiethnic group of Afghan Sunni *ulama* who subsequently chose to adopt the name "Nahdlatul Ulama Afghanistan." These Afghan religious scholars agreed to embrace and adhere to the principles of *tawaasuth* (moderation), *tasaamuh* (tolerance), *tawaazun* (balance/ objectivity), *i'tidaal* (justice) and *musyaarakah* (social solidarity), exactly as these principles are understood and practiced by Nahdlatul Ulama.

In Europe, Nahdlatul Ulama has launched a pioneering initiative with the University of Vienna, under the leadership of Rüdiger Lohlker, the noted expert and professor, to establish the Vienna Observatory for Applied Research on Terrorism and Extremism — known as Vortex — and thereby develop concrete strategies to address the threat posed by Islamist ideology and movements.

In Indonesia, the world's largest Muslim youth organization, GP Ansor (established 1934), opened its 15th National Congress on the morning of Nov. 26, 2015, with the screening of the film "The Divine Grace of East Indies Islam," which *The New York Times* hailed as "a relentless religious repudiation of the Islamic State and the opening salvo in a global campaign by the world's largest Muslim group to challenge the ideology of the Islamic State head-on."

The leadership of Ansor is closely aligned with the spiritual wing of its parent organization, Nahdlatul Ulama. Yaqut Cholil Qoumas was elected chairman of GP Ansor for the 2015-20 term. In his acceptance address, he said: "Islam Nusantara is at the very heart of our understanding of Islam, and our NU identity, as traditional Sunni Muslims. I believe you gentlemen are capable of safeguarding the universal love and compassion, and East Indies culture that lies at the heart of our Islam."

To prolonged applause from thousands of Ansor delegates, Syafii Maarif, former chairman of the central board of Muhammadiyah, Indonesia's second-largest Islamic organization, declared: "Frankly, I am full of doubt concerning the development of Islam in Arab nations. With their countries being destroyed like this, they need to learn from Indonesia."

Yahya Cholil Staquf conveyed the essence of the NU's worldview, and its relationship with those of other faiths and cultures, when he described Islam Nusantara as "Islam that does not arrive seeking to conquer anyone. Islam that does not come to destroy like those [extremists] do. But rather, Islam that contributes to developing a better civilization for *all* humanity, for as our Prophet — may the peace and blessings of God be upon him — said: 'I was sent for no purpose other than to perfect noble character and morality.' This is jihad to *build*, not destroy, civilization."

In May 2016, the NU hosted the International Summit of Moderate Islamic Leaders (ISOMIL) in Jakarta. Attended by approximately 400 traditional religious scholars from 30 nations, the event featured expert presentations and detailed discussion of the relationship between Islam and nationalism; the unchecked spread of religious extremism, terror, armed conflict in the Middle East and a rising tide of Islamophobia in the West; the role of certain Middle East governments in fostering the spread of sectarian hatred; and the need for an honest appraisal of, and response to, Islamist extremism and terror.

At the summit's conclusion, the Nahdlatul Ulama's Central Board promulgated a 16-point declaration that affirmed the mainstream nature of the NU's understanding and practice of traditional Sunni Islam; identified the salient factors driving Islamist extremism and terror worldwide; and committed the NU to develop a global alliance capable of addressing the twin threats of Sunni and Shiite extremism.

Widely covered by international media, the summit and NU declaration explicitly identified "specific modes of interpreting Islam as the most significant factor causing the spread of religious extremism among Muslims" (point 8); cast a spotlight on Saudi Arabia, Qatar and Iran for their role in having "weaponize[d] sectarian differences ... nurtured religious extremism, and stimulated the spread of terrorism throughout the world" (point 9); identified religious extremism and terror, among Muslims, as "directly contributing to the rise of Islamophobia throughout the non-Muslim world" (point 10); called upon "people of good will of every faith and nation to join in building a global consensus not to politicize Islam" (point 15); and explicitly affirmed that the NU "will strive to consolidate the global *ahlussunnah wal jamaah* (Sunni Muslim) community, in order to bring about a world in which Islam, and Muslims, are truly beneficent and contribute to the well-being of all humanity" (point 16).

Two days after the adoption of the ISOMIL Nahdlatul Ulama Declaration, Muslim, Christian, Hindu, Buddhist and Jewish leaders gathered in Jakarta to attend a Global Unity Forum co-sponsored by the NU's young adults organization, Ansor, and Bayt ar-Rahmah. This daylong event featured expert presentations and detailed discussion of the historic relationship between Muslims, classical Islamic law and those who adhere to other faiths.

As Yahya Cholil Staquf explained in his opening address, the Global Unity Forum was held as a direct follow-up to the International Summit of Moderate Islamic Leaders. "In its [ISOMIL] declaration, the NU firmly and honestly identified the salient factors most responsible for the emergence of this global crisis — i.e., factors rooted within specific elements of Islam itself... [the] forum convened today... represents a decisive 'first step' that demonstrates the NU is moving forward to implement its strategy. We shall not stop halfway nor abandon this path before we have reached our goal. We shall not return home [from the field of battle] until victory is in our hands."

At the forum's conclusion, Ansor issued a three-page declaration that included a call for religious scholars "to carefully examine and address those elements of *fiqh* [classical Islamic law] that encourage segregation, discrimination and/or violence toward those perceived to be 'non-Muslim.'"

International Response

While some Western journalists initially viewed Islam Nusantara as a clever marketing slogan, the term actually refers to a deep-rooted sociocultural and religious (i.e., phenomenological) reality that reflects the spiritual worldview embraced by the majority of Indonesian Muslims. As stated in the ISOMIL NU Declaration, "Nahdlatul Ulama offers the insights and experience of Islam Nusantara [East Indies Islam] to the world, as a salutary paradigm of Islam in which religion contributes to civilization, by respecting preexisting cultures and prioritizing social harmony and peace" (point 1).

The declaration continues: "Within the worldview of Islam Nusantara, Islam does not enjoin its adherents to conquer the world, but rather, to engage in the continuous development of *akhlaqul karimah*, or noble character and virtue, for it is only through *akhlaqul karimah* that Islam can manifest as Divine Grace for all creation" (point 5).

With this in mind, it is easy to understand the appeal of Islam Nusantara in a world increasingly gripped by savage conflict and atrocities perpetrated in the name of religion. Hence, the widespread favorable coverage of Islam Nusantara that has appeared not only in Western media, but also in the Arab Middle East.

As the Norwegian media outlet *Nettavisen* reported in April 2016: "While Islamic State has its base in the Middle East, the NU dominates the other side of the globe [i.e., the Malay Archipelago]." In fact, the NU enjoys great influence even beyond Indonesia's borders, says counterterrorism expert Magnus Ranstorp, director of Research at the Center for Asymmetric Threat Studies at Sweden's National Defense College, as reported by *Nettavisen*. "This organization projects strategic influence far beyond Indonesia, by demonstrating resistance to the Islamic State as an ideology, and by visibly opposing extremist forces. They are highly resolute in their approach [to this global threat]."

In a CNN report on the ISOMIL conference, filed by senior correspondent Ivan Watson, Ranstorp declared: "I don't see any other Muslim leaders coming to Europe, standing up like a tower and saying, 'Look, we are prepared to take this on.'" Ranstorp said Indonesian Muslim leaders are breaking new ground by proposing to make changes to Islamic law to better fit the modern era.

In an article titled "Political Horizons for Indonesian Islam," Muhammad Abul Fadel, deputy editor of *al-Ahram*, one of the oldest and most influential newspapers in the Arab world, described how "various entities, capable of exercising broad geopolitical influence, have begun to search for a genuinely tolerant face of Islam that may serve as a shield against extremist currents, after the failure of the Muslim Brotherhood [and its long-term influence operation in the West]."

As Abul explains:

> It is obvious that many Western leaders and communities are experiencing a problem with Muslims — not with Islam — due to jihadist violence and the subversive political agenda of Muslim interlocutors who were long perceived as "moderates." These pseudo-moderates sought to undermine Western culture, which has developed through the accumulation of historical experience over a period of many centuries. They have done so by seeking to impose a new lifestyle upon their European hosts, subverting and supplanting the West's hard-won values, such as individual freedom, tolerance, equality and justice, with their own lifestyle and values that [are based upon a narrow interpretation of Islamic law.]
>
> The spiritual essence of Islam does not reject the prevailing modes of government and social organization embraced by many Western countries, particularly those that promote the values of freedom, equality and justice. However, Muslims who claim to implement the "pure" teachings of Islam through widely publicized acts of violence have provoked panic and revulsion toward Islam among the general population of the West. Fortunately, certain members of the Western elite who recognize the spiritual essence of religion believe that Islam is more open and tolerant than commonly perceived.
>
> It's very difficult to exclude Islam from Western society, given that millions of European and North American citizens now adhere to this religion. Hence, the search has begun for a Muslim group whose understanding and practice of Islam constitutes a model of civilized behavior that does not contradict the fundamental values of Europe and the United States. The great Indonesian Islamic organization, Nahdlatul Ulama, which is also the world's largest, with 70 million followers, has begun to expand its operations internationally to fill this gap. The NU represents the most tolerant face of Islam, which is compatible with Western societies' values and traditions, and shows no sign of wishing to engage in conflict with the West.
>
> The Nahdlatul Ulama holds a view of Islam that its members describe as Islam Nusantara — East Indies Islam, or Indonesian Islam — which emphasizes the adaptation of religion to local culture, and firmly rejects the

ideology of extremist movements that have produced such a negative image of Islam in the West. This tolerant face of Islam, in Indonesia, accepts all the different religions and cultures that exist in the Malay Archipelago, and regards them as having a natural right to live side by side with Islam.

Given the facts described above, the profoundly spiritual and tolerant worldview embodied in the term Islam Nusantara has begun to expand beyond its local framework to a global environment. Many lines of communication have been initiated between the Nahdlatul Ulama and various Western governments. Spiritual leaders within the NU have begun to establish working relationships and operational nodes in many countries, operating under the organizational name, Bayt ar-Rahmah [Home of Divine Grace]. Each operational node propagates the model of tolerance embraced by the Nahdlatul Ulama, such as peaceful coexistence with others and respect for individuals' right to privacy, including freedom of thought and conscience. And each seeks to accomplish this by leveraging the profound humane and spiritual values that underlie and animate all religions.

These examples are merely the tip of the iceberg regarding what Nahdlatul Ulama has undertaken to date, and what must be accomplished if we hope to "defeat religious extremism and restore the majesty of Islamic teachings as a source of universal love and compassion (*rahmatan lil 'alamin*), which represents a vital key to building a just, prosperous and peaceful world." Whose words were these? Those of Abdurrahman Wahid, the late Indonesian president and revered Islamic cleric.

We invite others to join us in this effort, which we hold to be in service to God and humanity. I end by saying: "*WaLlahu A'lam,*" — or "God alone knows the truth of all things."

Invitation

KH. Yahya Cholil Staquf and Rev. Dr. Frank Hinkelmann

*Leaders
of the World Evangelical Alliance
and the Humanitarian Islam Movement
cordially invite you
to join in building a global alliance
founded upon shared civilizational values.*

*This alliance seeks to prevent the political
weaponization of identity;
curtail the spread of communal hatred;
promote solidarity and respect among the diverse
people, cultures and nations of the world;
and foster the emergence of a
truly just and harmonious world order,
founded upon respect for the equal rights
and dignity of every human being.*

APPENDIX

Biographies

Honoree

Bishop Thomas Schirrmacher
Secretary General & CEO of the World Evangelical Alliance

Descended from Huguenots who fled religious persecution in France, and raised in a family with a strong commitment to global Christian witness and mission, Bishop Thomas Schirrmacher has spent much of his life defending oppressed Christians around the world.

Bishop Schirrmacher's dedicated service to the persecuted global church both shaped his spirituality and brought him into contact with the World Evangelical Alliance (WEA). A prodigious author, Bishop Schirrmacher has written and edited 102 books, which have been translated into 18 languages.

Prior to his inauguration as WEA's Secretary General & CEO, Bishop Schirrmacher chaired the WEA's Theological Commission. He was deeply involved in producing *Christian Witness in a Multi-Religious World: Recommendations for Conduct*, a major statement jointly published by the World Council of Churches, the World Evangelical Alliance, and the Vatican's Pontifical Council for Interreligious Dialogue, which together represent more than 90 percent of global Christianity.

On April 22, 2020 — in his capacity at that time as WEA Associate Secretary General for Theological Concerns and Religious Freedom — Bishop Schirrmacher co-founded the Humanitarian Islam/World Evangelical Alliance Joint Working Group with spiritual leaders of Indonesia's Nahdlatul Ulama, the world's largest Muslim organization.

To mark the occasion, the editors of this volume issued a joint statement that included the following lines:

> Though we may always understand God and relate to God in very different ways, Humanitarian Muslims and Evangelical Christians agree that human life, family, faith, reason and property are fundamental human goods essential to comprehensive well-being in this world. We know these human goods are vulnerable and require protection from various threats, including both religious extremism and forms of secular extremism that seek to marginalize or even eradicate the presence of religion in social and public life. We therefore pledge to work together to strengthen and advance those social and legal norms, including basic human rights and liberties, that are essen-

tial to safeguard these fundamental human goods. We also believe in the existence of universal ethical standards, which will inform and inspire our collaboration in the realms of theology, politics, conflict resolution and education, and in the pursuit of shared humanitarian goals.

Inspired by Professor Thomas Schirrmacher, this *Festschrift* is testament to his extraordinary vision of a world in which Muslim and Christian believers reach across racial, religious, cultural, and political lines to strive for the equal rights and dignity of every human being.

Epigraph

KH. A. Mustofa Bisri

Former Chairman of the Nahdlatul Ulama Supreme Council, KH. A. Mustofa Bisri ("Gus Mus") is often called *Sang Kyai Pembelajar* — the Great Religious Scholar Devoted to Learning — by members of the world's largest Muslim organization. He is the co-founder and Chairman of Bayt ar-Rahmah; co-founder and Chairman of the Center for Shared Civilizational Values; and co-founder of the Humanitarian Islam movement, as well as its spiritual leader.

Widely revered as a religious scholar, poet, novelist, painter, and Muslim intellectual, Gus Mus has strongly influenced not only the 90-million-member NU but also the social, cultural and political development of Indonesia over the past fifty years — facilitating its transition from decades of authoritarian rule to an open, vibrant, and successful democracy.

A graduate of al-Azhar University in Cairo, which regards him as a highly distinguished alumnus, Mustofa Bisri's personal philosophy can be seen in the "Mata Air" ("Living Spring") interfaith community that he founded, whose membership is open to all who share its essential values: "Worship God; respect elders; treat those who are younger with loving kindness; open your heart to all humanity."

Numerous books and doctoral dissertations have been written exclusively about Mustofa Bisri, in addition to thousands of articles that reference his achievements in fields ranging from Islamic spirituality, theology, literature and the arts to education, the social sciences, and politics.

Editors

Thomas K. Johnson

Professor Reverend Thomas K. Johnson is a widely respected advocate of global religious freedom, with decades of experience working closely with major Christian and Muslim organizations. Following the collapse of the Soviet Union, Dr. Johnson and his family moved from the United States to Europe and lived there for 25 years — first in Minsk and later in Prague.

While teaching at Charles University in Prague, Dr. Johnson co-founded the Comenius Institute. Known as "the father of modern education" and "the teacher of nations," Jan Amos Comenius (1592 – 1670) was a philosopher, theologian, and bishop in the Moravian Church (*Unitas Fratrum*, or Unity of the Brethren), one of the oldest Protestant denominations in the world. Dr. Johnson established the Comenius Institute in order to "foster scholars who are convinced of the truth and importance of the biblical message, who attempt to live honestly before God, who are theologically balanced and well-developed, who can appropriate the best of historic Christian thought to carefully evaluate modern and postmodern trends, and who are active in church, society and education for the glory of God."

Throughout his years in Central and Eastern Europe, Dr. Johnson was deeply involved in teaching, studying, and promoting human rights, both in his university classes and with colleagues across the continent. After diving more deeply into the biblical and philosophical underpinnings of ethics and human rights, Dr. Johnson was appointed Senior Advisor to the World Evangelical Alliance's Theological Commission in 2012.

Dr. Johnson has served as the WEA's Special Envoy to the Vatican since 2016. In 2019, he initiated WEA's relationship with Nahdlatul Ulama spiritual leaders and in 2020 was appointed WEA's Special Envoy for Engaging Humanitarian Islam. Shortly thereafter, he and Bishop Schirrmacher joined NU leaders in establishing the Humanitarian Islam/World Evangelical Alliance Joint Working Group, which he co-chairs. In March of 2021, the WEA Theological Commission and Martin Bucer Seminary published the most recent of Dr. Johnson's many books, *Humanitarian Islam, Evangelical Christianity, and the Clash of Civilizations: A New Partnership for Peace and Religious Freedom*.

In the words of Paul Marshall, Wilson Distinguished Professor of Religious Freedom at Baylor University and senior fellow at the Religious Freedom Institute and Hudson Institute:

Indonesia has the largest Muslim population in the world, yet the country and its forms of Islam, especially Humanitarian Islam, are too little known. This is especially tragic since this may be the most important movement in the Islamic world, and it is engaged in active alliance with Christians and others. Here, Thomas K. Johnson gives us a clear, cogent, and crisp overview of its meaning and importance.

C. Holland Taylor

C. Holland Taylor is Chairman & CEO of LibForAll Foundation; Deputy Chairman & COO of its sister organization, *Bayt ar-Rahmah* (Home of Divine Grace); and Deputy Chairman & CEO of the Center for Shared Civilizational Values (CSCV). He also serves as Emissary to the United Nations, Americas, and Europe for Gerakan Pemuda Ansor, the five-million-member young adults movement of Nahdlatul Ulama, which itself has over 90 million followers and 21,000 *madrasahs*.

Mr. Taylor co-founded LibForAll (2003), Bayt ar-Rahmah (2014), the Humanitarian Islam movement (2017) and the Center for Shared Civilizational Values (2021) with spiritual leaders of Nahdlatul Ulama, including his close friend H.E. Kyai Haji Abdurrahman Wahid (1940 – 2009); KH. A. Mustofa Bisri, former Chairman of the NU Supreme Council; and KH. Yahya Cholil Staquf, the NU's current General Secretary.

These closely affiliated organizations derive their inspiration from the heroic example of President Wahid's 16th-century Javanese ancestors, whose deft use of soft and hard power defeated Muslim extremists and guaranteed freedom of religion for all Javanese, two centuries before the Virginia Statute of Religious Freedom and the U.S. Constitution's Bill of Rights.

In March of 2017, Gerakan Pemuda Ansor and Bayt ar-Rahmah launched the global Humanitarian Islam movement, which seeks to reform obsolete tenets of Islamic orthodoxy that enjoin religious hatred, supremacy and violence, by restoring *rahmah* (universal love and compassion) to its rightful place as the primary message of Islam.

Acting in his capacity as the COO of Bayt ar-Rahmah and GP Ansor's Special Emissary, Mr. Taylor has co-authored a number of historic documents with Nahdlatul Ulama General Secretary Kyai Haji Yahya Cholil Staquf, including the *International Summit of Moderate Islamic Leaders (ISOMIL) Nahdlatul Ulama Declaration* (2016); the *First Global Unity Forum Declaration* (2016); the *Gerakan Pemuda Ansor Declaration on Humanitarian Islam* (2017); the *Nusantara Statement* and *Nusantara Manifesto* (2018); and four resolutions unanimously adopted by Centrist Democrat International (2019 and 2020).

Mr. Taylor's unique combination of experience in the fields of international business, strategy, and the forging of cross-cultural relationships has enabled LibForAll to become "a model of what a competent public diplomacy effort in the Muslim world should look like" (*Wall Street Journal*). This work follows a career as a successful entrepreneur and global telecom executive, during which Mr. Taylor was credited by numerous leading publications as one of the essential catalysts in the deregulation of the global telecommunications industry.

In 2020, Mr. Taylor established the Humanitarian Islam/World Evangelical Alliance Joint Working Group with KH. Yahya Cholil Staquf and senior WEA leaders, including the co-editor of this volume, Dr. Thomas K. Johnson, and its Honoree, Bishop Thomas Schirrmacher.

Educated at the University of North Carolina — Chapel Hill and Princeton University, Mr. Taylor is fluent in English, Indonesian/Malay, and German.

Chapter Authors

Part I

H.E. KH. Abdurrahman Wahid

In a 2007 *Wall Street Journal* article titled "The Last King of Java," Pulitzer Prize-winning American journalist Bret Stephens described Abdurrahman Wahid as "the single most influential religious leader in the Muslim world" and "easily the most important ally the West has in the ideological struggle against Islamic radicalism."

Popularly known as "Gus Dur," Abdurrahman Wahid (1940 – 2009) was and remains one of the most influential religious and political figures in modern Indonesian history. Widely regarded as a saint among the 90-million-strong following of Nahdlatul Ulama, Gus Dur laid the theological foundations for the global Humanitarian Islam movement while serving as General Chairman of the Nahdlatul Ulama Executive Board (1984 – 1999).

During his brief term as Indonesia's fourth president (1999 – 2001), Abdurrahman Wahid restored civilian control of the military; eliminated the army's role in politics after 32 years of dictatorship; implemented regional autonomy and the establishment of Indonesia's anti-corruption agency; restored civil and political liberties to Indonesia's ethnic Chinese population; and preserved the political foundation of Indonesia as a multi-religious and pluralistic nation state in the face of serious challenges posed by Muslim extremists and their opportunistic political allies.

President Wahid's grave in Jombang, East Java, is visited by millions of pilgrims annually and is inscribed with the epitaph "Here Rests a Humanist" in Indonesian, Arabic, English, and Chinese.

Part II

KH. Hasyim Asy'ari

KH. Hasyim Asy'ari (1871 – 1947) was the founding Chairman of the Nahdlatul Ulama Supreme Council (1926 – 1947) and grandfather of Indonesia's fourth president, H.E. Kyai Haji Abdurrahman Wahid. In 1892 Kyai Hasyim traveled from Java to Mecca, where he studied with many of the leading Sunni Muslim *ulama* of that era and became renowned for his mastery of Islamic law, or *fiqh*, with a particular expertise in the Shafi'i school of Islamic jurisprudence and hadith scholarship. Upon his return from Mecca in 1899, Kyai Hasyim founded Pesantren Tebu Ireng in Jombang, East Java, which soon grew to become one of the largest and most influential Islamic boarding schools (*madrasahs*) in Muslim Southeast Asia.

In 1926, Kyai Hasyim Asy'ari joined with preeminent Islamic scholars from across the Dutch East Indies to establish Nahdlatul Ulama, or "Awakening of the Scholars." They were acting in direct response to the recent conquest of Mecca and Medina by Abdulaziz ibn Saud and his Wahhabi army, which massacred traditional Sunni Muslims and spread terror in its wake. Kyai Asy'ari's address to the inaugural meeting of Nahdlatul Ulama in Surabaya, East Java, articulates the ethical and theological framework embraced by the world's largest Muslim organization and remains the NU's foundational document to this day.

Nahdlatul Ulama united traditional Sunni religious scholars and quickly became one of the most influential organizations in the Dutch East Indies. Kyai Hasyim's son, Kyai Wahid Hasyim, would go on to serve as Chairman of the NU Executive Board and play a key role in drafting Indonesia's 1945 constitution, which enshrines the Republic of Indonesia's unique brand of inclusive, multireligious, and multi-ethnic nationalism.

Christine Schirrmacher

Dr. Christine Schirrmacher is a Professor of Islamic Studies at the University of Bonn, Germany and the Evangelical Theological Faculty in Leuven, Belgium. Since 2007, she has been a guest lecturer at the State and Federal

Authorities for Security Policy on an ongoing basis, and since 2001 she has taught annually at the "Akademie Auswärtiger Dienst" (Foreign Service Academy) of the Federal Foreign Office in Berlin. Dr. Schirrmacher regularly lectures on Islam and security issues at government institutions across Germany.

Dr. Schirrmacher is director of the International Institute of Islamic Studies (IIIS) of the World Evangelical Alliance (WEA) and its regional counterpart, the "Institut für Islamfragen" (Institute of Islamic Studies) of the German, Swiss, and Austrian Evangelical Alliance, as well as a frequent speaker and advisor on Islam for the WEA.

Dr. Schirrmacher has written 15 books and numerous scholarly articles in German, many of which have been translated into English, Spanish, Kiswahili, Romanian, and Korean. Her two-volume introduction *Der Islam — Geschichte, Lehre, Unterschiede zum Christentum* (1994/2003) *(Islam — History, Doctrines, and Differences from Christianity)* is widely used in seminaries and educational programs throughout German-speaking Europe.

Kyle Wisdom

Kyle Wisdom serves as Deputy Coordinator for Engaging Humanitarian Islam in the World Evangelical Alliance Office of Interfaith Relations. He is currently a Ph.D. candidate at Middlesex University in the United Kingdom, specializing in the relationship between Indonesian Islam and political philosophy, with a focus on applying insights from Indonesia to Western political discourse. Specifically, his work seeks to demonstrate the potentially vital contribution of religion's transcendental values to contemporary society.

After receiving his bachelor's degree in theology and a divinity degree, Mr. Wisdom moved from the United States to Indonesia. For eleven years, he worked with faith leaders, churches, and colleges, seeking to better understand the unique and complex relationship between religion and the modern nation state in the world's largest Muslim-majority democracy.

KH. Yahya Cholil Staquf

KH. Yahya Cholil Staquf is a distinguished Muslim scholar and co-founder of the global Humanitarian Islam movement, which seeks to recontextualize (i.e., reform) obsolete and problematic tenets of Islamic orthodoxy that may be readily weaponized to foster religious hatred, supremacy, and violence. Humanitarian Islam restores *rahmah* (universal love and compassion) to its rightful place as the primary message of Islam. As

General Secretary of Indonesia's Nahdlatul Ulama, Mr. Staquf is working systematically and institutionally to bring the civilizational wisdom and spiritual authority of *Islam Nusantara* (East Indies Islam) to the world stage, where a harsh, repressive, and all-too-often violent understanding of Islam has predominated for decades.

Mr. Staquf is descended from a long and illustrious line of Javanese *ulama* (religious scholars), including the renowned Bisri family of Rembang, Central Java. Educated from earliest childhood in the formal and esoteric (spiritual) sciences of Islam — by his father, grandfather, and uncle — Mr. Staquf later became a disciple of venerated Islamic scholar and Chairman of the Nahdlatul Ulama Supreme Council, Kyai Haji Ali Maksum (1915 – 1989), studying classical Islamic sciences under his direct tutelage at al-Munawwir Krapyak *madrasah* in Yogyakarta, Indonesia. KH. Ali Maksum was himself a disciple of Shaykh Umar Hamdan al-Makki (1858 – 1948) and Shaykh Hasan Masshat al-Makki (1900 – 1979) of Mecca, and he mentored several of Indonesia's most influential modern figures, including President Abdurrahman Wahid and KH. Yahya Cholil Staquf's uncle, the widely revered religious scholar, public intellectual, painter, and poet KH. A. Mustofa Bisri.

Inspired by President Wahid's moral and spiritual vision, Mr. Staquf co-founded *Bayt ar-Rahmah* (Home of Divine Grace) in 2014, and the Institute for Humanitarian Islam and Center for Shared Civilizational Values in 2021. Together, these closely affiliated organizations seek to prevent the political weaponization of identity; curtail the spread of communal hatred; promote solidarity and respect among the diverse people, cultures, and nations of the world; and foster the emergence of a truly just and harmonious world order, founded upon respect for the equal rights and dignity of every human being.

KH. Yahya Cholil Staquf serves as Gerakan Pemuda Ansor's Emissary to the Islamic World and as the Emissary for Indonesia's largest Islamic political party, PKB (which is rooted in the spiritual wing of Nahdlatul Ulama) to Centrist Democrat International and the European People's Party — the largest political networks in Europe and the world. He also serves on Policy Exchange's 16-member Indo-Pacific Commission, which is chaired by former Canadian Prime Minister Stephen Harper.

A former member of Indonesian President Joko Widodo's Presidential Advisory Council, Mr. Staquf is increasingly regarded by international observers as a potential linchpin in efforts to forge a global, values-driven alliance dedicated to strengthening the rules-based international order at a time of rising geopolitical uncertainty and widespread human rights abuse.

KH. Hodri Ariev

KH. Hodri Ariev serves as Chairman of Pondok Pesantren (*Madrasah*) Bahrul Ulum in Jember, East Java, and is an advisor to the Provincial Board of the Nahdlatul Ulama Association of Pesantren. He also lectures at the Annuqayah Islamic Sciences Institute in Sumenep, Madura, and at Sunan Ampel State Islamic University in Surabaya, East Java.

Kyai Ariev's father, grandfather, and great-grandfather were respected *ulama*, or religious scholars, trained in Islamic law and spirituality. In 1926 — in the wake of the Saudi/Wahhabi conquest of Mecca and Medina — Kyai Ariev's great-grandfather-in-law received the newly established NU's flag from Kyai Hasyim Asy'ari personally. He carried this banner by hand, travelling from village to village on foot across the island of Madura, summoning leaders of Islamic boarding schools throughout the heavily populated region to unite in preserving their traditional understanding and practice of Islam as *rahmatan lil 'alamin* (universal love and compassion).

Part III

Rüdiger Lohlker

Dr. Rüdiger Lohlker is a senior professor of Islamic studies at the University of Vienna and counter-terrorism advisor to the European Union and various Western nations. An expert in the field of modern Islamic movements and jihadism, the history of Islamic ideas, and Islam and the Arab world online, Dr. Lohlker also heads a Training Course for Imams at the University of Vienna (2010 – present).

In his capacity as head of the Vienna Observatory for Applied Research on Terrorism and Extremism (VORTEX), Dr. Lohlker led groundbreaking research into the Islamic State terror group (ISIS). This research, conducted with Dr. Nico Prucha and Dr. Ali Fisher, led to multiple briefings and discussions regarding ISIS with leaders of the world's largest Muslim organization, Indonesia's Nahdlatul Ulama, which convinced NU leaders of the need to accelerate their efforts to reform obsolete and problematic tenets of Islamic orthodoxy that underlie and animate jihadist movements worldwide.

James M. Dorsey

Dr. James M. Dorsey is a senior research fellow at the Middle East Institute of the National University of Singapore, non-resident senior fellow at the

Begin–Sadat Center for Strategic Studies of Bar-Ilan University in Israel, and co-director of the Institute of Fan Culture at the University of Würzburg in Germany.

Prior to entering academia, Dr. Dorsey was an award-winning, two-time Pulitzer Prize nominee veteran journalist, who covered ethnic and religious conflict in the Middle East, Africa, Asia, Europe, and Latin America for *The Wall Street Journal*, *The New York Times*, *Financial Times* and *The Christian Science Monitor*.

The author of several critically acclaimed books, *The Turbulent World of Middle East Soccer* syndicated column and blog, and numerous journal articles and working papers, Dr. Dorsey routinely advises governments, major financial institutions, corporations, and international agencies regarding developments in the Middle East and North Africa. He is a member of the advisory board of the European Water Partnership and has worked closely with the World Economic Forum, the World Water Forum, the World Water Council, the UN Secretary General's office, and the United Nations Foundation on conflict resolution, regional, and water issues.

Timothy Shah

Dr. Timothy S. Shah is Director of Strategic Initiatives of the Center for Shared Civilizational Values and Distinguished Research Scholar in Politics at the University of Dallas. From 2017 to 2020, Dr. Shah led an intensive project funded by Templeton Religion Trust on the religious freedom landscape in South and Southeast Asia. One of the project's major findings — that Nahdlatul Ulama spiritual leaders "represent the most theologically potent and operationally effective actors promoting religious liberty in the Islamic world today" — inspired Dr. Shah to join these NU leaders in establishing the Center for Shared Civilizational Values in 2021.

Dr. Shah co-founded the Washington-based Religious Freedom Institute in 2016, serving as its Vice President for Strategy and International Research and director of its South and Southeast Asia Action Team until 2020. Between 2011 and 2018, he was at Georgetown University, where he served as associate director of the Berkley Center's Religious Freedom Project and associate professor of the practice of religion and global politics in Georgetown's Department of Government. He was previously a senior fellow at the Pew Research Center and, from 2004 to 2009, a senior fellow at the Council on Foreign Relations, where he directed (with Walter Russell Mead) the Council's first program on Religion and Foreign Policy.

Dr. Shah is the author and editor of numerous books, including *Even if There is No God: Hugo Grotius and the Secular Foundations of Modern Political*

Liberalism (Oxford University Press, forthcoming); *Under Caesar's Sword: Christian Responses to Persecution* (Cambridge University Press, 2018); *Homo Religiosus? Exploring the Roots of Religion and Religious Freedom in Human Experience* (Cambridge University Press, 2018); *Christianity and Freedom: Historical Perspectives* and *Christianity and Freedom: Contemporary Perspectives* (both with Cambridge University Press, 2016); *Rethinking Religion and World Affairs* (Oxford University Press, 2012); *Religious Freedom: Why Now? Defending an Embattled Human Right* (Witherspoon Institute, 2012); and *God's Century: Resurgent Religion and Global Politics* (W.W. Norton and Company, 2011). Dr. Shah's articles on religion, religious freedom, and global politics, in history and in the contemporary world, have appeared in *Foreign Affairs, Foreign Policy, Journal of Law and Religion, Journal of Democracy, Review of Politics, Fides et Historia*, and elsewhere.

Dr. Shah received his A.B., magna cum laude, in 1992 and a Ph.D. in 2002, both from Harvard University.

Thomas Dinham

Thomas Dinham is an accomplished geopolitical analyst, journalist, author, and strategic communications professional who cut his teeth as a Middle East specialist covering events during the height of the Arab Spring. Described by the BBC's flagship current affairs program *From Our Own Correspondent* as "a witness to crucial days in the history of Egypt," Mr. Dinham has lived, studied, and worked in several of the region's key power centers, including Cairo, Abu Dhabi, Damascus, and Beirut.

Fluent in classical and colloquial Egyptian Arabic — both spoken and written — Mr. Dinham was hired by spiritual leaders of Indonesia's Nahdlatul Ulama in 2018 to assist in the expansion of NU operations worldwide. Supervised by NU General Secretary KH. Yahya Cholil Staquf and LibForAll/Bayt ar-Rahmah executive C. Holland Taylor, Mr. Dinham helped to draft the historic *Nusantara Manifesto*. Based in the UK, Mr. Dinham helps coordinate public communications, media outreach, and geopolitical engagement for the NU and its five-million-member young adult movement, Gerakan Pemuda Ansor. He also serves as rapporteur to NU General Secretary KH. Haji Yahya Cholil Staquf for the UK-based Indo-Pacific Commission, which is chaired by former Canadian Prime Minister Stephen Harper.

Mr. Dinham, a British citizen and a graduate of the University of Oxford, holds an M.A. from the University of Exeter. He has contributed commentary and analysis to academic journals, books, newspapers, and broadcast media — in both English and Arabic — including the BBC, *Financial Times, Strategic Review, al-Arab, al-Gomhuria, Global Security Studies Review, The Cipher Brief* and *Global Policy Journal*.

Invitation

Frank Hinkelmann

Dr. Frank Hinkelmann is an ordained minister of the Protestant Church of Austria and Vice Chair of the World Evangelical Alliance. An accomplished theologian, Dr. Hinkelmann studied theology at the German Theological Seminary (1989 – 1993) and at the Theological University of Apeldoorn in the Netherlands (2004 – 2006) before completing his Ph.D. at the Free University of Amsterdam in 2014 with a doctoral thesis on the subject of Austria's Evangelical movement.

From 1998 to 2007, Dr. Hinkelmann oversaw the Austrian ministry of Operation Mobilization (OM), before directing its European ministry from 2008 to 2017. He currently serves as OM International's Associate for Board Development. In 2014, Dr. Hinkelmann was elected president of the European Evangelical Alliance (EEA), and he is involved in theological training at a number of institutions. He also serves as President of the Martin Bucer Seminary in Bonn, Germany.

Dr. Hinkelmann has published several books on evangelical Christianity, including an exposition on the letters to the seven churches in the book of Revelation (2004); the history of the Austrian Evangelical Alliance (2006 and 2012); the history of the evangelical movement in Austria (2014); and an encyclopedia of Christian denominations in Austria (2009). Dr. Hinkelmann is also the editor of the German edition of Ruth Tucker's bestseller *From Jerusalem to Irian Jaya* (2007) and a series of books on Austrian evangelical church history.

Kyai Ariev completed his bachelor's degree in Islamic Law (*fiqh*) at Annuqayah Islamic Sciences College, graduating cum laude. He received his master's degree in Islamic Philosophy and Mysticism at Syarif Hidayatullah State Islamic University in Jakarta. Working with KH. Abdurrahman Wahid and C. Holland Taylor, Kyai Ariev helped to draft the seminal article "God Needs No Defense" and also helped to edit, research, and co-author *Ilusi Negara Islam* (*The Illusion of an Islamic State*), a book — published amidst the heat of Indonesia's 2009 national elections — that derailed the political aspirations of Islamist groups hostile to Indonesia's traditions of religious pluralism and tolerance, including the Muslim Brotherhood–affiliated political party PKS.

Kyai Ariev is also the co-producer, with C. Holland Taylor, of two film series developed under the supervision of NU spiritual leader KH. A. Mustofa Bisri: *Lautan Wahyu* (*Ocean of Revelations*) — filmed on location in Indonesia, Egypt, Germany, and the Netherlands — and *International Institute of Qur'anic Studies: Birth of a Movement*.

Permissions and Credits

In the Name Of, by A. Mustofa Bisri, appears by permission of the author and the poem's translator, C. Holland Taylor.

Introduction: "We Wish to Submit to the Dictates of Conscience," by Thomas K. Johnson and C. Holland Taylor, appears by permission of the authors.

Part I

God Needs No Defense, by Abdurrahman Wahid, appears by permission of LibForAll Foundation.

A Case for Ethical Cooperation Between Protestants and Humanitarian Muslims, by Thomas K. Johnson, appears by permission of the author.

Rahmah (Universal Love and Compassion), by Abdurrahman Wahid, appears by permission of LibForAll Foundation.

God's Universal Grace in Protestant Theology, by Thomas K. Johnson, appears by permission of the author.

Part II

Introduction to the Fundamental Principles of Nahdlatul Ulama *(Mukaddimah Qanun Asasi)*, by Hasyim Asy'ari, was translated into English by Thomas Dinham and C. Holland Taylor. Their translation appears by permission of Bayt ar-Rahmah li ad-Da'wa al-Islamiyyah Rahmatan li al-'Alamin.

Christianity and the Essential Characteristics of Democracy, by Christine Schirrmacher, appears by permission of the author.

Indonesian Islam and a Tradition of Pluralism, by Kyle Wisdom, appears by permission of the author.

How Islam Learned to Adapt in 'Nusantara,' by Yahya Cholil Staquf, appears by permission of Bayt ar-Rahmah li ad-Da'wa al-Islamiyyah Rahmatan li al-'Alamin.

The Primary Message of Islam: *Rahmah* (Universal Love and Compassion), by Hodri Ariev, appears by permission of the author.

Part III

Theology Matters: The Case of Jihadi Islam, by Rüdiger Lohlker, appears by permission of the author and the article's translator (from German), C. Holland Taylor.

Responding to a Fundamental Crisis Within Islam Itself, by Yahya Cholil Staquf, appears by permission of Bayt ar-Rahmah li ad-Da'wa al-Islamiyyah Rahmatan li al-'Alamin.

Gerakan Pemuda Ansor Declaration on Humanitarian Islam, drafted by Yahya Cholil Staquf and C. Holland Taylor, appears by permission of Gerakan Pemuda Ansor and Bayt ar-Rahmah li ad-Da'wa al-Islamiyyah Rahmatan li al-'Alamin.

The Battle for the Soul of Islam, by James M. Dorsey, appears by permission of the author.

Humanitarian Islam: Fostering Shared Civilizational Values to Revitalize a Rules-Based International Order, by Timothy Shah and Thomas Dinham, appears by permission of Timothy Shah and Bayt ar-Rahmah li ad-Da'wa al-Islamiyyah Rahmatan li al-'Alamin.

"Positive Deviance" Within the Indosphere & the Muslim World, by Timothy Shah, appears by permission of the author.

The Universal Values of Indonesian Islamic Civilization, by A. Mustofa Bisri, appears by permission of Bayt ar-Rahmah li ad-Da'wa al-Islamiyyah Rahmatan li al-'Alamin.

The editors wish to express their appreciation to Bruce Barron, Thomas Dinham, Timothy Shah, and Titus Vogt for their assistance in preparing this Festschrift for publication.

www.ingramcontent.com/pod-product-compliance
Lightning Source LLC
Chambersburg PA
CBHW070248230426

43664CB00014B/2442